GAME
DEVELOPMENT
ESSENTIALS
GAMEPLAY MECHANICS

Troy Dunniway

Jeannie Novak

DELMAR
CENGAGE Learning

Australia • Brazil • Japan • Korea • Mexico • Singapore • Spain • United Kingdom • United States

90460

Game Development Essentials:
Gameplay Mechanics
Troy Dunniway & Jeannie Novak

Vice President, Technology and Trades ABU:
   David Garza

Director of Learning Solutions: Sandy Clark

Managing Editor: Larry Main

Senior Acquisitions Editor: James Gish

Product Manager: Sharon Chambliss

Editorial Assistant: Sarah Timm

Marketing Director: Deborah Yarnell

Marketing Manager: Bryant Chrzan

Marketing Specialist: Victoria Ortiz

Director of Production: Patty Stephan

Production Manager: Stacy Masucci

Content Project Manager: Michael Tubbert

Technology Project Manager: Kevin Smith

Cover Design: *Crysis* courtesy of Crytek. All rights
   reserved. "Crysis" is a trademark of Crytek.

For product information and technology assistance, contact us at
Cengage Learning Customer & Sales Support, 1-800-354-9706

For permission to use material from this text or product, submit all requests online at **www.cengage.com/permissions**
Further permissions questions can be emailed to
permissionrequest@cengage.com

Library of Congress Control Number:

In-Publication Data has been applied for.

ISBN-13: 978-1-4180-5269-0

ISBN-10: 1-4180-5269-8

Delmar
5 Maxwell Drive
PO Box 8007
Clifton Park, NY 12065-8007
USA

Cengage Learning is a leading provider of customized learning solutions with office locations around the globe, including Singapore, the United Kingdom, Australia, Mexico, Brazil, and Japan. Locate your local office at:

international.cengage.com/region

Cengage Learning products are represented in Canada by Nelson - Education, Ltd.

For your lifelong learning solutions, visit **delmar.cengage.com**

Visit our corporate website at **cengage.com**

Notice to the Reader

Publisher does not warrant or guarantee any of the products described herein or perform any independent analysis in connection with any of the product information contained herein. Publisher does not assume, and expressly disclaims, any obligation to obtain and include information other than that provided to it by the manufacturer. The reader is expressly warned to consider and adopt all safety precautions that might be indicated by the activities described herein and to avoid all potential hazards. By following the instructions contained herein, the reader willingly assumes all risks in connection with such instructions. The publisher makes no representations or warranties of any kind, including but not limited to, the warranties of fitness for particular purpose or merchantability, nor are any such representations implied with respect to the material set forth herein, and the publisher takes no responsibility with respect to such material. The publisher shall not be liable for any special, consequential, or exemplary damages resulting, in whole or part, from the readers' use of, or reliance upon, this material.

Printed in Canada
1 2 3 4 5 6 7 11 10 09 08 07

CONTENTS

Chapter 3   Creating the Core:
the game's heart and soul. 63

Part III: Gameplay Strategies . . 213

Chapter 7   Creating Progression: ramping the player 215

Chapter 8   Creating Variety: involving the player 241

Introduction

Gameplay Mechanics:
creating fun

"Fun" is subjective, and game designers have a difficult job creating it. Each game we design is unique—with specific requirements and expectations; it's almost as if we must speak a different language each time we begin working on a new project. Most game designers assume that the game they create will provide hours of entertainment—but if this were true in all cases, why don't we enjoy every game we play?

The more objective you become as a game designer, the more you'll realize that the creation of fun can seem elusive. We have addressed this challenge by formalizing the steps necessary to achieve fun through *gameplay mechanics*—how players experience the game through a system of rules. In this book, we lay the groundwork, introduce the dimensions of breadth and depth, and guide you through various strategies that will result in the achievement of true player involvement.

The element of gameplay mechanics drives all aspects of a game, and strong mechanics can sometimes predict a game's success in the marketplace. This book contains numerous case studies that dissect well-designed games to determine the reasons for their success—allowing you to gain a deeper understanding of gameplay mechanics and the basis of the "fun factor."

This book will also help you design games that will not only provide players with short-term satisfaction, but that will keep them involved (and playing!) for the long run. It's not difficult to design a series of mechanics that try to accomplish everything—but it can be incredibly challenging to design a simple game with mechanics that can be combined in a powerful way.

As the game industry continues to mature, it's only a matter of time before the mysteries of game design are better understood. Until then, there is still a tremendous amount to learn. Gameplay mechanics encompasses the core of the game designer's role—creating fun through the intersection of art and science.

Troy Dunniway   Jeannie Novak
Simi Valley, CA   Santa Monica, CA

About the *Game Development Essentials* Series

The *Game Development Essentials* series was created to fulfill a need: to provide students and creative professionals alike with a complete education in all aspects of the game industry. As more creative professionals migrate to the game industry, and as more game degree and certificate programs are launched, the books in this series will become even more essential to game education and career development.

Not limited to the education market, this series is also appropriate for the trade market and for those who have a general interest in the game industry. Books in the series contain several unique features. All are in full-color and contain hundreds of images—including original illustrations, diagrams, game screenshots, and photos of industry professionals. They also contain a great deal of profiles, tips and case studies from professionals in the industry who are actively developing games. Starting with an overview of all aspects of the industry—*Game Development Essentials: An Introduction*—this series focuses on topics as varied as story & character development, interface design, artificial intelligence, gameplay mechanics, level design, online game development, simulation development, and audio.

Jeannie Novak
Lead Author & Series Editor

About *Game Development Essentials: Gameplay Mechanics*

This book provides an overview of gameplay mechanics—complete with historical background, dimensions, strategies, and future predictions.

This book contains the following unique features:

- Key chapter questions that are clearly stated at the beginning of each chapter
- Coverage that surveys the topics of gameplay mechanics concepts, process, and techniques
- Thought-provoking review and study exercises at the end of each chapter suitable for students and professionals alike that help promote critical thinking and problem-solving skills
- Case studies, quotations from leading professionals, and profiles of game developers that feature concise tips and techniques to help readers focus in on issues specific to gameplay mechanics
- An abundance of full-color images throughout that help illustrate the concepts and practical applications discussed in the book

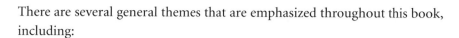

There are several general themes that are emphasized throughout this book, including:

- Distinguishing between games driven by gameplay, technology, art, and story
- Creating a balance between gameplay systems
- Design considerations for game characters, camera controls—and object, movement, and combat systems
- Exploring techniques such as emergence, freedom of choice, rewards, ramping, and variety
- Evaluating existing games with emphasis on the "fun factor" and how it was achieved

Who Should Read This Book?

This book is not limited to the education market. If you found this book on a shelf at the bookstore and picked it up out of curiosity, this book is for you, too! The audience for this book includes students, industry professionals, and the general interest consumer market. The style is informal and accessible with a concentration on theory and practice—geared toward both students and professionals.

Students that might benefit from this book include:

- College students in game development, interactive design, entertainment studies, communication, and emerging technologies programs
- Art, design, programming, and production students who are taking game development courses
- Professional students in college-level programs who are taking game development courses
- First-year game development students at universities

The audience of industry professionals for this book include:

- Graphic designers, animators, and interactive media developers who are interested in becoming game artists
- Programmers and interactive media developers who are interested in becoming game programmers
- Professionals such as writers, producers, artists, and designers in other arts and entertainment media—including film, television, and music—who are interested in transferring their skills to the game development industry.

Gameplay Mechanics: creating fun introduction

How Is This Book Organized?

This book consists of three parts—focusing on industry background, dimensions, and strategies.

Part I   Gameplay Groundwork—Focuses on providing a historical and structural context to gameplay mechanics. Chapters in this section include:

- **Chapter 1   Creating the Foundation: history of gameplay mechanics**—discusses the history of gameplay mechanics, the role of the "fun factor," and the evolution of platforms and tabletop games
- **Chapter 2   Creating the Process: the game's design path**—explores the elements of vision, restrictions, documentation, and driving factors in the game design process
- **Chapter 3   Creating the Core: the game's heart and soul**—reviews camera, object, movement, and combat systems
- **Chapter 4   Creating the Characters: the game's inhabitants**—focuses on character behavior, role, physical description, personality traits, and creation systems

Part II   Gameplay Dimensions—Focuses on how gameplay mechanics can provide both breadth and depth for the player. Chapters in this section include:

- **Chapter 5   Creating the Options: providing breadth**—discusses how gameplay mechanics can be used to create freedom of choice, immersion, and emergence for the player
- **Chapter 6   Creating the Connection: providing depth**—discusses how gameplay mechanics can be used to create rewards, advancement, and attachment for the player

Part III: Gameplay Strategies—Focuses on advanced techniques in gameplay mechanics such as progression and variety, along with thoughts on the future of gameplay mechanics. Chapters in this section include:

- **Chapter 7   Creating Progression: ramping the player**—explores blockade, navigation, dynamic difficulty adjustment, and load/save systems
- **Chapter 8   Creating Variety: involving the player**—explores the benefits and disadvantages of repetition, and methods for providing variety in a game's storyline and level structure
- **Chapter 9   Creating Cohesion: putting it all together**—highlights future predictions, career paths, and education related to game simulation development

The book also contains a **Resources** section, which includes a list of game development news sources, guides, directories, conferences, articles, and books related to topics discussed in this text.

How to Use This Text

The sections that follow describe text elements found throughout the book and how they are intended to be used.

key chapter questions

Key chapter questions are learning objectives in the form of overview questions that start off each chapter. Readers should be able to answer the questions upon understanding the chapter material.

notes

Notes contain thought-provoking ideas provided by the authors that are intended to help the readers think critically about the book's topics.

sidebars

Sidebars offer in-depth information from the authors on specific topics—accompanied by associated images.

quotes

Quotes contain short, insightful thoughts from industry professionals, observers, players, and students.

tips

Tips provide advice and inspiration from industry professionals and educators, as well as practical techniques and tips of the trade.

case studies

Case studies contain anecdotes from industry professionals (accompanied by game screenshots) on their experiences developing specific game titles.

profiles

Profiles provide bios, photos and in-depth commentary from industry professionals and educators.

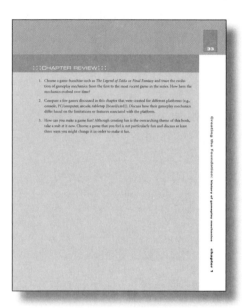

chapter review

Chapter review exercises at the end of each chapter allow readers to apply what they've learned. Annotations and guidelines are included in the instructor's guide, available separately (see next page).

About the Companion DVD

The companion DVD contains the following media:

- Game engines: *Torque* (Windows and Mac versions 1.5.1) and *Game Maker* (version 7)

- 3D modeling and animation software: *3ds Max* (version 9) and *Maya* (version 8.5 PLE)

- Game design documentation: GDD template (Chris Taylor/Gas Powered Games), *Sub Hunter* GDD (Michael Black/Torn Space), and *Uncivilized: The Goblin Game* [code name: Salmon] call for game design/submission (Wizards of the Coast)

- Game design articles: Harvey Smith/Witchboy's Cauldron and Barrie Ellis/One-Switch Games

- Game concept art: *Half-Life 2*, *Viewtiful Joe 2*, *Resident Evil 4* , *Devil May Cry 3*

- Game demos/trial versions: Take Two Interactive Software (*Prey*), Blizzard (*Diablo II*), Firaxis (*Civilization IV, Sid Meier's Railroads!*), Stardock (*Galactic Civilizations II: Gold Edition*), THQ (*Company of Heroes*), Enemy Technology (*I of the Enemy: Ril'Cerat*), Star Mountain Studios (*Bergman, Weird Helmet, Frozen, Findolla*), GarageGames (*Marble Blast: Gold, Think Tanks, Zap!*), Max Gaming Technologies (*Dark Horizons: Lore Invasion*), Chronic Logic (*Gish*), Large Animal Games (*Rocket Bowl Plus*), 21-6 Productions (*Tube Twist, Orbz*), CDV (*City Life, Glory of the Roman Empire, War Front: Turning Point*), Last Day of Work (*Virtual Villagers, Fish Tycoon*), Hanako Games (*Cute Knight*), Microsoft (*Zoo Tycoon 2: Marine Mania*), and U.S. Army (*America's Army*).

About the Instructor's Guide

The instructor's guide (e-resource, available separately on DVD) was developed to assist instructors in planning and implementing their instructional programs. It includes sample syllabi, test questions, assignments, projects, PowerPoint files, and other valuable instructional resources.

Order Number: 1-4180-5270-1

About the Authors

Troy Dunniway is an award-winning creative director, game designer, and producer with over 17 years of experience. He has had a lead role in companies such as Microsoft, Electronic Arts, Westwood Studios, Ubisoft, Insomniac Games, Midway, and Brash Entertainment. Troy was most recently Creative Director on *Tom Clancy's Rainbow Six Vegas* for the Xbox 360, PlayStation 3, and PC—and he was Lead Designer of *Ratchet & Clank Future: Tools of Destruction* for the PlayStation 3. Troy has won numerous awards—including Game Design of the Year, Best Game of the Year, and Best of Show. He has  shipped more than 45 games on almost every game console and the PC, and he has contributed to well over 30 additional titles. Troy has led many other titles—such as *Ratchet: Deadlocked, Munch's Oddysee, Fable, Command & Conquer 3*, and *Age of Empires 3*. He is the Chair of Gaming for the SIGGRAPH 2010 national convention and is working to expand the presence of gaming in the worldwide graphics industry. Before becoming a game designer, Troy worked on special effects for movies such as *True Lies* and *Lawnmower Man 2*.

Photo credit: Luis Levy

Jeannie Novak is the founder of Indiespace—one of the first companies to promote and distribute interactive entertainment online—where she consults with creative professionals in the music, film, and television industries to help them migrate to the game industry. In addition to being lead author and series editor of the *Game Development Essentials* series, Jeannie is the co-author of *Play the Game: The Parent's Guide to Video Games* and three pioneering books on the interactive entertainment industry—including *Creating Internet Entertainment.* Jeannie is the Online Program Director for the Game Art & Design and Media Arts & Animation programs at the Art Institute of Pittsburgh – Online Division, where she is also Producer & Lead Designer on a educational business simulation game that is being built within the *Second Life* environment. She has also been a game instructor and curriculum development expert at UCLA Extension, Art Center College of Design, Academy of Entertainment and Technology at Santa Monica College, DeVry University, Westwood College, and ITT Technical Institute—and she has consulted for the UC Berkeley Center for New Media. Jeannie has developed or participated in game workshops and panels in association with the British Academy of Television Arts & Sciences (BAFTA), Macworld, Digital Hollywood, and iHollywood Forum. She is a member of the International Game Developers Association (IGDA) and has served on selection committees for the Academy of Interactive Arts & Sciences (AIAS) DICE Awards. Jeannie was chosen as one of the 100 most influential people in high-technology by *MicroTimes* magazine—and she has been profiled by CNN, *Billboard Magazine,* Sundance Channel, *Daily Variety,* and the *Los Angeles Times.* She received an M.A. in Communication Management from the University of Southern California (USC), where she focused on using massively multiplayer online games (MMOGs) as online distance learning applications. She received a B.A. in Mass Communication from the University of California, Los Angeles (UCLA)—graduating summa cum laude and Phi Beta Kappa. When she isn't writing and teaching, Jeannie spends most of her time recording, performing, and composing music. More information on the author can be found at *http://jeannie.com* and *http://indiespace.com.*

Acknowledgements

The authors would like to thank the following people for their hard work and dedication to this project:

Jim Gish (Acquisitions Editor, Delmar/Cengage Learning), for making this series happen.

Sharon Chambliss (Product Manager, Delmar/Cengage Learning), for moving this project along and always maintaining a professional demeanor.

Michael Tubbert (Content Project Manager, Delmar/Cengage Learning), for his helpful pair of eyes and consistent responsiveness during production crunch time.

Sarah Timm (Editorial Assistant, Delmar/Cengage Learning), for her ongoing assistance throughout the series.

Christine Clark & Suzanne Davidson, for their thorough and thoughtful copyediting.

David Ladyman (Image Research & Permissions Specialist), for his superhuman efforts in clearing the many images in this book.

Gina Dishman & Patricia Shogren (Project Managers, GEX Publishing Services), for their diligent work and prompt response during the layout and compositing phase.

Per Olin, for his organized and aesthetically pleasing diagrams.

David Koontz (Publisher, Chilton), for starting it all by introducing Jeannie Novak to Jim Gish.

A big thanks also goes out to the people who contributed their thoughts, ideas, and original images to this book:

Barrie Ellis (One-Switch)

Brian Reynolds (Big Huge Games)

Chris Avellone (Obsidian Entertainment)

Chris Rohde (The Art Institute of Portland)

Chris Taylor (Gas Powered Games)

Deborah Baxtrom (The Art Institute of Pittsburgh – Online Division)

Farhad Javidi (Central Piedmont Community College)

Frank T. Gilson (Wizards of the Coast)

Greg Costikyan (Manifesto Games)

Harvey Smith (Midway Games)

Jason Bramble (Deadman Games, Inc.)

Jeremy McCarron (The Art Institute of Vancouver)

Jessica Mulligan (Sunflowers GmbH)

Jim McCampbell (Ringling School of Art & Design)

John Comes (Gas Powered Games)

Mark Skaggs (Funstar Ventures, LLC)

Mauricio Ferrazza (Univision Network; The Art Institute of Pittsburgh – Online Division)

Michael Black (Torn Space)

Milan Petrovich (The Art Institute of San Francisco)

Randy Greenback (Red Storm Entertainment/Ubisoft)

Roby Gilbert (The Art Institute of Seattle)

Starr Long (NCsoft)

Titus Levi

Tracy Fullerton (USC School for Cinematic Arts)

Travis Castillo (InXile Entertainment; Art Center College of Design)

Thanks to the following people and companies for their tremendous help with referrals and in securing permissions, images, and demos:

Ai Hasegawa & Hideki Yoshimoto (Namco Bandai)

Alexandra Miseta (Stardock)

Annie Belanger (Autodesk)

Brian Hupp (Electronic Arts)

Brianna Messina (Blizzard Entertainment)

Briar Lee Mitchell (Star Mountain Studios)

Carla Humphrey (Last Day of Work)

Casey Maloney

Chari Ong, Mark Morrison & Reilly Brennan (Midway Games)

Chris Brooks

Chris Glover (Eidos Interactive)

Chris Taylor (Gas Powered Games)

David Greenspan (THQ)

David Kwock & Gerilynn Okano (Blue Planet)

David Swofford (NCsoft)

Dennis Shirk (Firaxis)

Don McGowan (Microsoft Corporation)

Eric Fritz (GarageGames)

Estela Lemus (Capcom)

Frank T. Gilson & Greg Yahn (Wizards of the Coast)

Gena Feist (Take-Two Games)

Georgina Okerson (Hanako Games)

Jana Rubenstein, Makiko Nakamura & Eijirou Yoshida (Sega of America)

Jarik Sikat (KOEI)

Jason Holtman (Valve)

Jo-Ann Bryden & Helen Van Tassel (Hasbro)

Kate Ross (Wizards of the Coast)

Kathryn Butters (Atari Interactive)

Kelvin Liu & Mike Mantarro (Activision)

Laura Knight (Nickelodeon Family Suites)

Liz Buckley (Majesco)

Lori Mezoff (U.S. Army)

Margaret Adamic (Disney)

Mario Kroll (CDV Software)

Mark Overmars, Sandy Duncan & Sophie Russell (YoYo Games)

Mark Rein & Kelly Farrow (Epic Games)

Mark Temple (Enemy Technology)

Nintendo

Pete Hines (Bethesda Softworks)

Sophie Jakubowicz (Ubisoft)

Stephen Millard

Ted Brockwood (Calico Media)

Terri Perkins (Funcom)

Valerie Massey (CCP Games)

Vikki Vega (Sony Computer Entertainment America)

Yoh Watanabe (Tecmo)

Questions & Feedback

We welcome your questions and feedback. If you have suggestions that you think others would benefit from, please let us know and we will try to include them in the next edition.

To send us your questions and/or feedback, you can contact the publisher at:

Delmar Learning
Executive Woods
5 Maxwell Drive
Clifton Park, NY 12065
Attn: Graphic Arts Team
(800) 998-7498

Or the series editor at:

Jeannie Novak
Founder & CEO
INDIESPACE
P.O. Box 5458
Santa Monica, CA 90409
jeannie@indiespace.com

DEDICATION

To my wife Becky and sons Eric and Todd for their continual support of my long hours and crazy schedules in such an insane industry—and for putting up with me while I wrote this book.

—*Troy*

To Luis, who knows how to "play the game." Thanks for creating fun with me!

—*Jeannie*

Part I:
Gameplay
Groundwork

CHAPTER

Creating the Foundation

history of gameplay mechanics

Key Chapter Questions

- What is a gameplay mechanic?

- How is "fun" defined as it relates to games?

- How did the evolution of classic tabletop games affect the design of video games?

- What innovations were important in the evolution of console games?

- How did computer and arcade gameplay evolution differ from console gameplay evolution?

Designing games is one of the most rewarding jobs in the world, but it is also one of the most challenging. A great designer is part artist, scientist, author, director, cinematographer—and sometimes even a politician. You must shoot for the moon, but know you won't necessarily reach it. Game designers often work as part of a team—representing the central hub through which everything must function. Being a game designer means that you must be a jack-of-all-trades and master of all, defeating the stereotype that you can't be good at everything. There are many types of game designers: Creative directors hold the vision for a game, while the lead designers make it happen. Level designers build the worlds, while gameplay designers make the game fun by producing the game's core systems and defining how they work together to create the heart of the game. This book will cover all aspects of gameplay design: how the gameplay components fit together, how every piece of the puzzle is placed, and how to approach the seemingly simple but horribly complex task of making the game fun.

Gameplay Mechanics Defined

This book does not attempt to cover all aspects of game design and production. It is about how to design better *gameplay systems*—features of a game that need to function in order to ensure that a game is *fun*. Gameplay systems revolve around characters, movement, cameras, controls, combat, weapons, equipment, objects, enemies, magic, inventory, and other elements that most games must have in order to create and sustain the "fun factor." This book will give you ideas not only on how to make these systems work properly together and be cohesive, but also on how to ensure that they will be fun and innovative. We'll discuss how to do the following:

- Add variety to the systems in order to keep them from becoming repetitive
- Use emergence to allow systems to be combined in interesting ways
- Create interesting systems that hook players quickly
- Build addictive systems that will keep players engaged for a long time
- Advance the game's systems so that game difficulty and player interest are kept in balance

Game design is one of the toughest disciplines in the entertainment industry, and it relies on several factors to be successful. The smallest misstep can ruin a game for some players, even if you have done a million things right. Since it is impossible to do *everything* correctly, decide what you need to get right in order to be successful, and what can be a little weak if necessary. It is always about finding a balance. Even highly successful games have problems with some of their gameplay systems, but if the entire game experience is fun and captivating, fans tend to ignore these issues. However, a few gameplay issues combined with poor storylines, visual glitches, or technology problems can cause players and reviewers to be very harsh.

While this book cannot hope to teach you everything about how to design gameplay systems, it should inspire you to understand more about the systems you are designing. Remember that a solid knowledge of gameplay systems is only one piece in the massive puzzle involved in building a game. You still have to figure out how the gameplay systems you want will fit with the interface, story, technology, schedule, and many other factors.

Courtesy of Rockstar Games and Take-Two Interactive Software, Inc.

Grand Theft Auto III contains a variety of gameplay systems that make the game compelling and challenging for players.

The most general definition of a gameplay mechanic is a rule or feature that influences how the game is played. Every game uses a single gameplay mechanic or several different ones that either work independently or together to create new results. A good game designer must be able to define a gameplay mechanic, know how it is created, and apply this knowledge to the development of mechanics that are perfect for the game.

Courtesy of Midway Games, Inc.

Anything a player can do in the game, such as moving, jumping, shooting, fighting, or driving, is a gameplay mechanic. However, each large feature such as fighting consists of several small gameplay mechanics that work together to make fighting fun. Each player action that can be performed while fighting, such as punching, kicking, slicing, stabbing, shooting, or throwing, is a gameplay mechanic.

The more gameplay mechanics in a game, the more complicated it becomes. The job of most game designers, therefore, is not to just come up with new gameplay mechanics but to continually simplify and refine gameplay mechanics to make

Action games such as *Mortal Kombat: Shaolin Monks* contain a wide range of gameplay mechanics.

them easier for players to use. Game designers must also try to figure out how these mechanics can be combined and what additional gameplay will be created through these combinations.

Mechanics such as being able to walk and shoot could be combined in such a way that the player can do both at the same time. An emergent gameplay mechanic occurs when two gameplay mechanics are combined in a different way to create a new gameplay mechanic. If a player can spray gasoline from a pump and can also light a match, the player could create a flamethrower; even though the flamethrower is not specifically defined as a mechanic, it can result from both mechanics. (Emergence will be discussed in more detail in Chapter 5.)

Emergent mechanics are either predefined by the game designer or may result from smart players figuring out ways of utilizing mechanics together in a unique way. In *Munch's Oddysee*, the player controls two characters, Abe and Munch. Abe has the ability to pick up bombs and throw them. When bombs explode, they cause anyone nearby to fly up in the air. Players have figured out that the bomb explosions will not kill Munch, but only severely injure him. Munch has a limited ability to move, which creates many of the puzzles in the game as the player tries to get both Abe and Munch to the end of the level. However, players have realized that if they throw the bomb at Munch, they can send him flying and transport him to places he was not supposed to be able to access, therefore "breaking" the game. Several simple mechanics—picking up and throwing bombs, limited movement, and explosion knockback—could be combined to allow the player to do something unexpected.

Reprinted with permission from Microsoft Corporation

Emergent mechanics that are not predefined by the game designer occur in games such as *Oddworld: Munch's Oddysee*.

Designing for "Fun"

If a gameplay designer's job is to make a game fun, and fun is subjective, then how is it possible to reliably design for "fun"? Designing a really fun game involves both luck and skill. There are so many different features that must go into a game to make it fun that it is impossible to define "fun." If there were a magic formula for fun, every game would be a hit. Making a game universally fun is about as easy as making a comedy movie funny to everyone who watches it. Not everyone finds the same things funny or fun. It is very easy to make a game fun for yourself, but the real challenge is making a game fun for others; in order to accomplish this, you must first define your audience and determine what your players are looking for in a game. Some people play games because the gameplay itself is fun, and others prefer the storyline, experience, fantasy, challenge, or something else that fascinates them. Figuring out who your audience is, what they think they want, and what they really want will help you understand what they might find fun.

When we talk about mechanics, we are also talking about gameplay—since "mechanics" is more of an engineering concept, while gameplay is more of a design concept. To really understand the world of gameplay mechanics, it is important to look at how it has evolved.

Classic Gameplay

We have always looked for ways to entertain ourselves, whether with our voices and bodies alone, or with the help of paper and pencil, cards, or dice. Many classic games such as chess, checkers, cards, mah-jongg, cribbage, and backgammon have been around for thousands of years. Have you ever asked yourself why? What is it about these games that can keep people entertained day in and day out, year after year? Why do some video games sit on a shelf for a few months and are never heard from again?

Most classic games revolve around strategy and a complex set of interactions that flow from very simple rules and behaviors. The game of chess is a perfect example of simple rules creating complex behaviors. Each of the six different pieces have distinct movement rules. Some, such as the queen, are nearly unrestricted in direction or distance. Others are strictly defined—such as the pawn, which must move forward one square at a time and can only attack diagonally. When you combine all six different pieces and their movement rules with the confines of the chess board, there is a tremendous variety of ways to play the game. This could be defined as emergent gameplay mechanics, in that the game gives players a few very simple rules and abilities and then allows players to combine them to achieve many different abilities. For this reason, chess is easy to understand and teach to someone who has never played it but incredibly hard to master.

Big Stock Photo

We never seem to grow tired of classic games such as chess.

Board Games

Classic board games such as *Monopoly, Settlers of Catan, Life, Risk, Shogun, Candyland, Squad Leader,* and *Axis & Allies* have attracted players of all ages and range in difficulty from the simple pattern matching of *Candyland* to the sophisticated strategic thought required for *Risk.* While many board gameplay mechanics have not been translated into all genres of video games, there are still lessons to be learned. Board games often require puzzle solving and offer strategic learning. They are also really good at teaching us how to combine simple mechanics to form more complex behaviors. Most board games are extremely good references for strategy game design. These games utilize the simplest strategic components and are so entertaining and engaging that people have been playing them for many years. Like the game of chess, strategic board games have a lot to offer game designers.

Board games are played with pieces that represent either one or a group of objects or people. For instance, a single cube piece in *Risk* could represent an entire army. Pieces in board games usually are abstract representations, while the board itself could be divided into squares, hexes, or other areas for the pieces to move around on. If you look at early computer games, and even those of today, each unit or piece could represent one or many units in the game. This is especially the case in many turn-based strategy games such as *Civilization* or *Heroes of Might & Magic.* As many video games and genres have evolved, they have begun to use "pieces" that look more realistic.

MONOPOLY® & ©2007 Hasbro, Inc. Used with permission.

Relatively straightforward board games such as *Monopoly* (the first "tycoon" game, created as a response to the harsh economic reality brought on by the Great Depression) involve strategic decision making.

Pen & Paper Games

Another type of classic game that has had a significant impact on video games is the pen and paper role-playing game (RPG). *Dungeons & Dragons* is the most classic RPG and is still being utilized in game development to this day. Other RPG systems include *GURPS, Shadowrun,* and *Rifts.* More modern video game RPGs are based heavily on their pen and paper counterparts, using elements such as character levels, character stats, inventories, quests, hit points, modifiers, turns, and much more. Some modern video game RPGs are played in real time, but many games such as *Baldur's Gate* or *Star Wars: Knights of the Old Republic* still hold on to some of their pen and paper roots by having parts of the game take place in turns.

Pen and paper RPGs have also introduced us to social gaming and adventuring at a level yet to be reproduced by electronic games. Massively multiplayer online role-playing games (MMORPGs) such as *World of Warcraft* have attempted to capture the social gaming aspect of traditional RPGs by allowing players to not just play together but actually adventure together. When designing an RPG, consider using traditional pen and paper techniques to prototype the RPG mechanics. It is possible to mock up many of your gameplay mechanics and see how they work on paper before you spend time implementing them in the game.

Courtesy of Chris Brooks

Dungeons & Dragons being played at GenCon, a conference based in Indianapolis that focuses on tabletop games.

Console Gameplay Evolution

You can still learn a lot from traditional non-electronic games, which have dramatically affected the evolution of our industry. Let's take a brief journey through the last six generations of gameplay mechanics associated with video games. We will see how they have evolved to meet the changing market and the technological innovations we are developing for today.

There are many ways to measure the success of video games over the years. First and foremost, this is a business; to be successful, a game needs to be profitable. Most games never turn a profit. For inspiration, it is easy to look at what the gaming press hails as the greatest games of all time, but it is usually better to look at games that are profitable and try to understand what has made them financially successful.

A game designer's job is not always to look at the budget and care about it, but rather to come up with great ideas. However, it is important to understand how gameplay mechanics come together to make high-quality AAA games. One of the toughest things for game designers is to find a good balance of game systems that not only will be fun but will work well together. Never start to design a game that contains every gameplay mechanic; only half of the mechanics will actually make it into the game. Getting off on the wrong foot this way could cost you lots of time and money, or even your job. A skillful game designer must understand why certain games have been great over the years, what makes a game great now, and how gameplay mechanics have evolved.

Many games have been great because they were top selling (*Super Mario*), popular with reviewers (*ICO*), revolutionary (*Doom*), award winning (*God of War*), and the basis for movies (*Tomb Raider*). These qualities do not make any game better or worse than another, just different in its own way. Let's take a look at how a few seminal games have changed the way gameplay mechanics have been used throughout the years and brought us to where we are today. There are many other great games, but the sample mentioned here should illustrate how games have become much more involved and complicated over the years as technology has improved. You will also see how game designers have become better at designing games and players have become savvier.

It is hard to classify each generation or era of consoles because there is a tremendous amount of overlap between game systems. For instance, in the 2006 holiday season—even after the Microsoft Xbox 360 had been out for over a year and the Sony PlayStation 3 had just shipped—the Sony PlayStation 2 still managed to ship over one million units in North America alone, proving that many consumers are still driven more by overall console price and the selection of games than just by features alone. Consider this classification a general guide and overview, especially since a lot of games were released on multiple systems at various times. We are focusing on the bigger games that changed the industry in some way and not necessarily on which game first invented a certain mechanic.

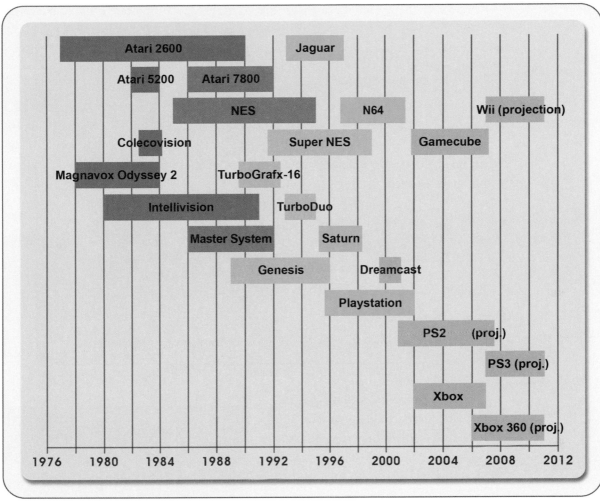

1ˢᵗ & 2ⁿᵈ Generations

Early video game systems were extremely primitive by today's standards but still contained some classic games that will probably stay with us in some form forever. Most first- and second-generation games had just a few gameplay mechanics, relying on a lot of repetition, pattern memorization, and timing skill to play. Most games were either restricted to a single screen (*Pac-Man* and *Donkey Kong*) or scrolling (*Pitfall!* and *Defender*). The Atari 2600 controller consisted of only a single joystick with one button, so games had to be very simple to control. Most action games allowed basic movement and shooting, but not much else. The games were designed to do a single thing and did not tend to utilize a wide variety of different mechanics; they just recombined the mechanics in different ways to make them interesting. Since the games were 2D, however, they were often much easier to control than today's 3D game equivalents.

Diagram by Per Olin

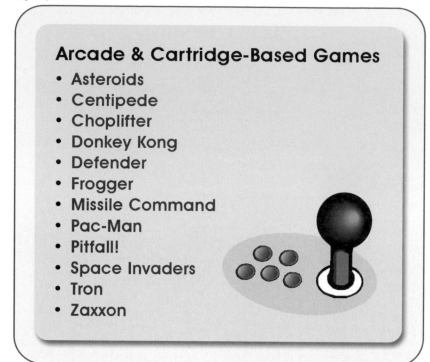

Arcade & Cartridge-Based Games
- Asteroids
- Centipede
- Choplifter
- Donkey Kong
- Defender
- Frogger
- Missile Command
- Pac-Man
- Pitfall!
- Space Invaders
- Tron
- Zaxxon

In *Pitfall!*, players could move side to side, jump, climb up/down a ladder, and swing from a rope. *Pitfall!* contained many hazards such as tar pits, quicksand, rolling logs, rattlesnakes, scorpions, walls, fire, and crocodiles for players to avoid while they tried to collect 32 treasures. It required players to learn how to time their jumps and do some basic problem solving to get past the obstacles.

Activision

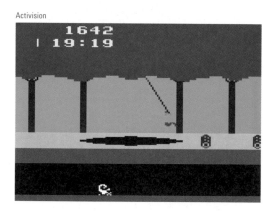

In *Pitfall!*, players could move side to side, jump, climb up/down a ladder, and swing from a rope.

Centipede allowed the player to move side to side, with some up and down movement, on a single screen; the player could also shoot the gun straight up. It was more like a classic arcade game that required quick reflexes and the ability to choose the best target based on strategic thinking. *Centipede*, like many other games, became more difficult by increasing the speed of the enemy attacks and movement. It also added more obstacles and some random attacks by other enemies to keep players on their toes.

Defender was one of the most successful early flying games, allowing the player to fly left and right along a side-scrolling world that eventually wrapped around on itself. The world featured hazardous mountains and cities of different sizes at the bottom (and the top in some versions) and six different kinds of aliens. Players could shoot normal weapons, use smart bombs, or teleport to a random location while protecting the humans on the ground from the alien enemies and progressing in the game. The enemies tried to either capture the humans, lay mines, attack players, or home in and kill players who took too long. The gameplay mechanics could combine these features into a number of variations, but it was still fairly simple in comparison to today's shooters.

Courtesy of Atari Interactive, Inc.

Courtesy of Midway Games, Inc.

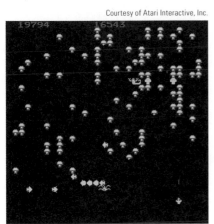

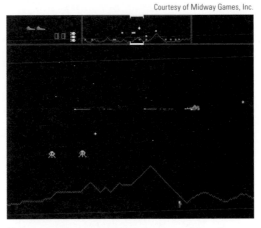

Centipede allowed players to move side to side, with some up and down movement, on a single screen and to shoot a gun straight up.

Defender was one of the most successful early flying games, allowing the player to fly left and right along a side-scrolling world that eventually wrapped around on itself.

The hundreds of games released during the first two console generations provided the foundations for many different game genres. Some of today's popular genres such as the first-person shooter (FPS), RTS, and sandbox had yet to be invented. The first few generations of games gave us a taste of different gameplay mechanics, but few games had more than a few solid mechanics available at any one time.

3ʳᵈ Generation (8-bit)

The third generation of game systems added tremendous power to what was previously available, allowing game designers to begin to spread their wings. Also, game designers were starting to learn from the first generation of games what players really liked. The Nintendo Entertainment System (NES), which dominated this era, saw the development of much more elaborate games than those found in the previous generation. No game, even if it came bundled with the system, has yet sold as many copies as *Super Mario Bros.* on the NES. Even *Super Mario 3,* which was not bundled with the system, is still the best-selling nonbundled game of all time with over 18 million copies sold. Another factor that contributed to the quality of the NES games was that for the first time a system had more than one button, as well as a D-pad instead of a stick, allowing designers to make games that were much more responsive and reactive to the player's actions.

Diagram by Per Olin

8-Bit Games

- Advanced Dungeon and Dragons
- Battletoads
- Bionic Commando
- Castlevania
- Contra
- Double Dragon
- Dragon Warrior
- Gauntlet
- Indiana Jones
- Joust
- Kung Fu
- Legend of Zelda
- Lemmings
- Mega Man
- Metroid
- Ninja Gaiden
- Pirates!
- Prince of Persia
- Spy Hunter
- Super Mario Bros
- Tetris

Super Mario Bros. was the first game to feature smooth scrolling levels, which made it a landmark in the video game industry. It is the game that basically defined what the platformer game genre was all about. The game introduced a wide variety of gameplay mechanics and began to allow players to combine them in interesting ways. Players had to think about how to kill enemies rather than just pushing a button and shooting a gun. Players could jump on some enemies to kill them or jump on shelled enemies to knock them on their backs, turning them into projectiles to hit other enemies. The game also allowed players to turn into giant fiery versions, which gave them special abilities. While the mechanics were fairly simple, they were used by players in a wide variety of entertaining ways. The game had 24 levels, which made the gameplay always feel fresh and interesting. *Super Mario Bros.* introduced bosses, secrets, coin collection, power-ups, and some other interesting mechanics. It remains one of the most pioneering and influential video game titles.

Double Dragon, released in 1987, was not the first beat-em-up game but it was probably the best known of its time and the first to introduce two-player co-op gameplay. It also was the first game that allowed players to take weapons from enemies and use them as their own. The game featured a system for buying new moves and upgrades, first seen in the game *Forgotten Worlds* a short time earlier but utilized very effectively in *Double Dragon.* The success of this game made the beat-em-up game genre popular for years to come.

Nintendo

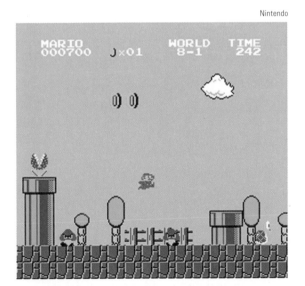

Super Mario Bros. was the first game to feature smooth scrolling levels, which made it a landmark in the video game industry.

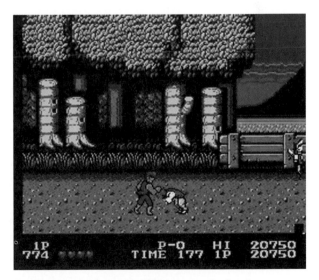

Double Dragon, released in 1987, was not the first beat-em-up game but it was probably the best-known of its time and the first to introduce two-player co-op gameplay.

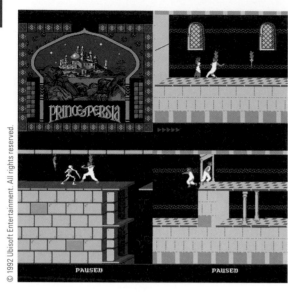

Prince of Persia, released in 1989, evolved platform gameplay mechanics significantly.

Prince of Persia, released in 1989, evolved platform gameplay mechanics significantly. The game captured the imagination of players with incredible animations and lifelike acrobatics. The game combined great swordplay combat, level design, and an immersive storyline. *Prince of Persia* made heavy use of time limits to keep the players moving and on their toes. It was also the first game to use a segmented health bar (called the power bar). Players would lose a segment of power by falling, getting hit by an enemy sword, or being hit by falling platforms. They could lose even more health by taking higher falls or falling on spikes—which would kill them instantly. Players could "refill" their power bars by drinking potions, and they could also increase the total size of their health bars by finding special large red potions. This new health system allowed the game to keep moving and did not require the player to be "perfect" all of the time—compared with some previous games, in which the player would die with each mistake. *Prince of Persia* advanced the platformer movement seen in previous games, allowing players to do more than just jump up and over smaller obstacles; it also gave them many more levels to jump to and ways they could move throughout the game.

All of the third-generation games made it possible to move more smoothly into the next generation of games and take even better advantage of the new systems. However, it took a long time to phase out the third-generation platforms, which remained popular.

4ᵗʰ Generation (16-bit)

The video game hardware once again improved during the 16-bit era. Games were still primarily two-dimensional and there was some graphics improvement from the Nintendo Entertainment System (NES) to Super Nintendo Entertainment System (SNES) eras—but it was the increased storage capacities of the new machines, improved controllers with more buttons, and even more savvy game developers that allowed games to be more complex than ever before. While the NES had sold around 60 million units and opened up the video game market significantly, the SNES sold only around 20 million units in the United States and 49 million worldwide, with increased pressure from Sega, which sold 29 million units of the Genesis. This fractured the market a bit, since for the first time there were two major players. Many publishers were forced to put out games on several systems now, which meant that game technology decisions were affecting the designs of some games.

Diagram by Per Olin

16-Bit Games

- Altered Beast
- Batman
- Chrono Trigger
- Donkey Kong Country
- Earthworm Jim
- F-Zero
- Final Fantasy
- Final Fight
- Herzog Zwei
- Indiana Jones
- Golden Axe
- Jungle Strike
- Lemmings
- Madden
- Mortal Kombat
- The Secret of Mana
- Shining Force II
- Sonic the Hedgehog
- Smash TV
- Super Mario World
- Super Metroid
- Super Star Wars Trilogy

Since many developers had a good understanding of how to build game engines and better tools—and many had engines from the NES era that could be easily tweaked to run on the SNES—developing for the SNES and Genesis became a little easier. There could be more games that utilized several different game engines. In the past, most games had run on a single engine that allowed them to draw only a single type of graphics (such as top-down or side-scrolling). With a 2D game engine, you can't simply move the camera around, as you can in 3D, to change the game. Many developers now had the ability to utilize several different game engines (or modes) in their games, which allowed players to experience a much wider variety of gameplay. The best example of this is the *Super Star Wars* franchise, which let the player run around in a side-scrolling action combat game, drive a landspeeder in a pseudo 3D engine, fly an X-wing through space, and much more. This era did not see a staggering amount of gameplay innovation, but some solid games emerged and pushed the boundaries of gaming excellence.

Nintendo

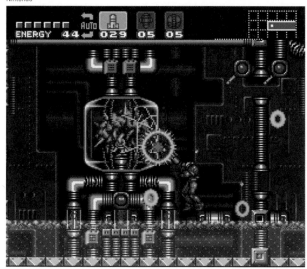

Super Metroid, released for the SNES in 1994, was a successful 2D action adventure platformer.

Super Metroid, released for the SNES in 1994, was a successful 2D action-adventure platformer. It provided the player with a very large, open-ended world that contained a nonlinear level design progression. This allowed the game to be played in almost any order. The game also had several hidden areas, making exploration a significant feature. The main gameplay revolved around players gathering power-ups in order to improve their characters, which allowed them to find and defeat the final boss. The game evolved some of the genre's weapon mechanics; players could use their weapons not only against enemies but to affect the environment as well. Players were able to use weapons to solve puzzles; since they could freeze enemies, for example, they could jump on them, using a wave beam to hit enemies through walls and activate switches from afar. *Super Metroid* also let players morph into "ball" mode and roll around to access a different set of abilities.

Sega's mascot for the Genesis was Sonic The Hedgehog, who appeared in his first game in 1991 and soon became the most recognized mascot in the video game universe. Sonic introduced the world to the adrenalin rush of games because the sheer speed of the gameplay had never been seen before. At its heart, *Sonic The Hedgehog* was a platformer, but it added new mechanics that made it stand out from the rest, such as loops, springboards, high-speed accelerators, and rings to collect. Sonic The Hedgehog's method of attack was also novel in the sense that he could curl into a ball and then smash into enemies either by rolling along the ground or by flying through the air. This had evolved beyond most games that involved shooting a weapon or attacking and jumping on enemies to kill them. *Sonic The Hedgehog*'s level design encouraged players to move quickly through levels. In addition it introduced the use of physics in games; players could build up speed going downhill, slow down going uphill, and experience drag through water. *Sonic The Hedgehog* allowed for underwater movement, but Sonic The Hedgehog could hold his breath for only a limited amount of time before he would die. The game's ring system was an innovative combination of health, lives, and scoring systems. If players were hit while not carrying rings, they would lose lives; being hit *while* carrying rings meant that all of them would be ejected. Collecting 100 rings gained players extra lives; in the end, this provided more points for a higher score.

Sonic The Hedgehog was a platformer, but it added new mechanics that made it stand out from the rest, such as loops, springboards, high-speed accelerators, and rings to collect.

Another game from this era that truly changed gameplay mechanics was *Final Fantasy IV* (*FFIV*), released in 1991. *FFIV* introduced several mechanics to the RPG genre, many of which are still used today; it is considered not only one of the best *Final Fantasy* games but one of the best games of all time. The game's "active time battle" system became the default system for most RPGs, and it also allowed players to battle with a large number of characters. The game had several different maps and screens on which the player would navigate and interact, including a world map, field map, and battle screen. During combat, the player had the option to fight, use magic or an item, retreat, change character positions, parry, or pause. The game offered a huge number of magic spells, along with the ability to summon monsters for assistance in battle. Players could also configure a team tactically, deciding who was in the front or rear of the group. All of these new gameplay mechanics—along with a solid storyline, great music, and polished look—made *FFIV* a leader in the RPG genre for many years.

While the 2D era for consoles was closing, this did not mark the end of 2D games. Even today, 2D games still occasionally occur on 3D generation consoles, and 2D games still dominate the Nintendo Gameboy and DS handheld markets, as well as current generation hardware for cell phones. It is difficult to say whether all handheld and cell devices will go to full 3D in their next generations. The PSP, the next-gen 3D handheld from Sony, has done poorly compared to the DS—showing that prettier graphics, especially with handheld devices, are not always needed.

5th Generation (32-bit)

As players woke up to the world of 3D games, many developers stepped forward hesitantly. The first generation of 3D games still looked fairly primitive; compared with some of the more recent 2D games, they ran slowly and were often much harder to control. However, the PS1 went on to sell over 100 million units and was in production for over 11 years. The Nintendo 64 had some of the most innovative and anticipated games on any console, but it managed to sell only around 33 million units. However, this didn't stop several of its games from becoming some of the all-time top-selling titles on any platform. Sony and Nintendo took the lead for a while, but as rumors of the next-generation systems began to circulate, the early fifth-generation systems such as the Jaguar sold only 150,000 units—and even the 3DO never sold more than 10 million units. As we entered the 3D era, many of the rules of gameplay mechanics had to change. Several factors contributed to the evolution of games during the fifth generation of consoles: the controller, the nature of 3D worlds (including navigation and camera control), and the increasing power of game hardware.

Diagram by Per Olin

32-Bit Games
- Banjo-Kazooie
- Crash Bandicoot
- Donkey Kong 64
- Goldeneye 007
- Kingdom Hearts
- Legend of Zelda: Ocarina of Time
- Legacy of Kain: Sould Reaver
- MDK
- Medal of Honor
- Metal Gear Solid
- Oddworld: Abe's Oddysee
- Panzer Dragoon Saga
- Perfect Dark
- Rayman
- Resident Evil
- Silent Hill
- Spyro the Dragon
- Star Fox 64
- Super Mario 64
- Tekken
- Tomb Raider
- Twisted Metal

The earlier attempts at 3D in games were clumsy and extremely hard to control. *Super Mario 64* came out in 1996 and changed all that, selling over 12 million copies. Nintendo spent a tremendous amount of time perfecting the controls and basic gameplay of *Super Mario 64*, and it showed. The company introduced analog sensitivity to the controls, along with freeform camera control. Players could walk or run based on how far they moved the analog stick. While *Super Mario 64* was not the first 3D platform game, it was so well done that it set the standard for all games to come.

Super Mario 64 introduced one of the most diverse sets of gameplay mechanics that had ever been seen. Game designers finally had the power and know-how to combine mechanics in a variety of exciting moves and abilities. Mario could walk, run, crouch, crawl, swim, climb, somersault, and jump to great heights and distances. Special abilities included the double jump, triple jump, long jump, wall jump, and backflip. The character had a variety of attacks including a punch, jump kick, lunge attack, power stomp, and slide kick, and he could crawl, pick up and carry items, and swim under water. Mario fought bosses, solved puzzles, raced opponents, collected coins and stars, and found keys to unlock doors. He could also collect power-ups, which would let him fly, become immune to damage, and take on an "immaterial" form so that he could walk through things. All of these abilities, combined with a huge open world, fun puzzles, intriguing secrets, interesting enemies, and friendly creatures added up to a revolution in game design on many levels. *Super Mario 64* changed the way future platform games would be created, and many action 3D games of the future would borrow ideas from it.

Nintendo

While *Super Mario 64* was not the first 3D platform game, it was so well done that it set the standard for all games to come.

Super Mario 64 introduced one of the most diverse sets of gameplay mechanics that had ever been seen in a game, giving players a variety of exciting moves and abilities.

Just as the *Mario* series made a spectacular transition from 2D to 3D, so did *The Legend of Zelda* series with the hit *The Ocarina of Time* in 1998; many critics consider it to be the best game ever made, period. *The Legend of Zelda: The Ocarina of Time* is one of the few games to have almost universally perfect review scores, and it has sold over 7.5 million units. *Zelda* had been reinvented on the N64, using many of the same features that made *Super Mario 64* so successful, but it then improved on them considerably and managed to reinvent the series. The controls, interface, level design, story, and gameplay mechanics worked smoothly together to form a highly polished experience. The game offered the player a tremendous number of weapons, items, potions, and much more. *Zelda* also utilized a mini-map to help the player navigate the confusing 3D world.

Many critics consider *The Legend of Zelda: Ocarina of Time* to be the best game ever made.

Metal Gear Solid (*MGS*), also released in 1998 to critical acclaim, sold more than six million copies. The game pioneered the "stealth action" sub-genre—taking the action genre to new heights, thanks to stellar graphics and gameplay innovations. One of the most cinematic games ever to be released, *MGS* showed players and developers that it was possible to fuse fun gameplay with a strong story and movie-like cinematography that had previously been impossible to accomplish. *MGS* introduced an innovative detection system that included both visual and audio elements. The player had to utilize stealth tactics and think twice about using a gun, even if it was silenced. If the player was detected visually or audibly by the enemy, alarms would be triggered—alerting more troops. This would force the player to hide until the alarm level was decreased. These systems could be used to the player's advantage with innovative gameplay devices (e.g., distracting enemies by making noises, hiding under a cardboard box and moving around inside it to avoid detection). The game also offered players a wide variety of gadgets to assist them, such as thermal goggles, C-4 explosives, rations—and even cigarettes, which could be used to detect traps with the smoke. *MGS* showed us that it was possible to do more with a game than just "run and gun."

6th Generation

With the sixth generation of games, it was less critical to come up with the next killer gameplay mechanic than to integrate the mechanics smoothly into the game experience. Many games also focused on creating a more stylistic, thematic, or cinematic experience into which the gameplay mechanics could fit. Some games still tried to create one new killer mechanic, such as *Black* with its destructible environments, but the games that prospered most were those that integrated many mechanics into a unique and highly polished game experience that captivated players.

Games such as *God of War* on the PS2 showed that tried and true gameplay mechanics combined in a very tight and properly executed manner may be just as successful as something new or different. *God of War* incorporates a highly addictive combat system with many moves, combinations, and mini-games to keep the player interested—as well as power-ups, puzzles, platformers, and bosses, all wrapped up in a satisfying package.

Diagram by Per Olin

64 & 128-Bit Games
- Beyond Good and Evil
- Black
- Crazy Taxi
- Fable
- Halo
- ICO
- Jak and Daxter
- Legend of Zelda: Windwaker
- Gran Turismo 3
- God of War
- Grand Theft Auto III
- Oddworld: Munch's Oddysee
- Mercenaries
- Okami
- Prince of Persia: Sands of Time
- Ratchet and Clank
- Resident Evil IV
- Shadow of the Colossus
- Shenmue
- Super Mario Sunshine
- Splinter Cell

Halo showed players that the most important aspect of a game is a highly polished set of basic features. Although none of its features were new, *Halo* was extremely well executed; it proved to many fans who had not played *Goldeneye* on the N64 that a console first-person shooter (FPS) could be successfully adapted to a current controller and could be fun as well as highly aesthetic.

Sony Computer Entertainment America

God of War incorporates a highly addictive combat system with many moves, combinations, and mini-games to keep the player interested.

Reprinted with permission from Microsoft Corporation

Halo showed players that the most important aspect of a game is a highly polished set of basic features.

Each genre is characterized by certain elements. The survival horror genre, dominated by the *Resident Evil* series, finally made a significant change with *Resident Evil 4* (*RE4*). Keeping everything that was good about the genre, *RE4* fixed all of the annoying features, such as bad cameras and difficult progression, that had plagued the genre for years. *RE4* also successfully transferred many new gameplay mechanics from other genres to survival horror games, reinventing the genre and opening it up to a whole new world of players. *RE4* showed how to thoroughly scare players without resorting to the cheap thrill techniques of the past and added a tremendous amount of adventure to the genre.

The *Grand Theft Auto* (*GTA*) series has become one of the best-selling franchises of all time. Although previous games, such as those in the *Mario Bros.* franchise, featured large open-ended worlds, no game had shown as much realism and style as *GTA*. Games in the *GTA* series became part of a new gameplay style known as "sandbox" in which players are put into a large open-ended world where they can do almost anything. This was a huge step forward in the evolution of gameplay mechanics design. While other games had been slowly evolving new gameplay mechanics with each new generation, *GTA* was busy revolutionizing gameplay mechanics.

© Courtesy of Capcom. Reprinted with permission. Courtesy of Rockstar Games and Take-Two Interactive Software, Inc.

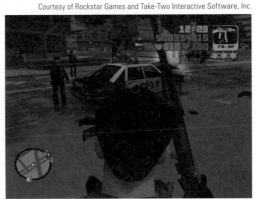

The survival horror genre made a significant change with *Resident Evil 4*.

With its innovative gameplay design, the *Grand Theft Auto* series (*GTA III,* shown) has become one of the best-selling game franchises of all time.

Other games offered player choice in various degrees, but *GTA* was the first to feel truly free and open. It also did an amazing job of providing choices that *made sense* within the context of the game's environment—such as stealing cars, fighting, blowing things up, and evading the police. Many players of *GTA* just "play around" for a very long time, occasionally going on missions or completing story-related tasks, always in a world that reacts to the player's "good" or "bad" choices. *GTA* showed the importance of having not just cool mechanics but *many different mechanics* that interact with the game in diverse but mutually beneficial ways—giving birth to the idea of *emergent gameplay mechanics*, a new form of compelling game design (introduced earlier in this chapter and discussed in more detail in Chapter 5).

Mature content also became more prevalent during this era. Many games included over-the-top violence, torture, drugs, gangs, sex, nudity (or close to it), and graphic language. These aspects are evident not just in the stories and cut-scenes but also in the gameplay mechanics. It seemed that game designers were looking for new ways to shock players by, for example, letting players kill other characters in a horrific and ultraviolent manner or have sex with prostitutes. Even many of the top games such as *GTA* took this controversial content to the limit. (Some might argue that this led to their overall success, as sales seemed to increase each time games like *GTA* were banned in countries such as Australia!)

7th Generation

It is a little too early to talk about the history of the seventh generation of consoles and associated titles. So far, the industry has seen a major split; the Nintendo Wii is changing the way games are controlled and forcing game designers to reinvent the way games are played at many levels, while the Xbox 360 and PS3 offer better graphics but little to no obvious gameplay mechanic enhancements out of the box. Some incredibly immersive games such as *Elder Scrolls IV: Oblivion* and *Gears of War* were released to huge fanfare, while other games such as *Tom Clancy's Rainbow Six: Vegas* have innovated in only a few areas but have been seen as groundbreaking for the same reasons that *God of War* and *Halo* were successful.

Tom Clancy's Rainbow Six: Vegas has innovated in just a few areas, but it is considered groundbreaking for its polish of several core gameplay features.

The increase in power associated with this generation means it will probably mimic the transition from the NES to SNES. There will be better looking games with marginal improvements in some gameplay mechanics, along with a smattering of extremely innovative titles that may or may not be top sellers or well-received by the public. However, this generation is still in the early part of its life cycle; there is still time to reach a tipping point that will force game executives to realize the value of making a game fun and innovative without focusing so heavily on visuals.

Diagram by Per Olin

Next-Gen & HD Games

- Assassin's Creed
- Dead Rising
- The Elder Scrolls IV: Oblivion
- Gears of War
- Lair
- Rainbow Six Vegas
- Wii Sports

Top-Selling Games

The following is a list of the 20 best-selling video games as of 2006 that were originally not bundled with a console. Notice that a very high percentage of these games are major franchises.

1. *Super Mario Bros. 3* (NES - 18 million)
2. *Super Mario Land* (Game Boy - 14 million)
3. *Grand Theft Auto: Vice City* (PS2 - 13 million)
4. *Grand Theft Auto: San Andreas* (PS2 - 12 million)
5. *Super Super Mario 64* (N64 - 11 million)
6. *Gran Turismo 3: A-Spec* (PS2 - 11 million)
7. *Grand Theft Auto III* (PS2 - 11 million)
8. *Gran Turismo* (PS1 - 10.5 million)
9. *Super Mario Bros. 2* (NES - 10 million)
10. *Gran Turismo 2* (PS1 - 9.34 million)
11. *Final Fantasy VII* (PS1 - 8.6 million)
12. *Brain Age: Train Your Brain in Minutes a Day* (DS - 8.51 million)
13. *Donkey Kong Country* (SNES - 8.30 million)
14. *GoldenEye 007* (N64 - 8 million)
15. *Super Mario Kart* (SNES - 8 million)
16. *Halo 2* (Xbox - 8 million)
17. *Tomb Raider II* (PS1 - 8 million)
18. *The Legend of Zelda: Ocarina of Time* (N64 - 7.6 million)
19. *Metal Gear Solid 2: Sons of Liberty* (PS2 - 7 million)
20. *New Super Mario Bros.* (6.76 million)

Source: NPD

Computer Gameplay Evolution

We cannot overlook the computer as a game platform. Many game genres developed on the PC because of its power, complex controls, mass storage, and advanced features that had never been possible on a console. Computer games evolved like their console game counterparts—from text adventures such as *Zork* to the graphically rich world of *Crysis*, which is too intensive for even the latest generation of consoles to play smoothly.

Diagram by Per Olin

Computer Games
- Age of Empires II: The Age of Kings
- Baldur's Gate II: Shadows of Amn
- Command & Conquer: Red Alert
- Deus Ex
- Doom
- Dune II: The Building of a Dynasty
- Fallout
- Grim Fandango
- Half-Life 2
- Master of Orion
- MechWarrior 2: 31st Century Combat
- Sid Meier's Civilization II
- Sid Meier's Pirates!
- SimCity 2000
- StarCraft
- Star Wars: TIE Fighter
- Star Control 2
- Syndicate
- System Shock 2
- Ultima VII: The Black Gate
- X-COM: UFO Defense
- Wing Commander II: Vengeance of the Kilrathi

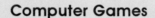

There are still many types of games that are popular only on the PC, such as massively multiplayer online role-playing games (MMORPGs; *World of Warcraft*), real-time strategy games (RTSs; *Age of Empires*), and simulation games (including flight simulators and process sims such as the *SimCity* franchise). Occasionally, these types of games will be ported over to a console, but they are rarely as good as their computer counterparts. Most of the top console RPGs come from Japan and were influenced by games such as *Final Fantasy*, whereas most PC RPGs are closer to American sensibilities and were modeled after *Ultima* and other U.S.-based RPGs.

The first-person shooter (FPS) began on the PC, and many computer gamers will swear a blood oath that playing an FPS on a PC is the only way to go. While the controls on the PC are superior, developers of console FPSs have added mechanics that have improved these games. Sales numbers of games such as *Goldeneye, Halo,* and *Call of Duty* ultimately suggest that the console FPS is the better, or at least the more popular, platform. This preference probably derives to some degree from the ease with which players can access Xbox Live to play online multiplayer games.

Electronic Arts, Inc.   Courtesy of Blizzard Entertainment, Inc.

The graphically rich world of *Crysis* is sometimes too intensive for consoles to play smoothly.

Massively multiplayer online role-playing games such as *World of Warcraft* are popular only on the PC.

We will continue to look to computer game developers for many graphical and gameplay innovations for many years to come. The computer is a much more open development platform, especially with the advent of Microsoft's XNA, and more indie game developers will continue to create new and experimental games on the PC in the hope of making names for themselves. The PC market also will continue to expand with contributions from the modding community and others who want to make their own game expansions or modules using game level editors shipped with most PC games.

Arcade Gameplay Evolution

Consider the influence that the arcade games had on video games. (Yes, there used to be places where we could play really cool games with our friends by putting quarters into machines!) Eventually, most arcade games were ported over to various consoles or computers, but they still influence the way that many games are developed.

Diagram by Per Olin

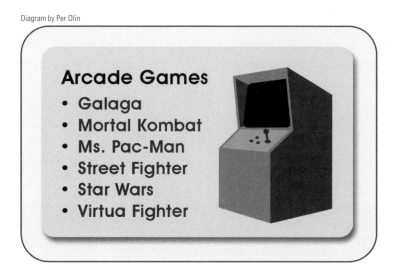

Arcade Games
- **Galaga**
- **Mortal Kombat**
- **Ms. Pac-Man**
- **Street Fighter**
- **Star Wars**
- **Virtua Fighter**

Arcade games, unlike console games, were designed to be played for a relatively short period and to be easily accessible but hard to master. Many arcade games were designed to keep players pumping quarters into them; this kept many from being particularly cohesive and caused their difficulty to ramp up significantly over time.

Courtesy of NAMCO BANDAI Games America Inc.

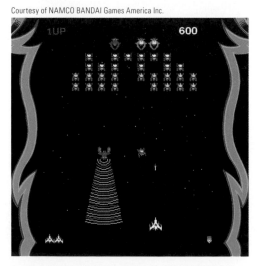

Arcade games such as *Galaga* were designed to be accessible yet difficult to master.

::::: The Evolution of *Zelda*

By looking at how the *Legend of Zelda* franchise has evolved visually over the years, you can see that the associated gameplay mechanics have changed drastically as well. What can you deduce from the images below? Note the differences in platforms as well as the times of release: *The Legend of Zelda*, *Zelda II: The Adventure of Link* (NES), *The Legend of Zelda: A Link to the Past* (GBA), *The Legend of Zelda: Majora's Mask* (N64), *The Legend of Zelda: The Wind Waker* (GameCube), and *The Legend of Zelda: Twilight Princess* (Wii).

Nintendo

Nintendo

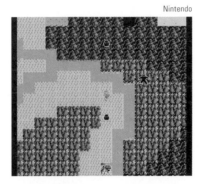

The Legend of Zelda (NES)

Zelda II: The Adventure of Link

Nintendo

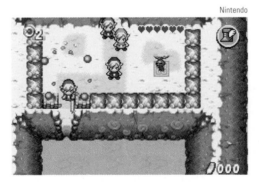

Nintendo

The Legend of Zelda: A Link to the Past (GBA)

The Legend of Zelda: Majora's Mask (N64)

Nintendo

Nintendo

The Legend of Zelda: The Wind Waker (Gamecube)

The Legend of Zelda: Twilight Princess (Wii)

It is fun to see how game graphics have evolved over the years. While this chapter is about changes in gameplay mechanics, it is important to realize that the power of the machines along with their graphics has led to the majority of the improvements and innovations in gameplay. Now that you have a background in the basics and the evolution of gameplay mechanics, let's take a look at the game design process.

:::CHAPTER REVIEW:::

1. Choose a game franchise such as *The Legend of Zelda* or *Final Fantasy* and trace the evolution of gameplay mechanics from the first to the most recent game in the series. How have the mechanics evolved over time?

2. Compare a few games discussed in this chapter that were created for different platforms (e.g., console, PC/computer, arcade, tabletop [board/card]). Discuss how their gameplay mechanics differ based on the limitations or features associated with the platform.

3. How can you make a game fun? Although creating fun is the overarching theme of this book, take a stab at it now. Choose a game that you feel is *not* particularly fun and discuss at least three ways you might change it in order to make it fun.

CHAPTER

Creating the Process

the game's design path

Key Chapter Questions

- Why it is important to establish a *vision* for the game early on?
- Why is it necessary to have a game design *process*?
- What are the four main areas of emphasis that *drive* game design?
- What types of *restrictions* might you face when designing a game?
- What are the components of a *project overview*?

When you design a game, it can be dangerous to jump right in and get started without laying the groundwork. While having great ideas is critical at the beginning, being able to properly execute the idea and make it fun is a lot more difficult. You can get away with being more loose and freeform if your development team is small, but a bigger project with more people makes it increasingly necessary to think about *how* you are designing the game and not just about *what* you are designing. It's critical to establish a development process early.

Getting Started with a Design

Every new game begins with a different set of needs, restrictions, goals, and requirements. Knowing where and how to properly begin a new game design can be very difficult. The game may be an original or a sequel, or it may be based on a license. Sometimes you have to take over a game that has been designed poorly. The game's genre will dictate the design, and each individual involved in the project might have a different opinion about the design direction. Even the tools and technology that will be used or developed will affect the way the design is approached.

Your game does not have to be as complex as *Gears of War* to require an established game design process.

Having an established game design process is an important part of being a good designer. It's rare to just sit down, get inspired, and turn an idea into a full-fledged game design. Although it has been argued that you can design a game any way you choose and be successful, the development of a distinct process is essential and will even prevent failure in most cases. This advice is especially true if you are trying to build a top-tier game. However, but it will help even a hobbyist to make a better game.

No matter what role you are playing in the design of a game, it is critical that you understand every design skill set. Many game designers have worked their way up from level designer to lead designer. Even if you are no longer building levels or working hands-on with the assembly of the game, you still must understand how the game is put together and how certain tools are used to create the game.

If you carefully analyze a game, you will see that many different systems, or mechanics, need to be designed; these include characters, quests, story, cut-scenes, environments, levels, and interfaces. Different team members will be responsible for preserving the game's vision. The only way to ensure that these systems remain cohesive is by preparing a game design document (GDD) to which the team can refer. The GDD details all of the proposed gameplay systems: How is the player going to move? What weapons and abilities does the player have? How does the player interact with the environment? How can enemies attack the player? How does the player take damage or heal? These and many other questions need to be addressed.

Every aspect of the game should be designed *before* another team works on it. For instance, in designing a game character it can be more beneficial to design the functionality of the character—a set of traits, abilities, and gameplay needs—before an artist draws up a concept.

The Enigmatic Gameplay Designer

The gameplay designer can sometimes be an "enigma" on the game design team because gameplay design is a specialization that is sometimes a mystery to the other members of the development team. Large (and sometimes small) teams tend to have dedicated gameplay designers whose job is to create gameplay systems that will be used by the player throughout the game. This role is sometimes filled by the lead designer or creative director, or by any of a wide assortment of other people. Even level designers and character designers may spend time designing the gameplay systems.

Designing games is about making compromises. It is rare to end up with a "perfect" game design—and the final game mechanics often differ greatly from those presented in the initial game design document. The team encounters problems that must be solved by making some sort of compromise. These problems may relate to technology, development, production, or simply an idea that was not fun and can result in severely changing a feature or cutting it altogether.

The original design for *Munch's Oddysee* called for the main character, Munch, to have the ability to transform into a giant raging monster like the Incredible Hulk, but this feature could not be added in time to finish the game on schedule. In making the first 3D

Reprinted with permission from Microsoft Corporation

An ability was cut from the title character in *Munch's Oddysee* in order to complete the project on time.

real-time strategy (RTS) game—*Armor Command*—for the PC, the technical problem of using a mouse in a 3D world as well as on a 2D interface heads-up display (HUD) was never solved; players could not click on the onscreen icons and had to use the keyboard to control the game's HUD, which made it very hard to use. In *Ratchet: Deadlocked,* the third-person camera and controls were removed in favor of the new lock-strafe controls that the team liked; however, the fans still wanted the third-person controls used in the previous games, so the team had to start over and reprogram the camera and controls.

The characters for *Tom Clancy's Rainbow Six: Vegas* were originally designed to be more undercover rather than hard-core military. They had to be redesigned once the reviews of *Tom Clancy's Rainbow Six: Lockdown* came out, revealing that playing as a special ops soldier was critical to fans.

Characters in *Tom Clancy's Rainbow Six: Vegas* were redesigned because fans preferred playing as a special ops soldier.

It is important to know the limitations of your tools, technology, and current abilities. Many poor decisions have been made because a designer was determined to do things a certain way. With more flexibility and compromise, the idea could have been implemented much faster and better. With every idea you turn into a feature, evaluate whether some small changes might make it much easier for the team to implement. The rest of the team also need to know that they are free to comment on the design and should not blindly implement it without thinking about the consequences.

K.I.S.S.

It may seem obvious, but the old adage "Keep It Simple, Stupid" really applies to game design. Keep asking yourself whether the design is too complicated. This goes hand in hand with your ability to compromise. As a designer, it is very easy to fall in love with your ideas and be unwilling to change them or to acknowledge the criticisms of others. Since we play the game a lot, and know its tricks and secrets, we become masters of our game and can't understand how difficult the game is to play. This means that weird idiosyncrasies and irregularities with controls, interfaces, and puzzles become impossible for the team to test objectively. However, you can continue to refine and reduce the complexity of the game mechanics as much as possible throughout the project, and you can watch how new players react to the game when they first play it. Learning how to keep the game simple contributes to understanding what is important in the game's design.

One of the toughest parts of being a game designer is trying to balance creativity with reality. On one hand, you need to be free to explore new ideas and try new things. On the other hand, you have a producer telling you "it has to be done by Friday." It is extremely hard if not impossible to schedule creativity, let alone innovation. Designers and creative directors want to make a great product and push the boundaries of game design. Unfortunately, this goal usually conflicts with that of someone else (usually the producer) who wants to get the game done within a certain time frame and budget. Although game development times vary widely, and games can take anywhere from 12 to 48+ months to develop, the designer has only a fraction of that. The rest of the team can't safely begin working until the gameplay systems designer, design lead, and creative director tell them what to make. This problem becomes more or less complex depending on several factors revolving around the technology, platforms, and team size required by the project.

Defining the Process

A design process is a series of steps that must be completed to refine an idea for a game and bring it to completion. Whether the game is designed by one person or a group, every feature of the game must be considered, refined, questioned, verified, and solidified before it can be implemented. As a designer, you control the content that goes into a project and determine the mechanics, moves, characters, special effects, levels, and much more. Be realistic about what is going into your game, and make sure from the start that everyone on the team understands what is in the game. Establishing a formal design process allows you to think about all aspects of the design and ensures that you cover all your bases up front.

© 2006 Bethesda Softworks LLC

The Elder Scrolls IV: Oblivion contains many different characters that use a wide variety of weapons, armor, spells, and other equipment. Gameplay systems needed to be carefully designed for flexibility.

You can have great art, technology, and design, but unless you have unlimited funds, a proper schedule is the most important part of any project. Since games are often one-of-a-kind propositions full of unproven content and technical hurdles, they are notoriously difficult to schedule; this is one reason so many games are extremely late. Having a design process provides a reality check for your schedule and game design. With a good understanding of the process, you are better able to gauge your own responsibilities and help the project's producer schedule the rest of the game realistically.

Failing to design key aspects of the game could cause major problems late in the development cycle. Therefore, a formalized game design process may be a huge advantage if you understand how to properly utilize it. With a little experimentation, you'll determine the process that works best for you and the game you are designing. Always set the bar high, and break down the process in as much detail as possible so that you have clear goals. Some might say that this approach is excessive, but if it gets you to think about the game development process and what really needs to go into it, then you have succeeded.

While there is no right or wrong way to design a game, there are many different ways to do it. This is both a blessing and a curse. We have lots of freedom, but finding the right process is very confusing. Many who write books and articles on game design and speak about it at conventions

Have two designers lead different processes. One designer reviews similar games already released and consumer reactions to their gameplay mechanics. The other designer holds blue sky brainstorming sessions for gameplay mechanics. Lead design then sorts them out through additional meetings.

—*Frank T. Gilson*
(Senior Producer, Wizards of the Coast)

have very strong opinions about what works and does not work for them, but they tend to preach it as the only solution. Some designers disagree with the way large publishers and big businesses work, and they will argue and rebel against any process until the bitter end. Some believe that game development has to be a completely organic process that can't be scheduled because the game needs to evolve into its final form. Other designers believe that it's best to have a game designed by a single visionary, while still others believe in design by committee. Whatever process you ultimately decide to use will have a great impact on the game's development. Let's discuss just a few examples of how a game design process might be driven.

Gameplay-Driven Design

A design driven by *gameplay* or a game mechanic is one where a unique or innovative gameplay feature, nor a single new or unique feature, will drive the entire game. Examples of this type of design include a simple game such as *Tetris*—or a more elaborate game such as *Katamari Damacy*, where players roll a ball that increases in size as it collects objects from the environment. This approach to game design usually focuses on making the game fun first, or trying to introduce something that has never been experienced before. Eventually, other mechanics or aspects may be added to the game, but usually the early emphasis is on a few key features.

Courtesy of NAMCO BANDAI Games America Inc.

Casey Maloney & Stephen Millard

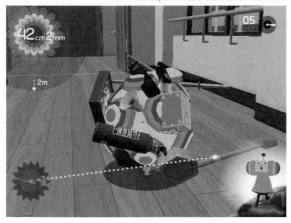

The *Katamari Damacy* series (*We Love Katamari,* shown) has a very innovative gameplay mechanic that has won lots of awards and attention.

Some gameplay-driven games may also evolve to utilize a special piece of custom hardware like the guitar in *Guitar Hero*.

Starting with the Player Experience

I begin by asking myself what kind of player experience I want to create—do I want something boisterous and fast, or should it be contemplative and creative, or perhaps strategic and serious, etc. Then I brainstorm types of activities and mechanics that might bring out that kind of experience. When I have an idea I like, I model it as a paper prototype and get some people to play it. Then I start making changes ... and playtest again, and again. When I think I've got something, I make a digital prototype (or several prototypes) and playtest again. A lot of times, there are prototypes for each of the various mechanics—it is often easier and faster to break things out in this phase.

—Tracy Fullerton
(Assistant Professor, USC School for Cinematic Arts,
Interactive Media Division)

Technology-Driven Design

In *technology*-driven design, a programmer sits down and develops a key feature or set of technologies and then makes a game out of it. *Blood Wake* for the Xbox is an example of a game where some incredible water technology was created; the designers were then driven to figure out how to make a game using impressive water physics.

Reprinted with permission from Microsoft Corporation

Reprinted with permission from Microsoft Corporation

Blood Wake has amazing water technology that makes driving boats a lot of fun.

Dungeon Siege II was created using a technology-driven approach by first developing a "sandbox" containing several technology features.

Another approach to technology-driven design is taken by a game series such as *Dungeon Siege*. The designers of these games had a strong programming background; they first developed what they call the "sandbox" and then thought about what they could make with it. In this case, the developer creates a whole series of features; once the technology is finished, the developer determines exactly what kind of game to make with the technology.

Art-Driven Design

Visual design is the process used by many developers who focus on art but have a tendency to de-emphasize game mechanics. Although the final product contains impressive visual style, some *art*-driven games lack a solid gameplay foundation. One of the biggest problems with art-driven design is that the visuals raise expectations that are often not supported by the underlying technology or gameplay mechanics. In general, it is easy to visualize a game in static storyboards or paintings (or even pre-rendered gameplay visualizations)—but very difficult to actually implement these visual ideas.

Okami is a game that emphasizes its rich and unique visuals.

Oddworld: Munch's Oddysee is driven by the need for a fantastic visual quality.

While art is a critical element in game development, it's important to ensure that it is kept in balance with the rest of the game. It's easy for art alone to take 100% of a system's resources, but don't forget that elements such as artificial intelligence (AI), physics, gameplay, and fun also have a role.

Story-Driven Design

Some game designers are making games to tell stories. A game series such as *Final Fantasy* focuses heavily on the game storyline. *Story*-driven games do have gameplay, but they tend to focus on the game's story at the expense of other elements.

Some adventure games such as *Dreamfall: The Longest Journey* are primarily interactive stories that place players deep into a story and immerse them in it. A story-driven game's script is usually worked on extensively near the beginning; the designers then figure out how to make it more interactive by adding gameplay.

> I generally take a simulationist approach—that is, either looking for mechanics that represent the subject material, or in some cases, striving for mechanics that replicate the feeling of the experience we're trying to impart (e.g., 'a game featuring outrageous cinematic stunts').
>
> —Greg Costikyan
> (Chief Executive Officer, Manifesto Games)

Funcom

Dreamfall: The Longest Journey puts the player in a carefully crafted interactive story.

Implementing a Design Process

You might start your design process with an idea such as "the game should have four-player split-screen multiplayer." Although you might be fairly sure that this is something you want to do, you must also figure out all the details. Discuss the idea with the other designers to get their comments and approval; you should also check with the programmers and the art department.

For more complicated or risky ideas, you might also need sign-off from marketing, testing/QA (quality assurance), and management. Each of these sign-offs is a necessary step in the design process. A designer can drive the vision of the game but cannot control it; other factors need to be taken into account before your idea can become a reality.

The design process can also help you identify several primary needs in your game production. A process should help you keep track of all of your ideas. It can also help account for all of the features in the game so that you don't forget any key features. The design process is closely tied to the schedule, which is an important constraint.

Making games is a team effort, and a design process can help your team work together more effectively. The design process helps to ensure that nobody on the team is implementing ideas without your consent. In addition to the project design process, each department should have its own development process (or pipeline) for features each are responsible for implementing. This helps keep proper communication channels open between team members and helps you adhere to your schedule.

It can be helpful to create a spreadsheet that lists every feature in the game in rows, with columns listing the steps of the design process. Creating a detailed design process spreadsheet serves several important functions:

1. The spreadsheet lists every important design feature, which helps ensure that no area is forgotten.
2. Continual updating makes it possible to track the progress of every design feature in the game and the progress of the game against its ship date.
3. The spreadsheet helps team members who must sign off on a particular feature locate the game in the design process.
4. The design process spreadsheet marks the beginning of a schedule, which is really the most important part of the project.

Feature	Priority	Date Due	Sign-Off: Concept	Design	Art	Programming	Producer	Marketing	Final Approval
Interface Design									
detail a									
detail b									
etc.									
Level Design									
detail a									
detail b									
etc.									
Units									
detail a									
detail b									
etc.									
Weapons									
detail a									
detail b									
etc.									
And So Forth									

Diagram by Per Olin

"Simple Fun Parts"

'Simple fun parts' is my generic term for small little activities, graphics and movements that people like to do or experience. For example, if you had a character that jumped like a pogo stick, a 'simple fun part' would be to have the player bounce the character to specific squares on a grid according to a pattern or even on beat with the music. It's simple and can be fun to do by itself and when the idea comes up, it goes on the list of 'simple fun parts' that can be used in the game. Brainstorming 'simple fun parts' is lots of fun and after doing it, you have a whole collection of elements that in and of themselves are fun to do. With a suitable review, you can then prototype these 'simple fun parts' in the game or even sometimes on paper to make sure they are fun and then to coax out additional fun from each idea. After you've prototyped the pogo jumper, for example, you might find that it's fun for the player to jump to squares that are at a different height or to move the target squares further apart to allow more air time. Whatever happens, prototyping the mechanic is good to do because it offers the opportunity to check your idea and discover even more fun from the 'simple fun part'. Then to build the full game, you simply integrate groups of these simple fun parts into the behavior/ability set of characters—and challenges the character must overcome across each mission, and then across the missions and a game as a whole.

—*Mark Skaggs*
(CEO & Executive Producer, Funstar Ventures, LLC)

Choosing a Design Process

A design process is set in place as a way for you to think about every aspect of the game early on, especially when it is time to set a budget and schedule. Industry professionals often do not work on critical components until late in the project, assuming that they will be easy. More often than not, this causes delays. Never assume that anything is easy.

Creation

A very small team should ideally be able to work by itself for at least six months before anyone else even joins the project. Initially, the designer roughs out the design. Once the basics of the design have been solidified, additional team members should be brought on board to assist with pre-production. By the time the design reaches the end of pre-production, the design should be fully realized and fleshed out so that when the project moves into full production, the team will have a blueprint of the entire game. Of course, some aspects of the game won't be fleshed out yet, but the preproduction phase should answer as many questions as possible. However, this ideal situation does not always occur. Often, you will have to work on projects that are already in full production and that have either no formal design or a weak design that needs to be fixed. The most challenging aspect of creating a formal design documentation procedure is that it needs to constantly change and adapt to every new project. It is impossible to create a set of rigid rules that are equally appropriate for every project.

Know the Risks & Rewards

The first, and most important, job is to determine what the game is. After that I come up with the categories of risk/reward systems I want to meet. Once I know what the game is and what risks and rewards I want to present the player, the mechanics come pretty easily. It's a matter of making every part of the game play speak to what the game is and what we want the player to feel. Then iterate until you get it exactly right.

—*John Comes*
(Lead Game Designer, Gas Powered Games)

Documentation

By formalizing your design process in documentation, you create a blueprint from which others can build the game. To communicate your intentions effectively, your documentation must meet certain standards of completion. The bigger your team, the greater the chance something will go wrong if your design is not thoroughly documented. A short-form design description might contain bullet points covering items such as theme, genre, platform, features, gameplay, and interface.

When you stake your name and reputation on the completeness and quality of document, you're placing a lot on the line. A designer's worst fear is to work on a project for an extended time with a large team and see it cancelled due to poor game design. As the lead designer, the fault would be yours.

A formalized design process will thoroughly document the steps needed to implement the game's features. In some ways, every design is documented—but if you're just writing down what comes to mind without thinking about the process and its implications, you're failing to formalize the document. A successful design process is planned in advance. This requires that you have some prior knowledge of game design and preferably some experience in designing the same kind of game. It also helps if you have a template to work with. A formalized design is finished when you, or any member of your team, can easily and realistically develop a game based on the information.

Working with Restrictions

Some of the toughest challenges in game design include knowing where to start and what restrictions are involved. These restrictions are often not evident until later in the project—but you should try to determine them, along with the questions you will need to answer to safely proceed, as early in development as possible.

Player & Genre Expectations

Most games are compared to similar titles on the market. If you are developing a game in a popular genre, such as a first-person shooter (FPS), you should know what the competition has done, is doing, or will be doing by the time yours is released. You also need to understand probable player expectations and then ensure that your game meets or exceeds them. This doesn't mean that you have to meet every expectation, but see that the total feature set you're delivering is appealing to the buyer. If you have only four weapons, five enemies, and a four-hour-long game in the crowded FPS market, you will most likely be in trouble.

Sequels

Making a sequel can be the easiest thing in the world, or the most difficult. If you are using the same tools, with few innovations and risks, the development of the sequel should be fairly straightforward and the design should be easy to manage. Existing tool sets can, however, lead to complacency and stagnation. If a sequel doesn't live up to the original and show at least small evolutionary advances in features and technology, you can easily alienate a loyal fan base.

::::: The Evolution of *Tom Clancy's Rainbow Six*

Tom Clancy's Rainbow Six: Vegas was a challenge to design; although it was the fifth game in the series, the team had to innovate and reinvent the genre as much as possible. This was no easy task; it was like trying to design a whole new game—especially since it was to be the first next-generation game in the series. Facing requirements to incorporate features that made the franchise great and the fans happy, the team had to constantly evaluate whether it was taking things too far. In this case, it was the best and worst of both worlds.

Intellectual Property Owners

Unless you are lucky enough to be developing an original concept, there is a high probability that someone owns the rights to your game's intellectual property (IP), which could be from a book, movie, television show, comic, game, or any other source. This IP owner will have a say about the content of the game.

Bruce Lee: Quest of the Dragon for the Xbox was originally published by Microsoft, which licensed the Bruce Lee IP from Universal, which, in turn, had licensed the rights from the Bruce Lee Estate. There were multiple levels of approvals to work through at each stage of development. At one point, around 25% of the female enemies had been modeled for the game when someone decided that Bruce should not be fighting women, because he never did in real life. No women enemies could then be used in the game, even though the team had spent a great deal of time and money creating the models and didn't have time to replace them. Eventually Bruce's daughter, Shannon, decided that Bruce would have stayed current and contemporary. She believed that if Bruce were alive at the time of the game's development, he might have agreed to fight women— so she let the team keep the female enemies in the game. Working with a licensor can be incredibly satisfying but also very dangerous and unpredictable.

Electronic Arts, Inc.

The Lord of the Rings: The Battle for Middle-earth II was published by Electronic Arts, but was licensed from New Line Cinema.

Publisher Expectations

Management and marketing executives at a publisher will often expect certain things from your game. A publisher's management style can be either very hands-off or heavy-handed once the company signs off on the initial concept. If you have never worked with them in the past, it is best to make sure you properly communicate the game's vision and major changes to the publisher as they occur, so that no red flags are raised late in the project.

Marketing expectations can take many forms. For example, in analyzing similar titles to make sure your game will be competitive in the marketplace, marketing often plays the numbers game. Marketing executives may believe that consumers want more and more in a game—more guns, enemies, levels—but this is only partially correct. Too often, developers are in the process of designing a single-player game when marketing suggests something like, "Just throw in a multiplayer mode, it shouldn't be too hard. Oh, and make sure it's competitive with *Battlefield 2*."

The marketing team always has good intentions, but it doesn't always understand how difficult some features are to develop. Keep in mind that top marketing executives at many publishers often have enough power to decide the fate of the game's development, so you should always factor in what they have to say.

Electronic Arts, Inc.

A game such as *Command & Conquer 3: Tiberium Wars* requires a tremendous amount of work to develop all of the different gameplay modes.

Developer Expectations

In addition to expectations from the publisher, expectations from your team or the executive management of your development studio can affect the project. Some managers take a very hands-on role in the creative aspects of the game, while others just want to make sure it is delivered on time and within budget. Each will have some impact on the overall design of the game, so it is especially important to get their sign-off early.

Resource Limitations

Most game designs are overly ambitious and require far too many resources (such as people or time) to create. While it is good to be ambitious in order to create a great project, it is also good to know your limitations. If you have only a short time or a small team, you may need to make certain choices; facing both kinds of restrictions will require you to make a completely different set of design choices.

Partial Design

It is very common to be hired, transferred, promoted, or thrown onto a project in which the design may be only partially complete or the vision for a project may have been established by a creative director, designer, publisher, or management team. At Midway, a very short new game concept (which may have been written by anyone at the company) is focus tested for feasibility; then executives decide which projects to work on. At Ubisoft, new game ideas are established by its editorial board in France before design teams may begin. Every publisher has a different way to get its ideas approved before a team can move forward.

The risk is that if the initial design concept is flawed in any way, the development of the game may be very difficult or challenging. This will force the team to spend a lot of time working on features that aren't feasible, fun, or appropriate. This problem may be obvious to the development team, but it may be hard to sell the publisher or management on a design change.

Psychonauts was originally cancelled by publisher Microsoft Game Studios and then picked up by Majesco.

Where to Begin . . .

With all of this confusion, how do you know where to begin and what to do? Unfortunately, there are no easy answers; experience and luck are the only things you can count on. The best advice is to lay out all the different expectations and get approval from all of the parties involved as early as possible before spending time designing elements that may not be viable. This involves working with the creative director to determine the proper vision for the game, incorporating input from the team, and then seeking approval of the design concept from upper management.

You have to find a balance in your game designs; too little or too much may lead to problems. Every game has some level of design documentation, but the question is what level is right for you and the project. As a general rule, you should expect to write a minimum of 100 pages. An epic story may require writing a lot of backstory, character development, and other details to flesh out the narrative. However, if your design document is nearing 500 pages and the game is not yet playable, it is time to re-evaluate your project.

A formalized design process helps you nail down a project's goals. It is not enough to say that you want to create "the best FPS on the market." Your goals need to be measurable, distinct—and you must summarize how you plan to achieve them. A proper game design process will usually start with outlining the high-level goals and features of the game so that you can explain them to others.

If you are not sure about where to begin, think about the game design as a giant jigsaw puzzle. You can put the puzzle together one piece at a time, working on some obvious places in the puzzle where everything makes sense and coming back later to the hard parts. The easiest place to start is with the border of the puzzle, which hopefully has a flat edge and is easy to find. The flat edges in your design are your various restrictions and requirements, and they are a natural starting place.

Can You Overdesign?

There comes a point in every paper design when more planning is not advisable. If you design too much of the game before it is playable, you run the risk of designing features that are not fun and thereby lose the soul of your game. It is very important to strike a balance between documentation and implementation. Some games need to have a design completed early, but you usually cannot design a game from start to finish. Think of designing a game as a military operation. You do not want to just gather all your troops together, and tell them to attack. Although this is sometimes necessary to win the war, it is not the safest thing to do, especially if your troops are green. A good military operation requires proper training, practice, intelligence, and preparation before execution. Until a military unit knows exactly what the terrain and the opposition are like, it can't plan the specifics of the battle. Then while drilling for combat, it may change the initial plans before finally committing to battle. Game design is similar: You have to design a lot of general features early on, using broad design strokes. As you learn how your game is shaping up, you will know more about how to refine your ideas to create an excellent game. By building a prototype you may find that different design elements should be substituted before you move into full production. This analogy shows that no matter how well you plan, you still need to evaluate the game design before committing to it. As bad strategy can result in losing the war, a bad game design can get the project cancelled. Moreover, victory is sometimes bittersweet if there are too many casualties. Likewise, an inadequately designed project might get out the door, but everyone involved may be burned out and frustrated when the game sells poorly.

Begin with what you know and work outward from there. Ask others on the team for their opinions; find out what information others will need immediately and focus on that. Programmers need specifications for the code they will write; artists need to know about the types of characters that will be in the game; and executives might want information about key features.

If you are new to a company or know you will be working with a specific publisher, ask for examples of other project documents to see what standards you are expected to meet. Some publishers will take whatever you give them, while others will demand a wide variety of documents that they may or may not have clearly defined.

Brian Reynolds on the Prototyping Process:::::

Brian Reynolds is a 15-year industry veteran recognized as one of the most talented and productive game designers. Honored by *PC Gamer* magazine as one of 25 "Game Gods," Brian has masterminded the design of an unbroken stream of hit strategy games, including the multimillion-selling *Civilization II*, *Alpha Centauri*, and *Rise of Nations,* as well as such new games as *Rise of Legends* and *Catan Live.* He is also highly regarded for his mastery of the art of programming. Brian's dual specialty gives him the substantial advantage of being able to bring his own visions to life, and he has built a reputation for finely tuned strategy games. As CEO of Big Huge Games, Brian concentrates on the creative side of the company, devoting most of his time to hands-on development of new game concepts and prototypes.

Brian Reynolds
(Chief Executive Officer,
Big Huge Games)

We try very quickly to get a basic prototype of simple gameplay up and running. By very quickly I mean preferably within a month. Then we play the prototype and iteratively/incrementally improve it: each time we play, we discover which things work well and which things aren't working. The things that work well we improve further or make more central to the gameplay; the things that aren't working we either find a way to fix or we take them out. Then, often only a few hours later, we've bashed together the next version of the prototype with our changes in it, and we can play that. The game gradually accretes new parts and becomes more and more fun.

Creating the Project Overview

Before you jump in and start designing various game systems, consider how the game should be structured. Once you have a vision for the game and can establish the process, create a high-level overview of the project to get a good sense of what you want to create, why you are going to create it, and what will be involved in its creation. This can often be completed in just a few pages, using bullet points to high-light the key project facts and figures. The foundation for the game relies on plan-ning, research, thinking, structuring, and summarizing the game's features.

Platform

It is important to establish the platform(s) on which the game will be released. The design for a cross-platform game will differ from one that is exclusive to a single console or platform. If the game is going to be on the PC, you should also consider establishing goals for the minimum and recommended system specifications.

Big Stock Photo

Reprinted with permission from Microsoft Corporation

Sony Computer Entertainment America

Nintendo

Will the primary platform for your project be PC, Xbox 360, PS3, or Wii?

Genre

Establish the kind of game you are trying to make at the beginning of the process. Some designers don't like to classify their games, which can be fine in some circumstances—but if you are trying to create an FPS, make sure you state this early and embrace it. You should then consider what features are required or expected for the genre, and what other genre features you plan to incorporate.

Is your game based on a license or IP? This can be very important for some projects such as the *Tom Clancy's Rainbow Six* series—which is characterized by a modern, realistic, military stealth genre. The designers need to understand that fans are buying the game not just because it is an FPS, of which there are many, but because they like the fantasy of playing a special forces operative and having access to realistic weapons, equipment, and gadgets. This fictional genre requirement drives many of the design decisions in a game such as *Rainbow Six: Vegas.*

Will your game be a massively multiplayer online game set in a fantasy world, such as *World of Warcraft*?

Audience

Several decisions need to be made regarding your audience:

1. Choose the game's rating—which will determine whether it is for children, adults, or another specific age demographic.
2. Think about what types of players you want to attract—hard-core players, casual players, or some mix of the two.
3. Define additional target demographics or psychographics such as gender, occupation, or religious affiliation.

You should also define the interests of your audience. Are you going after players who enjoy science fiction, fantasy, or modern realism? This is not necessarily the

same as defining the genre. An FPS could be based in either a futuristic or contemporary world, for example, and a role-playing game (RPG) doesn't always have to take place in a fantasy world.

If your game is based on a license, its fans should also be included and properly understood to make the game successful. You might even list fan statistics if they are known, such as Nielsen (television viewer) ratings or film box office numbers. The *WWE Wrestling* franchise reportedly has around 80 million fans in the

United States alone and upwards of 500 million fans worldwide. These numbers are exponentially higher than those of any other wrestling license or martial arts event. Understanding what has made these fans so loyal over the last 20+ years has helped many wrestling games to succeed.

Competition

It is important to acknowledge the competition and how it relates to the game. This will help you to both further target your audience and identify ways in which you can improve on games that are already successful in the marketplace. *Saints Row* is clearly a competitor to *Grand Theft Auto (GTA)*, and the audience for *GTA* might be an ideal target. Identifying your game as similar to an already-existing title is actually helpful and, to some, essential. Having no competition, in contrast, puts your project in uncharted territory.

Eidos Interactive Ltd.

Just Cause could be referred to as *"Mercenaries* and *Grand Theft Auto III* meet James Bond."

Gameplay Goals

Establish early whether your game is going to be revolutionary, evolutionary, innovative, or a clone. It is good to look at any areas you plan on adjusting and ask yourself if you are planning more than your team can possibly accomplish. You may want to rethink some of your design based on your overall gameplay goals, time, budget, and resources.

Try to understand whether the features you would like to innovate involve technology or gameplay. Adding boats to your game may not be a huge risk if your programmers already have a great water simulation system. Changing the fundamental way that combat works in your game, however, could prove to be extremely risky and would need to be evaluated before you spend much time and resources on implementing it.

© 2006 Ubisoft Entertainment.

Electronic Arts, Inc.

Ubisoft's *Assassin's Creed* implements a new design for player movement, interaction, and combat using as few buttons as possible.

First-person melee combat was minimized in the final version of *Goldeneye: Rogue Agent*, after time and resources were spent on the concept.

The danger with innovation is that if it fails, the rest of the project can suffer. The team working on EA's *Goldeneye: Rogue Agent* for the Xbox and PS2 spent a lot of time trying to get first-person hand-to-hand combat working, but it ultimately proved not to work and was severely minimized in the final game. Trying to develop the concept was not necessarily a bad decision; if it had worked, it could have evolved the FPS genre a great deal, but it also cost the team and project valuable time that could have been used at the end of the game for polish.

Gameplay Modes

As early as possible, you should determine which gameplay modes need to be in the game. Some game modes are part of the barrier to entering the market and will be required by most fans and reviewers. For example, having a multiplayer mode in an open world, *GTA* type of game is not really required, even if some fans have been asking for it, but not having it in an FPS or real-time strategy (RTS) game could be a huge problem.

Courtesy of Rockstar Games and Take-Two Interactive Software, Inc.   Courtesy of Rockstar Games and Take-Two Interactive Software, Inc.

The *Grand Theft Auto* franchise contains several game modes, such as riding a motorcycle and flying a helicopter in *Grand Theft Auto: San Andreas*.

You also need to decide on the priorities for these modes and where the main emphasis of the game will lie. This will help you understand where the bulk of your resources must be placed. It will also help you make the correct design decisions when conflicts arise between different modes and when compromises must be made to make both modes work correctly. Understand what the competition is doing, and be realistic about which modes you will support and how much you will support them; otherwise, you may end up doing many things poorly and not doing any one thing very well.

Electronic Arts, Inc.   Electronic Arts, Inc.

A mostly multiplayer game such as EA's *Battlefield 2* (left) has a huge emphasis on multiplayer mode, with support for some single-player gameplay, while a game such as EA's *Crysis* primarily focuses on the single-player experience, with multiplayer added.

Hooks

Beyond the vision for the game, it is also important to define its key hooks; these might be key selling points, or what sets the game apart from the competition. It is a good idea to focus on the new features that will attract players to the game. You generally want to avoid specifying how many levels or weapons are in the game, unless there is something remarkable about this. Establishing the hooks for the game should help keep you focused on its most important elements.

Project Goals

Setting measurable and definitive goals for the project is one of the designer's most important tasks. For instance, a project goal could be to "create a game with a 90+ *Metacritic* (*http://www.metacritic.com*) rating in 18 to 20 months for $20 million." This statement establishes many factors that will help to define the scope and scale of the project. Avoid vague goals such as "fun," which is both difficult to measure and very subjective.

Having an early project scale benchmark is crucial. For better or worse, many teams that have flexible ship dates and budgets tend to come up with many crazy ideas that are impossible to implement. Although flexibility might allow you to come up with some revolutionary ideas, consider the amount of time and risk it can take.

You might begin by setting goals only for the prototype or concept phases of the game, which will give you more latitude than attempting to define all the project goals from the start. This usually works best if you aren't given a ship date, fixed budget, or other restrictions.

Team Goals

Besides the goals you set for the project, you should also set team goals and make sure they are clear from the beginning. You can then compare the project goals with the team goals and ensure they are compatible as you move forward. This can be a little difficult to establish but can be very helpful to the team's accomplishment and morale. A team goal could be to avoid crunch time on the project and to work only 50 hours a week.

Technology Base

It is also important to establish the technology base for the project. You might be working on a sequel with a fairly complete engine already in place, starting from scratch, or using a licensed engine such as Epic's Unreal 3 engine. If you already have technology in place or any key technology decisions have already been made, it can be important or at least helpful to verify that these decisions and goals have been set. Some companies such as EA have purchased existing engines such as Criterion's Renderware and have several internal engines and tools but have still chosen to license an engine such as Unreal 3 because they feel it is better to license an engine than to modify one they already have. No matter what path the technology takes, you should have an idea of how your engine should work and how you can maximize its use.

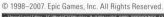

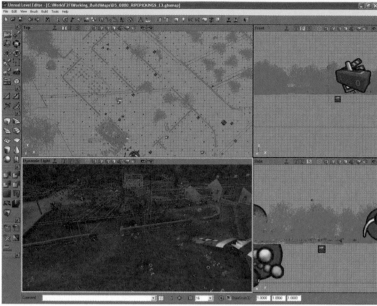

You might use a licensed engine such as Epic's Unreal 3 to create your game rather than work from scratch.

Core Theme

Establish the core theme for the game by asking yourself a series of questions such as these:

- What is the essence of the game?
- Who is the player?
- What does the player do?
- How does the player do it?
- Where does the player do it?
- What does the player do it with (e.g., gear, tech)?
- Who does the player do it with (e.g., adversaries, allies)?
- Why does the player do it?
- What are the game's stand-out features?

These questions will become the basis for some of the elements you need to address in detail throughout the design of the game. Spending some time creating an overview of these features at an early stage can be extremely helpful, save you a lot of time later in the project, and add cohesion to the design.

In this chapter, you have learned about the importance of the design process in gameplay mechanics. Now let's take a look at some basic elements—including movement, camera, controls, and combat.

:::CHAPTER REVIEW:::

1. Play three electronic games of different genres and discuss the most likely type of game design (art, gameplay, story, technology) that was emphasized in the creation of each game.

2. Create a project overview for an original game idea, using the format discussed in this chapter. Be sure to conform your design to the needs of your audience, and consider how you might create strong mechanics through gameplay modes.

3. How would you change your development process for your original game idea if you had to deal with a number of restrictions, some based on expectations from partners and other outside influences? Choose at least two types of restrictions and discuss how these might affect your original process.

CHAPTER 3

Creating the Core

the game's heart and soul

Key Chapter Questions

- What types of *camera* systems are used in games?

- Why are *controls* and *object* systems important?

- What are the best ways to design character *movements* in a game?

- What are the different systems associated with *combat*?

- How do you make all of the *systems* in your game work together?

At the heart of every game is a series of gameplay systems revolving around core features such as camera, controls, and movement. If players have trouble with the most basic actions in a game, what chance do they have to enjoy the rest of the game? For a character action game, especially one using a third-person camera, the character, camera, and controls must be polished to perfection. The same applies to a racing game, where the "character" is a vehicle. The moment-to-moment core gameplay also includes character interactions such as combat in most games. Every combat system must work seamlessly and smoothly with the rest of the gameplay systems—one of the most critical components in making the game fun. Players repeat actions associated with core gameplay systems over and over again; if these systems are created incorrectly or their associated actions are difficult to perform, not even the best graphics or storyline can save your game.

Camera Systems

Every game uses either a first-person or third-person camera of some kind. First-person cameras always reflect the perspective of the player character, while third-person cameras can be positioned at almost any height, angle, or zoom. Most games also have a wide variety of secondary cameras to use in different gameplay modes, cut-scenes, or other areas. No matter what kind of camera you are using, you will have to deal with many potential problems. Cameras, just like controls and interfaces, seem like the simplest elements in the world to design, but they can be extremely complicated and are important to perfect. Even adjusting the camera's field of view can make a big difference in how a game plays. With high-definition and widescreen becoming standard on most systems, designing a camera system and interface that works for 16:9 and 4:3 is also becoming increasingly difficult.

The most difficult cameras to design are for third-person character games, so let's look at some associated design choices. This doesn't mean that first-person shooter (FPS) or other cameras are easy, but they are typically much more straightforward than a third-person camera. Most third-person cameras have the added difficulty of allowing for player control. An FPS or first-person camera can rotate in place and will never concern itself about colliding with the environment, whereas a third-person camera usually spins around the central character and has to move properly in the environment without clipping through objects or getting stuck.

Camera systems: third-person from *Devil May Cry 4*; first-person from *Call of Duty 3*; lock-strafe from *Tom Clancy's Ghost Recon: Advanced Warfighter*; and fixed from *God of War II*.

Some games have a cinematic third-person camera. *God of War* utilizes fixed cameras that the player can't control. Designing a third-person camera that is easily controlled by the player and also feels natural is extremely hard to do, but the solution is usually more technical in nature. Deciding where to place your third-person camera is also very challenging. A variant of the third-person camera includes lock-strafe, which functions like a first-person camera but is pulled back behind the head of the player character. One of the problems with a third-person camera is that as the player moves the camera, the character turns and moves; this makes it impossible to continue shooting at an enemy in front of the character while also moving around, unless some additional functionality is included.

The solution many games use is to have a lock-on or lock-strafe button or mode that causes the player to always face a certain direction when active. This is a very necessary feature in most action games, but it is especially critical if you have medium- to long-range guns or weapons. It may be possible to avoid using lock-strafe if your game is closer in range and utilizes more melee types of weapons or ones that require less precise aiming. A third-person camera gives the player little control over precise aiming. With lock-strafe, it is easier to aim more precisely—but a lock-on system allows the player to lock onto a particular object but not to decide where on that object to attack or interact. Some games have tried to utilize a sub-targeting or precision-targeting system that allows the player to target a specific location; for the most part, these have been more difficult to use and must be carefully considered.

You may need several cameras in the game. Two different cameras may be required if the character can drive a vehicle and talk to non-player characters (NPCs), for example. Make sure you fully design all of the cameras you will need at an early stage if possible, so that they can all be programmed into your game correctly and will not have to be tacked on later.

Control Systems

How many games have you played in which it was difficult to control the player well, drive the car without crashing into walls, or make a jump or other required move? Every genre and type of game must be controlled in a completely different way. Making sure your games have great controls is one of the most difficult gameplay design problems. In many games, almost every aspect is designed up front except for the controls—because the team thought they would be easy to design! Great controls take a lot of time to get right, especially if the player is directly controlling a character's every action.

First-person control schemes are typically easier to pull off than most, but they still take a great deal of finesse to get right. Even if you decide to blatantly copy a great game such as *Halo*, don't underestimate the amount of time and resources it will take to ensure that the controls are well designed.

Control schemes in first-person shooters such as *Halo 2* are more straightforward to design but can still be tricky to get "just right."

You must design most of the core features before you finalize the control scheme, and you should continually revisit the control scheme to make sure that all of your new features are feasible. Many great ideas have been thrown out because they were impossible to implement with a console or a PC controller. When you are dealing with multiple platforms, make sure that you design for the least common denominator if possible.

Another important consideration when you design the controls is to understand your audience. It is very easy to make a control scheme too difficult to use and impossible to master. Understand who is going to play your game, and run playtests as soon as possible to evaluate the controls. One of the most difficult skills in game design is making things easy, so spend a lot of time continually refining the controls as you work on the game.

Before you begin designing any of the systems in the game, determine how you want the controls to work and measure them against the moves or attacks you want to include. Alternately, you can come up with a large "wish list" of things you want the player to be able to do and then determine how they can work together in a unified control scheme.

> I tend to think about the core gameplay systems in terms of how they will integrate or impact the core mechanics—so, how much visual information a player needs about an environment will affect camera controls, what controls are likely to be used together or in succession affect how they are arranged, etc. It is critical to me that these systems add to, rather than interfere with, the player's interaction with the central game mechanics.
>
> —*Tracy Fullerton*
> *(Assistant Professor, USC School of Cinematic Arts, Interactive Media Division)*

Movement Systems

Whether you are designing an action, racing, sports, or any other type of game, the most significant part is the central character. It doesn't matter whether the character is a real person, a fantasy character, or a vehicle. How the player moves when controlling the "character" is among the most important aspects of most games; this requires a tight connection to the controller, possibly some context-sensitive actions, and a supporting camera. Some real-time strategy (RTS) or sports games don't let the player directly control the character, but only dictate some of the character's actions or location, while the computer interprets the rest.

On one extreme, a game such as a first-person shooter (FPS) typically has very limited moves, which might include simple undetected movements or basic jumping. On the other extreme, many platformers are mostly about jumping in different ways and include hardly any other moves. However, as games mature, we're seeing a lot more moves that are barriers to entry. The latest trend is to include many context-sensitive moves that you can perform only at specific locations in the environment. The types of moves that can be performed will be limited mainly by your camera and controller. It is extremely difficult to jump accurately in a first-person game, which is why all platformers use a third-person camera. Yet it is hard to achieve accurate object targeting, control, and placement using a third-person camera. You want to avoid constantly moving the player between different cameras and control schemes, but you also need to make sure that the movement system is in alignment with the rest of your core systems.

To design your movement system, you must first determine the type of game you are making and the game's allowed moves. Trying to design even the basic moves of a character can be challenging. Can the player walk, run, sprint, crawl, duck, or waddle? The player might have to carefully walk a narrow beam or tightrope as in *God of War* or *Prince of Persia*. How does the player easily perform these maneuvers? Is the player going to use lock-strafe or lock-on in a third-person game?

Sony Computer Entertainment America

Platformers such as *Ratchet & Clank* contain a great deal of jumping but not many other types of moves.

Sony Computer Entertainment America

The player character (Kratos) walks a narrow beam in *God of War*.

A vehicle-based game will probably have fewer movement systems to design, but the finesse and controls of the basic movement system will typically be tighter and incorporate more responsiveness than in a character-based movement system, since even a small press on the controller in the wrong direction could be hazardous. Once you have determined the basic movements, you can start adding more elaborate ones, which will be determined by the type of game, level of realism, and goals.

Most platformers have a fairly standard series of moves—such as jump, double jump, flip jump, side jump, and wall-to-wall chimney jump. There can be many different variants if this is important to the game. *Tomb Raider* also has acrobatic low moves such as dive rolls. *Prince of Persia* and some others have started adding a large number of context-sensitive platforming moves such as wall runs and wall flips. There are also a fair number of interactions in the environment—especially actions such as climbing up and down ladders, swimming, and moving around on ledges (walking on, flipping off, hanging from, and climbing up from them).

Electronic Arts, Inc.

Eidos Interactive, Ltd.

There are usually fewer movement systems in racing games such as *Burnout: Revenge*, but they must incorporate much more responsiveness than in most other types of games.

Tomb Raider: Legend contains climbing and low acrobatic moves such as dive rolls.

Interviews with Shigeru Miyamoto have revealed how he approaches game design. Miyamoto starts by implementing the most basic feature, such as running, and makes that fun; he then adds jumping and makes it fun before adding the next action. While this design approach may not work for everyone, the philosophy behind it shows why his games are so masterful and fun to play; Miyamoto cares about the user experience and knows that it is critical to ensure that the core of the game is fun *before* layering on lots of complexity. You will also notice that his games are very responsive. The more fast-paced your game is, the more responsiveness needs to be considered; responsiveness is especially critical for fighting games. This concept is most evident in considering whether or not to allow players to activate new moves while in the middle of performing another, or whether a character animation sequence needs to run before players can input the next move. Responsiveness will play a major role in helping you decide how your animation systems function, how your combos will work, and what types of moves are possible to make in the game.

When you are deciding on the types of moves to add to the game, also look at the character's world interaction rules. Consider the following:

- How far can the character fall before dying?
- How high and how far can the character jump?
- How far and how fast can the character run?
- What blocks the character's path?
- Where can the character go?
- Does an obstacle such as a small wall that is only 1–3 feet high block the character's path?
- Where else can the character go that won't be immediately obvious?
- How much air control and movement is allowed when the character jumps in the air?

Not allowing the player to complete simple actions will break the continuity of the immersion. Some games have included context-sensitive moves to react to material in the environment, such as a quick hop or flip over a short wall, jumping over a railing and flipping around to hang onto it, and climbing up a pole and jumping from it. Other games have added advanced combat features that allow the player to take cover behind objects in the environment and use them in combat.

::::: Context Sensitivity

A *context-sensitive* action is one that triggers a certain result based on the player's situation, time, location, or button press. Context sensitivity is most commonly used to activate objects in the game such as an elevator button, door, or switch. These are usually triggered by distance from the object, such as a wall run in *Prince of Persia*. Many games, such as *Assassin's Creed* and *God of War*, now tend to use more context-sensitive moves that allow the character to interact with the environment, other characters, or objects in the game. These moves might be triggered when the player is close to an object, wall, location, or even several items combined; they might be triggered when an enemy is in a specific location, using a certain weapon, or has a certain health value. *God of War* has incredible finishing moves that the player can perform when many of the enemies have low health.

Games such as *Assassin's Creed* use context-sensitive moves.

Over the last 10 to 20 years, all player actions required in a game have become exponentially more complicated. It is now almost impossible to complete very complex moves, such as a wall run, by using a normal controller without context sensitivity. Some context-sensitive moves require the press of a button, while others can occur automatically. The drawback of many context-sensitive moves is a reduction in responsiveness. Since many of them are highly contextual, it would seem odd if players attempted to break out of them halfway through an animation.

The other drawback to using context-sensitive actions is that they require the game to interpret the player's actions, which can lead to player frustration when the results are unexpected. For instance, let's say that the player is running around fighting an enemy in a room and is feverishly pressing the attack button. What happens if the player gets close to a wall, and the game determines that the player should take cover along the wall or even run up it and flip off? Causing the player to lose control for even half a second in some games could result in player death, not to mention frustration.

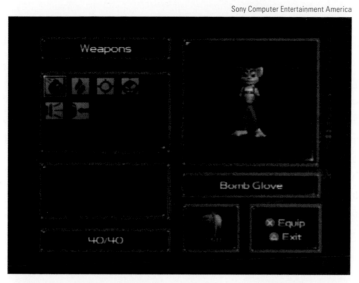

Weapon selection menu in *Ratchet & Clank*

Vendors are located far away from combat in *Ratchet: Deadlocked* to minimize their accidental use.

Context-sensitive moves and actions are very important to games today, and are probably unavoidable in most games, especially if you are trying to keep the controls and interface simple. However, you need to understand how to control them and minimize player frustration. In *Ratchet: Deadlocked*, it was clear that the vendors could pose a problem during combat, so they were located as far away from any combat as possible to minimize their accidental use. You can also adjust the sensitivity of contextual actions, ranges they can trigger, and timings required to activate them so that normal play doesn't result in their accidental activation—unless you want it to. It is important to make an early decision on whether or not to use context-sensitive actions in your game.

Games such as *Ratchet & Clank* are famous for using a wide variety of gadgets to assist players in moving through the environment, which can add a lot of movement variety to the game. *Ratchet & Clank* incorporates recurring gadgets such as Swingshot, which allows the player to swing like Tarzan from circular orbs; Grindboots, which allow the player to skate along railroad rails at high speed; MagnaBoots, which allow the player to walk on metal surfaces (even upside down); and Jetpack, which allows the player to hover and fly around in a limited manner. In some cases, it is best to allow the player to use such equipment anywhere and at any time, but in other cases, it is best to control the action. Try not to force players to pause the game, find the item, equip it, and then use it quickly before they have to flip back to their weapons. Make sure that using gadgets to traverse or otherwise interact with the world is as seamless and context sensitive as possible.

Sony Computer Entertainment America

Courtesy of Rockstar Games and Take-Two Interactive Software, Inc.

Ratchet & Clank: Going Commando incorporates various gadgets that provide assisted movement to players.

Vehicular movement is prevalent in the *Grand Theft Auto* series *(Vice City,* shown)—in which players can control cars, motorcycles, planes, and boats.

Besides movement on foot, many games also use vehicles exclusively, a combination of foot and vehicle movement, or linear vehicle gameplay. Vehicles may drive on the ground, roll along it, fly above it, and travel through the depths of space or the ocean. There is no limit to the types of vehicles in the game; technically, even a skateboard or snowboard could be classified as a vehicle—since each require specific control schemes, behaviors, and reaction models to be fun. Not all vehicle movement needs to be directed by the player either. The player may just ride along on a vehicle for transportation or may shoot at targets while the vehicle provides transportation in a "rail shooter" segment of gameplay. The player's movement may be limited, such as in a car going down a "track" with only one path to follow, or unlimited in a vehicle that will go almost anywhere. In *Mercenaries,* it is possible to run around on foot, drive ground vehicles, and pilot helicopters. *Grand Theft Auto* also allows the player to operate a plane, boat, motorcycle, or bicycle. Just like a character, a vehicle needs a lot of work to get the movement, physics, and controls just right, which is *much* more difficult than you think! Airplanes, cars, boats, spaceships, and other vehicles have very different movement needs.

Jeremy McCarron on Core Gameplay Mechanics ::::::

After graduating from the classical animation and 3D animation programs at the Vancouver Film School in 1995, Jeremy worked for Mainframe as a production assistant. He then became a character animator for the next five years on productions such as *ReBoot, Beast Wars*, and *War Planets*. Jeremy was a senior animator for the direct to DVD *Casper's Haunted Christmas* and a supervising animator for the *Heavy Gear* and *Action Man* television series. He briefly ran the department as the head supervisor of animation before leaving to join Radical Entertainment as an art director. There, he worked on the *Simpson's Road Rage, Monsters, Inc.*, and *Scarface* games. He returned to Mainframe as a CG supervisor and animation director for *Barbie's Fairytopia* (I & II) and *Barbie & The Magic of Pegasus* direct to DVDs. Jeremy is currently working toward his MBA at Simon Fraser University in Vancouver.

Jeremy McCarron
(Academic Director,
The Art Institute of
Vancouver)

I really like the *Splinter Cell* series for its game mechanics. The control scheme is very intuitive, and it just 'feels' right. The key for good mechanics is responsiveness. If you hit a button or the D-pad, the onscreen response has to be immediate and smooth. I feel as though Ubisoft really nailed the transitions between animations on those games, too. The overlapping action is strong and the interaction with the on-screen character is very satisfying.

It's becoming almost standard for next-gen games to contain some kind of forward or inverse kinematics (IK) system, which typically allows the programmers to control a character and adjust its movement to fit the situation. Programmer-driven animation is never as good as animated motion, but it is getting better all the time with programs such as Natural Motion's Euphoria taking procedural animation to the next level. Using IK to control a character is especially handy if the character is hit by an explosion or other physics system and needs to accurately react. The trouble that most systems have, though, is transitioning between IK and animated systems smoothly. Therefore, it is difficult to rely on using IK to solve all your problems. If you want to use IK to perform radical moves where characters end up in an awkward position, it is best to make sure they will be dead when they stop moving and don't have to get back up again. Make sure that your animation system allows you to properly transition between different states without awkward popping and glitches.

::::: The Problem with Space

If you give players the ability to fly in space and in the air, it is *very* easy for them to become disoriented and wind up upside down, backwards, and completely confused. The classic game *Descent* and its sequels allowed for moving with six degrees of freedom in tunnels and sometimes in space, but it also tended to cause many players to get "motion sickness." Space combat is even more confusing and difficult to design well. Some games such as *Star Wars: Rogue Squadron* solved some of these problems, but a lot of time and resources went into getting it right. Many other games have tried to incorporate freeform space combat and space flight and have done it poorly. Be careful when designing a game using flying vehicles; one solution is to use a tube-driven flying mechanic, where the player's ship always moves forward and is constrained inside an invisible tube.

Courtesy of CCP Games

EVE Online

Adding lots of moves to a game and giving players the freedom to move anywhere they want sounds like a good thing, but keep in mind that, with more movement options, players can get into more trouble. Freeform movement not only makes movement more challenging but can drastically increase the difficulty of navigating in 3D space, where players tend to get lost and not know where to go. Our game worlds are typically facades that we want the player to stay inside of. If you give the player the ability to jump up high, then he might be able to exit a level. This gets even worse when you give the player the ability to move objects around and then jump on them. In *Ratchet & Clank,* players may use a jump glide to fall slowly and a charge boot to move quickly. Players learned they could get to places where they weren't supposed to go by using these two abilities together in unanticipated ways—so the design team had to find all of these locations in the game and build art to restrict their movement and stop the abuse.

In *Munch's Oddysee,* many floating platforms contain thin walls and a door. Players have the ability to maneuver in the air while jumping, and they learned that they could jump out toward the wall and then quickly maneuver themselves back to the platform on the other side of the wall, bypassing the door and a puzzle that was set up for them. This broke many areas in the game, so the design team was forced to add short walls along the edge of each wall where it intersected with the platform, ensuring that players couldn't jump around the wall. (This maneuver was so difficult that only some of the skilled testers could consistently perform it.) Consider the abilities you are giving the player and how they will interact or could be exploited—and have the testing team look for movement exploits early in the project.

In *Deus Ex,* the player has a lot of freedom, including the ability to place wall mines as traps. Players learned they could place the mines on the wall and then jump up them and out of the level.

In *Oddworld: Munch's Oddysee,* the player has the ability to maneuver in the air while jumping.

It's best to create small representative sections of the game world, with the levers and design controls that allow you to quickly test and tweak your ideas. For example, in an RTS, the camera height, the scale of the units, the scroll speed, and unit movement speeds all need to be nailed down. Thinking through how it should work in your mind only gets you so far; seeing it live and 'in game' allows you to make sure what you're doing works for the player.

—Mark Skaggs
(CEO & Executive Producer, Funstar Ventures, LLC)

Creating the Core: the game's heart and soul   chapter 3

Object Systems

An object system includes the objects that will be in the game; which of them will be used by the player; how they will be used; how they are acquired; and how multiple objects are managed. This system will also help you understand the capabilities of your combat system.

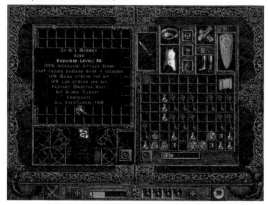

Peter Jackson's King Kong contains a simple object system that allows the player to hold one gun and the ammunition or a spear only, and not have to manage any additional inventory or worry about how to switch weapons. In contrast, *Diablo II* has a traditional role-playing game inventory area holding items of all sizes that can be rearranged and manipulated in many different ways.

Some games have thousands of weapons and inventory items, while others have only a few. Obviously, the number of objects in the game is directly related to the game's complexity. If your goal is to create a simple game that is very accessible to new players, avoid incorporating a complicated object system. Remember that the player needs to be able to easily find and use objects. If you have dozens or even hundreds of items that will be accessed regularly, make sure that the interface supports the rapid selection and use of items.

Ratchet: Deadlocked contains a wide variety of items that players may use.

Ratchet: Deadlocked contains a wide variety of items that players may use. In previous games, the mode was single-player, so it was acceptable to pause the game while the player brought up a quick-select menu and chose a new object. However, *Deadlocked* focuses more on multiplayer and co-op, requiring that the game never be paused, so item selection has to be quick and easy.

When you design your object system, it is important to classify the types of objects in the game and the gameplay functions they fulfill. Weapons and usable objects are those that the player must actively select and utilize.

Passive objects always work automatically; they are given to players to give the perception that they are collecting more items. A quest item can also be found by players or given to them when they are told to do something with it, such as deliver it to a particular location. It is important to distinguish quest items from others, since players can't or shouldn't buy, sell, use, or lose them. Some games also allow for the creation of new objects by combining other objects. Beyond the standard objects used by players, such as weapons, health packs, energy restorers, and armor, there are many additional items that you might consider putting into your game—such as power-ups (which increase character statistics), keys, and maps.

:::: *The Legend of Zelda*: A Pioneer in Object Systems Design

Miyamoto succeeded in creating a game system that has withstood the test of time. If you look back to the original *Legend of Zelda* on the NES and compare it to more recent iterations of the game you'll see that it is mostly unchanged, retaining the core gameplay mechanics from way back in 1986. Today, the latest in the series is still fun, challenging—and, most importantly, entertaining and will undoubtedly be popular for years to come.

At the center of the game is the player, who is allowed to explore the game world while battling enemies to acquire items that will provide access to new areas that were not accessible before. The process repeats over and over again, becoming increasingly more challenging—but the game always adds appropriate items/abilities to the players' repertoires so that they have what they need to succeed. It offers a variety of action-oriented gameplay, puzzles, RPG mechanics—all mixed into a great adventure with a story open enough that players can place themselves into it easily. It's a pure and simple design that has been mimicked successfully in so many games that it's impossible to count them. Surely it was not the first game ever to take this approach—but it was the most polished and successful, allowing it to influence designers across the world.

—*Randy Greenback*
(Creative Director, Red Storm Entertainment)

Nintendo

The Legend of Zelda: Twilight Princess

Combat Systems

Whether you like it or not, most action games revolve around combat. Some games use only one type of combat, while others use many different weapons or attacks for combat.

Courtesy of Rockstar Games and Take-Two Interactive Software, Inc.

PCJ-600

Grand Theft Auto: Liberty City Stories contains a variety of combat systems.

The types of combat in a game can include hand to hand, melee, ranged, and vehicular. Melee combat involves any type of short-range hand-to-hand combat using weapons such as swords, axes, or spears. Ranged combat can occur at several distances (close, medium, long) and typically has different rules at each distance. Close-range weapons typically include flamethrowers, shotguns, and other weapons that fire only a short distance. Medium-range weapons include most ballistic pistols, rifles, submachine guns, rail guns, laser rifles, bows and arrows, and crossbows, and thrown objects such as grenades, Molotov cocktails, or spears. Long-range weapons include sniper rifles, rocket launchers, and artillery weapons. In vehicular combat, players can use the vehicles as weapons or use any type of mounted weapon. Vehicular weapons tend to be heavier, more powerful, and longer in range than handheld weapons. It doesn't matter how the weapons are classified, as long as the rules are consistent. The less realistic your game is, the more freedom you will have to focus on making the game fun rather than worrying about details.

Targeting Systems

It's important to finalize your general weapon targeting system early in the process. First-person shooters are fairly straight-forward, but they often still need help targeting weapons such as grenades and showing the player where the grenade will be thrown. Third-person, fighting, and vehicular combat games often do not allow the player to easily move, target enemies, and perform all of the necessary attacks. This can become even more complicated if the player can flip between multiple types of combat.

First-person shooters require that the player use both hands at once to move the character and to look around or target the enemy. While players are becoming savvier every day, and games such as *Halo 2* have shown that many people will buy a great FPS, new players have trouble using both of the analog sticks and firing their weapons at the same time. First-person games are great for ranged combat, but they are horrible for any hand-to-hand and most melee combat. Third-person games excel at short-range, melee, and hand-to-hand combat, but they have difficulty handling most long-range combat. Most third-person games also let the players switch to an optional "look" mode or first-person view while using some weapons, but it is awkward to force players in and out of this mode on a regular basis.

The most common solution adopted by third-person games that use ranged weapons, and by some first-person games (such as *Metroid Prime*) is a lock-on targeting system. The use of strafing in third-person games still doesn't solve the targeting problem. Lock-on targeting systems come in several varieties. Soft-lock is an automatic lock-on that does not require the player to press a button and typically locks on to the most obvious target (or a series of targets in some cases). It is impossible for the system to know exactly what the player is trying to attack, which can cause frustration. In *Ratchet: Deadlocked* the player may quickly press a button to cycle through possible targets if the target that was automatically selected was wrong.

Reprinted with permission from Microsoft Corporation

Nintendo

A targeting cursor in first-person shooters such as *Halo: Combat Evolved* helps players of all levels target their opponents.

Some first-person games such as *Metroid Prime* have adopted a lock-on targeting system.

Nintendo

The Legend of Zelda: Twilight Princess has an excellent hard-lock system known as z-targeting.

The second type of lock-on is called a hard-lock, which requires the player to either press and hold a button or press a button to toggle it on or off. When a hard-lock is activated, the targeting cursor locks on to an enemy, and all shots are usually sent to that location, making it easy for the player to hit the target. Another common feature of the hard-lock system is auto-strafe. When locked onto a target, the player begins to circle strafe around the enemy, making it possible to hit the target while moving. At some levels, hard-lock systems require less skill, since combat is not about aiming anymore. However, lock-on combat can be skill based because it requires the player to use the right weapon at the right time, maneuver in the world while fighting, and do anything else that requires some finesse.

Melee or hand-to-hand combat systems often don't require targeting because players are usually engaging a single target directly in front of them. However, some games might allow the player to throw an object quickly and thus need to use lock-on.

Electronic Arts, Inc.

THQ

James Bond: From Russia with Love incorporates a sub-targeting system, which allows the player to lock on to an enemy and select a targeting location on that particular enemy. While this system can often be difficult to use, it can allow players to perform head shots or other specialized actions.

Full Spectrum Warrior has an innovative grenade targeting system that allows the player to accurately lob grenades and use them more effectively.

Sony Computer Entertainment America

Sony Computer Entertainment America

In *Ratchet: Deadlocked*, a ground targeting cursor is used for lobbed weapons that stayed at a fixed distance away from the player, showing where lobbed weapons would be landing. However, the ground targeting cursor also has some lock-on and gravitates toward any nearby targets.

The Mark of Kri has an innovative combat system allowing the player to sweep the right analog stick around to select multiple opponents. The types of combos that can be performed vary depending on the number of characters selected by the player. The system then allows the targets to be close or far away and for the player to interact with them in different ways.

Other games such as *Bruce Lee: Quest for the Dragon* attempt to let players fight multiple enemies by using the right analog stick to control the direction in which the player is attacking, thus allowing the player to throw quick punches and kicks in any direction. Fighting multiple enemies in a melee system is extremely challenging and there is still no perfect solution for handling all of the problems.

Melee Combat

At the simplest level, a melee combat system is short ranged and usually deals with characters attacking each other with their hands, feet, or weapons they are holding. Melee combat doesn't apply to vehicles, unless you consider smashing your vehicle into another one to be melee combat. Most melee weapons do damage by blunt force (bat or stick) or slicing and stabbing (sword or axe); these weapons vary widely in size, shape, and specialized use. Some weapons are designed to allow the player to do light damage but move the weapon very quickly (rapier or foil); to move slowly but deliver devastatingly powerful attacks (battle axe); to be longer or shorter in range; or to be used for offensive or defensive purposes. Most melee weapons are derived from medieval combat or martial arts; for example, the lightsaber from *Star Wars* is a futuristic sword with an energy blade that can slice through almost anything.

Melee combat systems can vary greatly in scope and scale. Even some FPSs such as *Medal of Honor* allow for a single strike that can be performed when an enemy gets very close. In this case, the player is attacking the enemy with the butt of the rifle, using a butt stroke attack. In its simplest form, a melee attack consists of the player delivering a single short-range hit—whether by hand, foot, or weapon.

Courtesy of Midway Games, Inc.

Melee combat systems are common in fighting games such as *Mortal Kombat: Armageddon*.

Combos

For a game to have a true melee system, you need to do more than allow for a single attack or just a few basic attacks. Depth and complexity are necessary for a true melee combat system. A combo allows the player to press the same or different buttons in rapid succession or simultaneously to perform different attacks. Even if a melee weapon attack, fist attack, and kick are placed on separate buttons, the combat would be very simplistic unless you allowed for combos. Hitting the X button several times in rapid succession to perform an attack, which results in the game simply performing that attack over and over again, is not a combo. However, if the player hits X three times in succession to make two simple attacks, and follows this with a more advanced or different attack after the third button press, this would be considered a three-hit combo. There is no limit to the number of hit combo sequences you can chain together.

© Courtesy of Capcom. Reprinted with permission.

Tecmo

Combo systems are essential in action games involving a lot of melee combat, such as *Devil May Cry 4* and *Dead or Alive 4*.

Designing a combo system for a game such as *Ratchet & Clank* is exponentially easier than for a fighting game such as *Soul Calibur* or *Mortal Kombat*. It is not difficult to string together a series of attacks and make the player press many buttons in various patterns and timings. Designing combos that are logical and easy to remember and that require mastery is difficult. You need to reward players who are able to achieve longer and longer strings of button presses, but you can't create imbalance in the game by making the latter attacks too powerful to be stopped. Finding a balance and making sure your melee combat system is satisfying is much harder than it seems. To make a successful combo system, you often must design an extremely responsive game where the player can instantly chain together moves and quickly transition from one move to another without having to wait for animations to finish.

Reprinted with permission from Microsoft Corporation

In *Kameo: Elements of Power*, there are enemies that, while stunned, reveal their exposed chins on which the player may perform an upper cut to do damage.

The one exception might be wrestling games, whose elaborate combos often tend to be slower in pace and timing than those of traditional fighting games. Some of this is because a real wrestling match is much slower than a real martial arts match. Martial arts games take place exponentially faster than real life matches as well and are exaggerated to make them fun and not terribly realistic. It is possible in a wrestling game to get caught up in a series of moves by an opponent and be almost helpless to break out of the combo for even a minute or two unless you are very skilled, whereas martial arts combos usually don't last more than a few seconds.

Besides just pressing the buttons, combos and most melee combat systems also require proper timing. Players must learn not only how to execute their attacks or moves—but, more importantly, *when* to execute them. For example, players may need to perform a specific move when the enemy is in a distinct state. This is especially common in boss fights, where players must do something to stun the boss; they then have a few seconds to perform a specific attack in order to directly damage the character.

THQ

Complex moves are common in wrestling games such as *WWE Smackdown! Vs. RAW 2006*.

Sony Computer Entertainment America

God of War takes context-sensitive moves and makes them into mini-games or specialized attacks. The player must weaken enemies and then has the option to perform specialized moves requiring a special set of button presses. If the player performs such a move correctly and in the time required, it often results in major damage or death to the enemy.

Many games use melee moves that are also range dependent; the game could perform different moves based on the distance between the enemy and the player character. The player would also have to learn how to judge distances from enemies and which moves may be performed based on these distances. Not every game has moves that vary by distance; however, since many games don't actually lock on to a specific target, players don't know if the target is close or far away. Determining the distance from an enemy is a basic form of context-sensitive move adaptation.

Context-sensitive moves can occur in many different melee combat systems. Games can track how much the enemy is damaged, where the enemy and the player are located, how many enemies are available, and what weapons the player or enemies have. A wrestling game might have different moves if the player or opponent is against the ropes, in the corner, lying down, pinned, turned away, severely injured, using a weapon, running, jumping, interacting with the environment, against a wall, or close to an object. You can incorporate many context-sensitive melee combat moves that you can incorporate into a game.

Controlling Combat

The greatest complexity in designing a melee system involves the controls; it is not easy to map 100 or more different moves onto a controller that has only eight usable buttons and two analog sticks. The first thing to determine is the audience for the game. Most fighting games appeal to a smaller, hardcore audience that have grown up playing them and want them to be similar to other games they have played. However, a hardcore fighting game doesn't appeal to the mass market audience. It is very difficult to make both audiences happy. The most basic melee system uses only a single button for melee attacks. Some games may have separate buttons for melee or ranged attacks, weapon or hand-to-hand attacks, or attacks using hands or feet. You must decide how the attacks with multiple buttons will be presented to the player. The simplest system is to use a weak or strong attack, a fast or heavy attack, or some level of power differentiation between the two attacks.

Classic 2D fighting games such as *Street Fighter* allow the player to attack an opponent high, mid-range, or low. This combat is also fairly easy for players to understand, since they need only to remember where on the opponent they want to attack. This system makes the player focus more on the opponent. In 3D, however, this system does have a few problems, since it often requires the use of the analog stick to point the attack in the desired direction. It doesn't work well in a full 3D fighting game where the player can move anywhere in the arena. This option is used by classic games such as *Tekken* but incorporates a left-right stance, which means that the player character stands with one foot forward, and the type of move that can be performed is based on which foot is forward. This system is pretty hard-core and forces players to really understand the game well to be successful.

Classic 2D fighting games such as *Street Fighter* (*Alpha Anthology*, shown) allow the player to attack an opponent high, mid-range, or low.

Fighting games such *Tekken 5* use a left-right stance.

Modified Attacks

An attack modifier button is a common way to give the player an additional variety of moves. Some games utilize a button that modifies other buttons when toggled or held down. You could have one attack button and an attack modifier button. The player presses attack to make the player character perform a normal attack or holds down the attack modifier button and presses attack to make the character do something different. While this may not make sense with only a single attack button, it can be useful for other things as well, especially if you have several attack buttons. The modifier button might also be pressed for movement as well as attacks—allowing the player to jump higher, run faster, or perform other special moves. The modifier button can be an effective way to add some depth to an otherwise simple system.

The most common type of modifier found in games containing melee combat is the jump button, which may be used for all kinds of melee moves and not just for platforming. Some games also utilize a duck or dodge button that allows the player to go down and not just up. Besides simple ducks, these moves might include dive rolls and other more aggressive maneuvers. While ducking itself isn't an attack, many different moves can typically be triggered by being in a lower position. Dive rolls, ducking, and jumping are not the only possible ways for players to avoid being hit by an attack.

Blocking is a major part of most melee combat systems. Deciding how you want the player to be able to block is harder than you think. How much, how quickly, and how long can really affect the way the game is played. Too much blocking might make the game too easy, but not enough blocking makes it useless and frustrating. Allowing the player to move while blocking or performing other attacks may also allow the game to be abused. Consider whether the player takes any damage while blocking; some attacks can get through a block, or the block may be effective only if the player is facing in the right direction. It may be important to decide how the player character is going to respond to and defend against an attack.

Courtesy of Midway Games, Inc.

Mortal Kombat: Shaolin Monks uses complex modified moves such as blocking.

Besides blocking incoming enemy attacks, another choice involves reversals and counters—fairly sophisticated systems that have begun to appear only recently in games. Instead of blocking an enemy attack, the player now has the ability to use an enemy's attack against him. These are most commonly found in wrestling and martial arts games and hand-to-hand combat, but the principles could be used in almost any kind of melee combat system. A counter is like a block and a strike rolled into one; it can take almost any form and may be as simple as pressing a button, but timing it properly can be tough in most games.

Grappling is extremely close range hand-to-hand combat, where one person grabs another. This type of attack has been avoided by most games until recently because of its complexity. It is extremely difficult to have two computer-controlled characters accurately interact, and most game engines still find it difficult to accurately detect every limb and how they should all intertwine.

A throw is the simplest form of grappling that tends to be used in games; players often enjoy being able to grab enemies and send them flying in another direction. It is possible in a melee combat system to have any number of additional special moves, which might be context-sensitive or finishing moves designed to kill an enemy. The only limit to the types of special moves you might add is how to easily activate them.

Grappling is common in wrestling games such as *WWE Smackdown! Vs. RAW 2006*.

Players must find special moves exciting and easily accessible. If the game requires memorizing a lot of rules before it can be played, the system may be too complicated. The trick to designing a successful melee combat system is figuring out how complex it needs to be and then trying to simplify it as much as possible. If you're designing a full-fledged melee system, you need to make sure there is enough depth to allow the players to master it.

Courtesy of Midway Games, Inc.

Electronic Arts, Inc.

In *Mortal Kombat: Shaolin Monks*, the player may activate a stun attack when an enemy is almost dead. The attack brings up a special screen, allowing the player to enter a five-direction key press that will activate any one of a number of different finishing moves.

Def Jam: Fight for New York allows the player to earn finishing moves by gaining experience from fighting and then buying them at a "training" facility. The player can then map up to four different moves to the D-pad and may execute them when a special meter is filled.

Ranged Combat

Once combat moves farther out, it can be considered ranged—even if the distinction between melee and ranged is a little vague at times. It is important for a designer to understand the differences between the two types of systems and what they mean to the player. You can easily have a combat system that utilizes both ranged and melee combat or only one of them. In ranged combat, the player uses some sort of weapon, magic, power, or special ability to attack an opponent.

THQ

Ranged combat is the emphasis of 3D shooters such as *The Outfit*.

Many different categories of weapons can be used in ranged combat. The most basic type of ranged weapon is a projectile gun, which includes anything that shoots a projectile straight at an enemy. The effect of the projectile once it hits can vary tremendously. Even a missile can be considered a projectile—one that explodes. A lobbed weapon is thrown or shot in an arc; this could include grenades and any other item that can be thrown. Streaming weapons are those that shoot out a stream made of liquid, fire, or other viscous material. Guided weapons are those that track an enemy. It is possible to have other types of weapons as well, but this is one way to characterize the basic types or classes of weapons. You can also classify many weapons as light, medium, or even heavy—depending on how much damage they do.

It doesn't matter how you classify weapons; what is important is that you do classify them somehow. You should have different categories of weapons, each of which fulfills a different function in the game. Even if your game is realistic, a weapon such as an M-16, AK-47, or H&K 91 doesn't mean much to many people. Players need to know that each weapon has a different function and very distinct uses that are obvious to players who know nothing about weapons. This problem is most difficult for realistic games, but it can still occur in sci-fi or fantasy games as well.

Weapon Functions

What are the different functions that should be associated with your game's ranged weapons? There are weapons that are short range but very powerful, or fast firing, such as pistols. Some short-range weapons, such as shotguns, can hit multiple enemies. Fast-firing but semi-inaccurate weapons such as submachine guns contain a lot of ammo. There are general-purpose, medium-range, high-firepower weapons such as assault rifles, and there are slow-firing but long-range weapons such as sniper rifles. You can also consider more specialized weapons, such as those that fire quietly by using a sound suppressor, are guided, stun but don't kill, or have an area of effect. Having a weapon to fill each of these needs is not critical, but you have to understand the differences and why you should or shouldn't support certain types of weapons.

Many weapons can use very similar combat models and technology, but some of the weapons require additional support and features to make them work well. You must avoid allowing the player to find a dominant strategy, one particular tactic so powerful that the player can win the game just by using it. Balancing a game well enough to avoid all occurrences of this is often difficult, but necessary. An example is the inclusion of a sniper rifle or another kind of long-range weapon. Being able to shoot targets from a distance before they can react would be a dominant strategy. In most cases, there are several ways to avoid this abuse; you can limit the amount of ammunition you give players, or you can make the artificial intelligence (AI) respond when someone is shot so that subsequent kills using the sniper rifle are exponentially harder to accomplish. There may be other ways to keep a sniper rifle in check, but it is important to understand how devastating a gun like a sniper rifle can be in some games if left unchecked.

Activision

Press and hold X to swap M1 Garand for MP40

Weapon selection screen in *Call of Duty 3*.

Allowing the player to silently kill an enemy opens up a can of worms, requiring you to have an entire stealth system if it is to work well. It can also be troublesome if the player can always sneak up and silently kill people but the AI never responds. Some action games have suffered by including stealth mechanics or weapons because players don't know if they should go in with guns blazing or sneak in

Games such as *Tom Clancy's Splinter Cell: Double Agent* are often built almost entirely around the principle of stealth.

quietly. If you include stealth weapons, make sure they are properly and fully supported throughout the game. Nonlethal weapons have a similar set of problems and need to be fully realized before they are included. Levels must be designed properly to fully support specialty weapons; a sniper rifle is of little use in tight corridors, while a stealth weapon is of little use on a sunny day in the desert.

You need to make sure that the player can easily access various weapons, combine them, or switch between them easily. Be careful if you have a tendency to mix up types of enemies. If some enemies are "immune" or invulnerable to a specific weapon or require the player to use a particular weapon—or if you mix close-range enemies with those that are far away—make sure the player can easily switch between various weapons in order to maximize their combined effectiveness.

In *Kameo: Elements of Power* for the Xbox 360, the different "weapons" are the various forms your character can transform into. The player can easily alternate among four different forms at any time. This is especially important because most of the enemies in the game require that you use more than one form against them in a fight. After spraying an enemy with fire, the player character may need to

Team selection screen from *Kameo: Elements of Power*.

switch to a different form that can throw rocks, or use another form to knock off the enemy's shield before switching back in order to directly damage the enemy. The way you design enemies could have a major impact on weapon design and should be considered before you finalize the design of your weapons. It is important to think through the control scheme and interface goals of the game while you design the weapon systems to ensure that they are all in alignment and will not conflict with each other.

Weapon Attributes

All weapons rely on different abilities and statistics, and most share a number of common attributes that must be carefully balanced to make sure they are fun and worthwhile. Some weapons have additional attributes or abilities that set them apart. At the most basic level, most weapons have a value for damage, armor penetration, velocity, ammunition, rate of fire, accuracy, spread, knockback, clip size, and reload rate. These values will reveal important information about a weapon. Major attributes of every weapon include how much damage it does, how fast it shoots, and how much ammunition it has. Other factors such as how much it knocks back an enemy and if it penetrates armor are important, but they have more to do with the specialization of a weapon than its base functionality.

Even seemingly small factors such as whether the weapon has a clip size and if the player has to reload can have a major effect on the game. A weapon that holds only six shots and takes a very long time to reload may be a big concern in a game that constantly throws lots of enemies at the player, even if those six shots are incredibly powerful. With a clip system, you also have to determine how the ammunition in the game is going to work.

Activision

Reloading in military first-person shooters such as *Call of Duty 3* can have a major effect on the game.

In *Tom Clancy's Rainbow Six 3,* each clip could hold a different amount of ammunition. This was designed to be hyper-realistic, but it could lead to confusion because players might see that they have six clips left without realizing they have only 12 actual shots, since some clips may have contained only a few rounds. The game does not automatically reload if the player runs out of shots; the player must press a button to manually reload. While this system is very realistic, it could be frustrating for casual players who may not notice in the heat of battle that they are out and wonder why they are no longer able to shoot.

In *Ratchet & Clank: Size Matters,* the shots from a projectile weapon curve slightly to make sure they hit their targets—and the red circle shows that anything within it is being hit.

Accuracy is another major differentiator in some game weapon systems. Aiming accurately, especially in a third-person game, is very difficult. Some games have no real weapon accuracy at all; the weapon just hits the target if fired. Most FPSs utilize some kind of targeting reticule, which is often circular, expanding and contracting depending on what the player is doing. Some reticules might change if the player is moving, kneeling, tired, or distracted in some way. There are two common ways to represent accuracy. Some games use a circle to show that anything within it is being hit, while others use it to show the player's spread of bullets. There is no right or wrong way to show accuracy, and it is not critical that you utilize accuracy for weapons. However, understand that feedback to players about the accuracy of their shots is critical and must be properly defined and explained.

Alternate Weapon Modes

Some weapons have an alternate mode or use. For instance, a sniper rifle might be shot from the hip (less accurate) or used with a scope (more accurate, allowing the player to zoom in on the target). A scope is an alternate way to fire a rifle in some games. The more wide open your game is, the more important a scoped rifle and long shots become.

Some games may also have an alternate fire (alt-fire), which could be anything from a different attack (such as a grenade launcher) to different ammo or faster rate of fire. Alt-fires are more commonly associated with science fiction weapons, but anything is possible. Alt-fire can provide some needed functionality to a weapon or it could add unneeded complexity. Examples of alt-fire include allowing players to: fire weapons in normal or silenced mode; launch a straight or guided missile; shoot a machine gun on burst or full automatic; or release normal or armor-piercing ammunition.

Far Cry: Vengeance contains vast levels with long draw distances that contribute to the use of a sniper rifle.

Another kind of alternate fire, commonly found in platform games, is a charge-up attack. This typically requires that the player hold down the attack button for some time while the attack builds up power and then release the button to shoot it. In some cases, the player may be able to release the attack early but at a lesser damage level or ability. Some players want the immediacy of being able to trigger an attack instantly, while others will argue that the finesse of being able to time the use of a charge-up attack is half the fun. A charge-up attack may be designed in many ways, but you must consider whether or not your audience will understand it and be able to fully utilize it in the heat of battle.

Damage Systems

When you deal with almost any kind of game, it is important to define its core failure states. How does the player character take damage and die? Players may be able to fail in other ways, but the damage system failure state is usually the most important, especially in understanding how the player gives and receives damage. This might sound like a simple and straightforward system, but it is one that can become very complex very fast. In designing a game's damage system, you should address the following questions:

- Do the players and enemies have hit points (HP)? Do objects in the environment have HP?
- Do characters or objects have armor? How do armor and HP interact?
- Do characters have individual HP on different limbs, sections, or parts?
- How does the player heal? Are enemies able to heal?
- How is damage distributed?

At the most basic level, the player character and enemies have some HP. When a weapon or attack hits them, HP are instantly removed. In some cases, the HP of the player may be represented by a number, a graphical bar representing percentage, discrete chunks, or any other type of graphical representation. Some games have only a single HP—if you get hit once, you die. Other games try to represent HP more naturally and show it through the animations and graphics associated with the player character. There are several ways to represent health in the game, but regardless of how you do it, make sure the player can easily understand it.

Character picking up armor in *Unreal Tournament 2004*

Health becomes a little more complicated if the character has armor. A shield may be considered a temporary piece of armor. In some cases, armor may be treated like additional HP; weapons first damage the player's armor, then

Electronic Arts, Inc.

In *Mercenaries 2,* the player may target the rotor blades of a helicopter to bring it down quickly and make it crash.

the player's health. However, it may be possible to have actual armor-piercing weapons that can negate the armor and directly remove HP from the character. In some cases, the character or vehicle may have location-specific armor that can be removed to allow certain locations to be damaged.

Other locations, such as a character's head, may be considered a weak point. It is possible that—despite having armor—if the player or enemy is shot in the head, the result is direct damage to HP as well (and often an instant kill).

Weak points can be used for purposes besides head shots. A large enemy may have a weak point that can be targeted by the player to disable some function of the unit. There are many ways to use armor and weak points to make your player character or enemies more interesting or tougher to kill. Just keep in mind that these systems do make the game more complicated, especially when you consider representing the armor value to the player.

Hit Reactions

If the player or enemy is damaged in the attack, some kind of reaction should be triggered so that the player knows that damage was done. It shouldn't matter whether the hit affects the health of the unit or just its armor; some reaction needs to be immediately evident. A hit reaction could include special animation sequences, spark or particle effects, a flashing interface, a reduced health bar, the player character recoiling, or an armor piece flying. Many more games are using physics and IK to simulate more realistic weapon hits. You do have to be careful with this because it is not always possible to have a smooth blend between IK animation and traditional character animation. Most IK systems still are not sophisticated enough to get a character to stand up from an awkward position smoothly. You must ensure that the transitions to the hit reactions you specify are smooth, especially when the character isn't dead and is expected to do something else afterwards. For the latest next-generation games, it is becoming more critical for enemies to react to the players' actions in better ways.

You can also take more advanced considerations into account when you design a damage system. It is possible to use damage over time; this could take the form of acid, fire, poison, or some other effect that will continue to damage the player or enemy over time as long as it lasts. In some cases, the effect may stop after a length of time, or it may stop only if the player "cures" the effect by doing something. If you use a system that has damage over time, make sure players understand the effect this has on the player character or enemy.

Being damaged by the environment is becoming more common in games. In the past, a player character might have been damaged by falling in some water, lava, or other substance. It is now more common for dangerous environmental conditions including spikes, breakables, and other hazards to cause damage. In addition to being damaged by the environment, the player might also use the environment to attack enemies through physics, knockback, or additional techniques other than the use of weapons.

Damage may occur as a result of falling from a height, whether due to a weapon hit or just a movement mistake. You must decide how far the player character can fall before taking damage and how much damage the character can take at various levels. In *Ratchet & Clank,* there is no penalty for dropping off most cliffs; instead, the game teleports the character back to the edge after falling off instead of allowing the character to die.

It can also be very important in next-generation games to show damage visually, which can enhance the game's realism and provide feedback to the player. Be careful about depicting blood in games localized for some overseas markets (such as Germany). Limb damage may be shown by disabling the use of a limb or even removing it entirely. It could be dangerous to show limb damage on a player character if it will impede the character's performance. Decreasing the player's abilities could create a snowball effect—making the game more difficult to play as the player takes on more damage, resulting in increased player frustration. Damage can be used in many ways; make sure that the damage system fits the game and your vision for it.

Courtesy of Midway Games, Inc.

An enemy impaled on spikes in *Mortal Kombat: Shaolin Monks* is just one way that a character can take damage from the environment.

Courtesy of Midway Games, Inc.

Damage to a character in games such as *Stranglehold* may be shown visually.

Creating the Core: the game's heart and soul   chapter 3

Healing

Just as important as taking damage is repairing it. You can make the game too easy if you give the player too much health, but giving the player too little health can make it too difficult. How player characters heal or recharge their armor or energy may drastically affect the game experience and pacing.

The most common way to heal is to use a health pickup. The easiest pickup is one that is not stored in inventory but is just picked up and used when needed. This pickup could take the form of a health pack, crate, colorful icon, or anything else that either fits seamlessly into the game world or looks out of place but is easy to recognize. This simple system has several advantages. Designers may place health pickups in the optimal locations, such as before or after key battles, to ensure that the player will always get health when needed. This is also the easiest system to manage, since no inventory is required. The drawback to this system is that it does not require skill or strategy. Players will usually understand that they simply need to survive and find the next location.

Nintendo

Health pickup in *The Legend of Zelda: A Link to the Past*.

Another type of health pickup is one that the player can pick up and save for when it is needed. The advantage of this system is that it requires some skill from the player, since the player must determine the right time to use the health pack. The drawbacks are that the player has to micromanage the health packs and can run out of them at a key point. Health packs can be found, given away, or purchased, so they can also be placed in key locations for the player to find if you want to ensure that health will be available to the player at key times (such as before a boss battle).

A similar form of healing involves using spells, magic, or devices. The player might use something like mana or energy to heal, which is broader than using a specific health restoration item. Using the same energy to attack the enemy and to heal the player character can create problems, although it can also lead to interesting tactics and choices that the player must make in the heat of combat.

It is also possible to use a dynamic difficulty health-spawning system that can automatically spawn new health pickups or items if the player is doing poorly. This can be best hidden in a game that uses crates or other breakable objects that store random items. The system can then determine how well a player is doing and decide to heal the player if necessary.

Another variant involves a key location that heals the player—such as a body shop, person, or health pad. The advantage of these systems is that they fit into the world very well and can be controlled by the designers. They may also be used to repair vehicles and larger items that may not normally be repaired or healed with a health pack or some equivalent object.

Eidos Interactive, Ltd.

Healing device in *Deus Ex*.

It is also sometimes necessary to automatically heal a player, whether before a boss battle, at the start of a level, or at another key location. Otherwise, it may be virtually impossible for you to balance the game; if players go into the situation damaged, they would have little chance of survival.

Some games such as *Halo* allow players to heal over time so that they can duck out of danger, heal, and get back to the action. While this system works almost perfectly for *Halo,* it is easy to get wrong. If you rely on the player recharging health over time, you can easily disrupt the pacing of the game and force the player to wait, run away, and retreat often. If you want the player to heal *only* over time, make sure you do it carefully and work to minimize any waiting.

Death

If all the health is removed with a hit, the player or enemy can be considered dead. It may also be possible to "die" for other reasons such as not completing an objective before the time runs out, being trapped or captured, being seen (in a stealth game), or failing any number of other objectives. The consequences for all of these failure states can be the same or different in nature.

Whether it is the player or an NPC that is dying, you need to have some kind of death animation and possibly an effect to go with it. Vehicles and some enemies will typically blow up when destroyed. It is also common to use physics to send characters or vehicles flying after they have been killed or destroyed.

To help put your health back up to normal you can eat food, use health pick-ups or you can protect yourself by wearing body armor.

Courtesy of Rockstar Games and Take-Two Interactive Software, Inc.

In many games, players can respawn after dying (such as outside the hospital in *Grand Theft Auto*).

A designer must make some tough decisions about the cost of dying. Is the game over, or can the player load the last save or checkpoint? Does the player teleport somewhere in the level? Does the player have a limited number of lives? Does the death cost the player any money, experience, or something else? In *Ratchet & Clank,* the player has unlimited lives and respawns at the start of the level or a checkpoint after dying. In *Grand Theft Auto,* the player is taken to a hospital or police station and is then respawned outside of it and must pay money to be healed or freed. Therefore, the number of lives that the player has is directly related to how much money the player has in the game. Players can come back from death as long as they have money. When players die in *Ratchet: Deadlocked,* they respawn—but their ammunition isn't replenished, which means that the player must spend money (bolts) on more ammunition and restart the level or section as a penalty for death. In a few cases, dead players might have to go to another level (such as "hell") and fight their way out. You need to determine the cost and limits for dying; there should be a penalty for death, but you also want the player to be able to pass an area without giving up.

One aspect of controlling death is called *act tuning*, which can be used as part of a dynamic difficulty adjustment system throughout the entire game or just in specific locations that are hard to tune. Act tuning involves lowering the difficulty of an area, enemy, or challenge based on how well the player is doing. If the player is facing a difficult boss, you can subtly adjust the difficulty of that boss each time the player dies to make success easier and easier. Act tuning can be an important part of balancing player deaths and penalties, but it isn't the only system that adjusts the game based on player performance.

What role do all of these variables play in creating your game? You must consider your game's goals and genre. Every type of game will have a wide variety of needs when it comes to designing core systems. An FPS can have a camera, guns, and fighting—just like a third-person shooter. However, a third-person camera is far more complex to create because it has to move within the world independently of the controls, along with the player's manual override of its location. The same applies to first-person vs. third-person movement. Each system requires you to weigh the differences and take full advantage of them.

When you examine all of the conditions that go into making core gameplay systems work, you will realize that designing the systems alone won't be enough. Even the design of the levels will be greatly affected by the decisions you make about core gameplay systems. The way a level is built should take advantage of the camera, controls, and other core systems—while placement of enemies and how they attack the player will also impact how the rest of the game is designed. For instance, in a third-person game, you can see all around a player—it is easier to allow the player to fight all around and quickly attack enemies on any side than in an FPS, where the player has a more limited point of view.

> *Grand Theft Auto, Prince of Persia* (the later series), and *Lego Star Wars*. The way each of these games flow, by managing the concept of "player death," is pure genius. I think that for all the advancements that games have made, the death penalty (if I can call it that) has always been too harsh. These are all great examples of how this has been radically improved, and they really solve one of the biggest remaining challenges we have in games today: the challenge of making games fun for everyone.
>
> —*Chris Taylor*
> *(Creative Director & Owner, Gas Powered Games)*

While none of these techniques will require a massive amount of rework, you should be aware of what additional work and systems may be necessary to support your decisions. For instance, if you decide that the player can heal by using health packs, you must come up with the following:

- A way for the player to carry them
- The number that can be carried
- Whether they can stack in the inventory
- How to pick them up, use them, find them, and/or buy them
- Whether the player can quickly or easily use them with a keyboard shortcut or quick button
- Where and how they will be hidden or placed in the world for the player to find
- How much health each health pack gives the player
- How fast can it heal the player
- Whether the player can heal others with it
- Whether there are multiple sizes of health packs

Many additional issues could revolve around what seems to be a simple decision to include health packs in the game.

Making the player character move well, fight well, and be fun to play is an extremely challenging job. There is no right or wrong way to design a movement and combat system, but many existing games definitely have some serious design flaws. Don't underestimate the difficulty of creating great core systems that work well with your games.

:::CHAPTER REVIEW:::

1. Play an electronic game that uses a specific camera system such as first-person, third-person, lock-strafe, or fixed. If you were to redesign the game so that it uses a different camera system, how would it affect the gameplay?

2. Design a movement system for your original game idea. How will you incorporate context-sensitive moves?

3. Why is there relative complexity in combat system design? Play a game that utilizes one or more combat systems and discuss the associated target, melee, ranged, and damage systems. If applicable, design one combat system for your original game idea.

CHAPTER

Creating the Characters

the game's inhabitants

Key Chapter Questions

- What are some ways of *conceptualizing* game characters?

- How do character *roles, movement, and objects* impact a character?

- What are some character *behaviors* and how do they relate to the character's role, physical description, and personality traits?

- How do *character creation systems* affect gameplay?

- What are some techniques for designing a memorable *enemy* character?

Designing characters for games can encompass everything from visual appearance and personality to sociology, psychology, history, behavior patterns, and core abilities. Different design processes may be used for player characters and non-player characters depending on how similar they are and whether the player has the ability to "inhabit" multiple characters. Game character design may also include the creation of a wide assortment of creatures, monsters, aliens, robots, vehicles, and other nonhumans. These characters may not speak or have the same qualities as other characters in the game, but they can be just as challenging to design. This chapter focuses primarily on how to create interesting, compelling, challenging, and dynamic characters for your game. It is not going to tell you how to design a detailed AI (artificial intelligence) system for your characters, but it will help you shape a plan for your character's AI needs.

Conceptualizing Characters

Almost every game contains characters. The definition of a character is not exclusive to human beings. Your game could have aliens, creatures, animals, or any assortment of living things that could be classified as characters. Even a machine could be a character, but this begins to stretch the definition (unless the machine has intelligence, personality, or other traits that make it seem more alive). It is up to you as a designer to decide what is classified as a character in your game.

You may find it helpful to create a classification system for the characters in your game. This becomes important because custom programming for every character in your game can be cumbersome. In order to develop characters efficiently,

For further reading on this topic, please see *Game Story & Character Development* (Krawczyk/Novak), part of the *Game Development Essentials* series.

you need to classify them into categories that might allow them to share skeletons, animation, weapons, or other features. Many games have customizable characters that allow the designers to create a wide variety of characters with a smaller assortment of pieces.

Sony Computer Entertainment America

Most games feature or star a memorable character such as Kratos in *God of War II*.

It is becoming incredibly time-consuming to create next-generation, photorealistic, or highly detailed characters. Many developers now spend time designing characters up front and making sure they are happy with them before commiting a tremendous amount of art, animation, and programming resources.

After you decide on the core systems of your game, it is a good idea to work out the characters. Start with the central player character(s), followed by the rudiments of the other characters in the game. Ask yourself questions about the types of characters you would like to see in the game and what roles they would play. Are all the other characters in the game enemies? Can the player interact with characters in ways other than combat? No matter how you begin designing the characters, be sure to begin with the player character(s) as early as possible.

Sony Computer Entertainment America   Sony Computer Entertainment America

Even creatures, animals, and aliens can be considered characters, such as in *Ratchet & Clank* and *Crash Bandicoot*.

Character Asymmetry

In a game with a lot of enemies, it is most important to make them all as different from each other as possible, and also as different from me as possible. I call this the principle of asymmetry, that the more asymmetric your game characters are, the more interesting they will be. Try to find as many clear-cut ways as possible that characters can be different from each other—not just their stats and weapons, but also their AI algorithms and strategies.

—Brian Reynolds
(Chief Executive Officer, Big Huge Games)

Visual Development

It is becoming more critical for characters to be first conceptualized by a designer and then drawn by a concept artist. Characters need to fit into the overall game design, be fun and interactive, have sophisticated AI, and follow some fixed rules. As a designer, you must work closely with character artists to ensure that all characters are visually appropriate. You may also want to approach problems from several angles and let the character artists also come up with concepts that can inspire the designers.

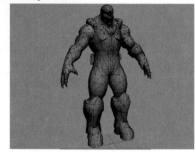

Visual character development includes sketches, concept art, wireframe, flat shaded model, textured model, and finished color model (Locust from *Gears of War,* shown).

chapter 4   Creating the Characters: the game's inhabitants

Once the character concept is approved, the character model can be created. This process is much more elaborate than it was just a few years ago. We now typically have to create several character models of different polygonal complexities: a high-poly version used to create the bump and displacement maps that make it look more detailed than it really is, and a low-poly in-game version.

Nintendo Nintendo Nintendo Nintendo

Multiple drawings of the same character (such as Link from *The Legend of Zelda: Twilight Princess*) can show signature poses, action moves, and angles.

After the character model is created, it is mapped and the texture details are applied, along with the higher-end maps. This usually includes adding gloss maps and others. (Characters rarely have just a single texture map anymore.) The character's completed body model then needs to be boned and skinned with either a custom skeleton or a specific class of skeleton. The next step is animating the model and then the programmers take over.

Art by Jason Bramble Art by Jason Bramble

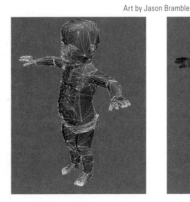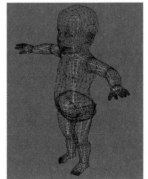

Different model complexities are created for every character—which, once modeled, must be rigged with a skeleton before it can be animated.

At some companies, characters are assembled by programmers who set up all the different states, animations, reactions, events, and AI that are needed to drive the characters. As the complexity of characters increases, this job falls into the hands of experienced technical designers. In the past, a complex non-player character (NPC) might have had a few dozen animations; now characters with over 500 animations are common—especially if the game focuses on melee combat, as in *Mortal Kombat: Shaolin Monks*.

Courtesy of Midway Games, Inc.

Mortal Kombat: Shaolin Monks has a very sophisticated melee combat system.

No matter what character development process you choose, it is important to realize that you will need to work on a character at its start and finish. Ultimately, it is up to you to make sure that your design is solid enough to work properly.

Characters need to start out as full 'beings.' Any screenwriting course will talk about three-dimensional characters. Game characters deserve no less treatment. Where did they come from? Who were their parents/creators? What was their existence like prior to our encountering them? And so on. Lay this foundation at the very least.

—Frank T. Gilson
(Senior Producer, Wizards of the Coast)

Brainstorming

Before you come up with specific character designs for your game, it is good to do some high-level brainstorming that results in a *very* short description or set of bullet points. This will not only help you see how far you want to push your character designs, but it will also provide a forum for the design team to talk about the types of characters they would like to see in the game. Here is an example of an initial list covering only three characters:

- **Reaver:** Big powerful creature, shoots fire from hands, heavily armored, slow, loud shriek calls other nearby Reavers
- **Shrieker:** Small creature that can burrow in the ground, moves very fast—and emits an ear-deafening scream that damages enemies, shatters glass, and causes you to have a hard time seeing
- **Invisio:** Can turn invisible, cannot be shot when invisible, has giant energy sword for melee attacks, hunts in packs

Nintendo   THQ   Activision

There are many different possible character types in most games (*Mario Party 6, Destroy All Humans!,* and *Call of Duty 3,* shown).

You should classify the characters in your game by form or function in order to avoid the risk of making all of your characters unique. At some level, all characters should share something, whether base geometry, skeleton, animations, or artificial intelligence (AI). Since creating characters for next-generation platforms is exponentially more expensive than before, the goal of having unique characters is not feasible for most developers.

Mauricio Ferrazza on Character Archetypes :::::

Mauricio Ferrazza
(Instructor, Art Institute
of Pittsburgh—Online
Division; Designer &
Computer Animator,
Univision Network)

Since age 17, Mauricio has been working in theatre, TV, and cinema production. His theatre experience taught him a great deal of sensibility and introduced him to the great playwrights of all time—including Ibsen, Shakespeare, Pirandello, and Miller. Mauricio then worked behind the scenes as an art director, production manager, associate producer, and writer—which showed him the complex and extraordinary roads and avenues that one navigates when producing and creating any theatre/cinema/TV production. Mauricio has a BA in Advertising & Marketing and an MFA in Computer Animation from Miami International University of Art & Design. While pursuing his MFA, he specialized in dynamics and particle simulation—which creates computer-generated simulated images to replicate and illustrate natural forces and effects widely used by the film and game industries. He has also been deeply involved in the production of short animated 3D movies, exploring mostly character animation and its fundamentals.

In 1949 Joseph Campbell released his book *The Hero with a Thousand Faces* and made a big impression in the field of mythology. The book was based on the pioneering work of German anthropologist Adolph Bastian, who first proposed the idea that myths from all over the world seem to be built from the same "elementary ideas." Swiss psychiatrist Carl Jung named these elementary ideas "archetypes," which he believed to be the building blocks not only of the unconscious mind, but of a collective unconscious. In other words, Jung believed that everyone in the world is born with the same basic subconscious model of what a "hero" is, or a "mentor" or a "quest," an "enemy," and that's why people who do not even speak the same language can enjoy the same stories.

A character may be based on a particular archetype, which is a common character pattern: Jungian archetypes are modeled after mythology, legend, and folk tales. For example, both Puck from the Shakespeare play *A Midsummer Night's Dream* and Bugs Bunny are examples of the Jungian trickster archetype because they defy established standards of behavior, fulfilling a particular role in a story

Campbell's contribution was to take this idea of archetypes and use it to map out the common underlying structure behind religion and myth. He proposed this idea in *The Hero with a Thousand Faces*, which provides examples from cultures throughout history and all over the world. Campbell eloquently demonstrates that all stories are expressions of the same story-pattern, which he named the "Hero's Journey," populated by archetypes that would become characters that people from different countries, continents, languages would identify themselves with. The archetypes are defined by their actions and decisions, resulting in the composition of their core personalities:

The Protagonist: "Pursue" and "Consideration," the Hero; the Antagonist: "Prevent" and "Re-consideration," the Shadow; the Guardian: "Help" and "Conscience," the Wise Man and so on. A single character may fulfill more than one archetypal role, depending on the plot of the game and the complexity of the storyline.

Creating characters to be interesting, compelling, challenging and dynamic is a result of the psychological study of archetypes, placing them coherently within the story line, creating an appealing conflict, placing the "Hero" in the path of his "Journey." In games, an interesting phenomenon occurs when the Antagonist many times emulates a greater fascination than the Protagonist, or the Hero. This fascination creates conflict and urgency, necessary to set up the perfect stage for the "Hero" to complete his "Journey," the cycle, the game.

Types of Characters

Not every non-player character (NPC) needs to be an enemy. It is important to describe the various types of NPCs and their abilities. Here are some possible types of NPCs at the highest level of classification:

- **Allies:** Characters who help the player, could be characters who fight alongside the player or help in other ways
- **Civilians:** Generally neutral characters, usually have limited interactions
- **Background:** Characters seen only at a distance or not interactive
- **Story:** Characters who are used in a cut-scene or other game story event
- **Vendors:** Characters who perform a function in the game to buy/sell or perform other transactions needed by the game systems
- **Enemies:** Characters who are hostile to the player character, typically intelligent
- **Creatures:** Hostile or neutral characters, but generally less intelligent; include various animals, swarmers, monsters, or other types of characters
- **Vehicles:** Not always considered characters—but are usually controlled by characters and may have some character traits

You may have more or fewer types of characters in the game. Once you have defined the various types of characters you need, it is time to define the role each character needs to play within each type.

Character Roles

It is good to spend some time thinking about what abilities you need your characters to have. Brainstorm a list of generic verbs for your characters, as well as a list of functions or roles you need them to fill. A more realistic game such as *Call of Duty* will have a different approach than a game such as *Lord of the Rings: The Battle for Middle-Earth II* or another RTS.

A real-time strategy (RTS) game has very distinct roles that characters need to fill in order to make sure the game is balanced and fun. Its characters need to do very specific things to be properly balanced against the player units. A historical shooter may just try to re-enact a specific battle or event with the units that were there, so its character design relates more to the personalities of the units. Defining the function of your characters may be challenging and depend on the game genre, but it could break down to look something like this:

- **Armorer:** Repair and sell armor and weapons
- **Sorcerer:** Buy and sell magical items
- **Trader:** Buy and sell general equipment and supplies

Vendors are in *The Elder Scrolls IV: Oblivion* to provide items or services to the player.

Enemy types might include:

- **Melee:** Fights close in
- **Grunt:** Serves as a general purpose infantry type
- **Heavy:** Uses heavy weapons
- **Ranged:** Performs like an archer
- **Long Range:** Performs like a sniper
- **Indirect:** Can lob attacks
- **Defensive:** Is heavily armored and less aggressive
- **Specialized:** Fights in an unusual or specific way
- **Leader:** Helps other units

Most games such as *Gears of War* contain enemies that attack or compete against the player

Creature types might include:

- **Swarmer:** Dangerous creature that bites
- **Animal:** Harmless creature that runs away
- **Insect:** Creature that moves along paths in the world

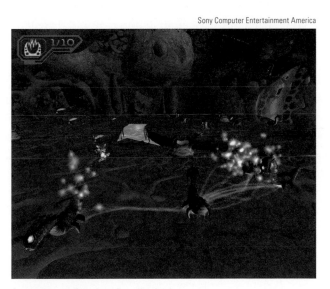

Swarmers in *Ratchet: Deadlocked.*

Vehicle types might include:

- **Transport:** Vehicle for carrying units
- **Tank:** Heavily armored attack vehicle
- **Jeep:** Unarmored fast attack vehicle
- **Bike:** Two-wheeled cycle

Courtesy NCsoft

Vehicles are an important part of most games such as *Auto Assault* and may appear to have personalities and other character traits.

Characters can fill many additional roles. Deciding what types of roles you need characters to fill is a very important step in character design because it will help ensure that your characters have enough diversity and that all of their associated functions will be filled.

> It's important to steer clear of stereotypes and clichés—which is often easier said than done. Putting yourself into the situation of your characters and making them react to outside influences is important to keeping things dynamic. Assuming you put your characters in interesting situations, make them come out of that situation changed—for the better or worse or both.
>
> —John Comes
> (Lead Game Designer, Gas Powered Games)

Character Movement

Not every character has to move like a human. Having characters move in new and more interesting ways can improve how they are perceived in the game. Adjusting how fast a character can move will make a big difference. Some possible character movement choices include: on the ground or in the air; fast or slow; jumping or bounding; teleportation; and wheeled, legged or multilegged/multilimbed. No matter how a character is going to move, you need to weigh how this movement affects the game's balance, AI, and technology.

Despite all of the improvements in inverse kinematics (IK) and animation systems over the last few years, most games still lack a sense of kinetic motion. Characters still run around and stop suddenly. In a first-person shooter (FPS), where players do not see their characters, this is not a problem for the player character but it applies to NPCs. Are you tired of seeing the player character run down the road at a sprint, only to run into a wall and come to a complete stop in the next frame? Are you tired of being stopped by a small bump ahead or watching enemies run around and change direction constantly? Many situations make our characters look less appealing when moving in the world.

What we are missing in games is momentum or kinetic motion. Besides just making the game look better, momentum and other advanced movement techniques can be used in a variety of emergent gameplay situations. This could be especially useful in a game that relies on melee combat. It can be very useful to know that an enemy is charging full steam ahead and cannot stop in time, or that two enemies running at each other will collide. Having characters run at a wall, slam into it, and look as if they hit it would be an improvement, but having a character smash into the hood of a car and go flying would be an exciting option and could be very useful as well.

Making characters more dynamic in the way they move is important for most next-gen games such as *Prince of Persia: The Two Thrones*.

Extending the move set to include more moves as in *Prince of Persia: The Two Thrones* could also be a good first step in making your game more exciting. Ask yourself what else in the environment could be more interactive. Can your character flip off walls, jump over objects, climb over walls, or do other interesting things?

Human Spider-Men

For some incredible examples of character movement that is possible, even for a normal person in real life, take a look at the sports of Parkour Free Running and Russian Climbing. There are some incredible videos on the Web showing unbelievable footage of human spider-men. Video game characters have a long way to go before recreating these abilities. Any form of acrobatics or gymnastics can serve as inspiration for what could be possible in games someday. (See *Parkour Free Running* at http://www.foucan.com and *Russian Climbing* at http://video.google.com/videoplay?docid=515642196227308929)

Another aspect of extending the move set is to add comedic elements, perhaps simply characters making mistakes. Having an NPC trip and fall, slip, run into something, shoot a friend, or do other such things is often a great next step. There are many examples of physical comedy and plenty of ways it could be used to make games more interesting and exciting.

Weapons & Attacks

If your game involves combat, you will be designing characters who attack, use weapons, or fight in some way. Define the type of attack and then determine how it will be performed. The way a character fights is just as important as the attack itself most of the time.

Sony Computer Entertainment America

There are many possible weapons that might exist in any game (such as those in *Ratchet & Clank,* shown).

Characters can use weapons that they pick up in the world or a weapon that they are carrying; they can also use their bodies, magic, or technology as weapons. Designing the weapons or attack abilities for a character that can fight is just as important as designing the rest of the character.

It is more important to consider the type of weapon your character will use. Players need to see major differences in the function of their weapons, not subtle differences (unless the game is very realistic). This point relates to the character roles mentioned earlier; each weapon or attack should be useful for a distinct purpose. Attacks can be very short range to extremely long range, with almost no limit to the types of weapons or attacks. Possible weapon types include machine gun, crossbow, spear, missile launcher, flamethrower, hand grenade, and magic spell (such as a fireball). Possible attack types include melee (punch, kick, or claw slash), bite, tail whip, and ram. You should define the types of attacks your characters might make early in the project. If your game requires a lot of creativity and unique storylines—such as those in science fiction or fantasy settings—you may want to brainstorm an extensive list of ideas and narrow it down to the best ones.

Beyond just defining the weapons, you also need to consider other factors that will make your weapons and attacks interesting. Unless you are trying to model a real-world weapons system, it is not necessary to account for all of the following factors in your weapons. However, it is important to realize their effect on your weapon and how the player uses it in the game. Here are just a few of the possible weapon properties:

- **Rate of Fire:** How fast can the weapon fire? Can you hold down the button to fire several shots, or is it a single shot only?
- **Accuracy:** How well does the attack work at different ranges, while moving, or under other conditions? Does the accuracy change over time?
- **Guidance:** Is the ammunition guided in any way?
- **Penetration:** How does the weapon penetrate its target? Can it penetrate armor, pass through multiple targets, or pass through environmental objects?
- **Additional Damage:** Does the weapon do any additional damage after it hits, or can it give the character it hits something like acid or fire that damages over time?
- **Targeting:** How is the attack targeted? Can the player zoom in, lock on, or do anything else to improve the chance of hitting the target?
- **Range:** How far can the weapon shoot?
- **Spread:** How tight (single shot) or loose (shotgun) does the weapon shoot?
- **Area of Effect:** Does the weapon damage only a single character or can it damage multiple characters?
- **Reload Speed:** How fast can the weapon reload if it has a clip?
- **Clip Size:** How many attacks can the weapon perform before it needs to be reloaded?
- **Ammunition Type & Availability:** How often can the attack be used?
- **Upgradcability:** Can the attack be upgraded in any way?
- **Change Weapon Delay Time:** How long a delay is necessary to change to a new weapon?
- **Movement Restriction:** Can the character move while attacking? Is the weapon or something else fixed while using it?
- **Sound:** Is the weapon quiet or noisy to shoot?
- **Streaming:** Can the weapon attack continuously, like a flamethrower?
- **Knockback:** Does the weapon push away things it hits?
- **Attack Combos:** Can the attack be combined with any other attack to do something else?
- **Charge-Up:** Does the attack trigger instantly or does it require a delay or time to build up its power?
- **Secondary Abilities:** Does the weapon have any additional abilities?

There may be even more factors to take into consideration as you design your weapons or attacks. Most weapons will have some combination of these behaviors that vary and make the weapon unique.

Chris Rohde on Character Integration :::::

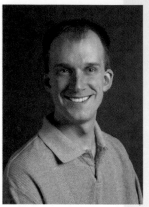

Chris Rohde
(Assistant Director,
Game Art & Design,
Visual & Game
Programming, The Art
Institute of Portland)

Chris Rohde is an assistant director for the Game Art & Design and Visual & Game Programming academic programs at The Art Institute of Portland in Portland, Oregon. He has several years of professional experience as a 3D modeler for virtual simulators and as a character modeler, character rigger, and character animator for online children's games. Chris continues to teach various game courses at The Art Institute of Portland.

There are a lot of ways to ensure that game characters are interesting, compelling, challenging, and dynamic, but the best way I know is to integrate the character into the story behind the game. A character never just 'drops in' to a game. A character always comes from somewhere and is going somewhere. Each character should be unique in a special way. Stereotypical 'special powers' have proven to work in certain games, but developed personalities and attitudes along with strong ties to the story have also worked. All characters in a game should play a particular role, such as the typical 'hero' and 'villain' roles. Characters that do not have a purpose should be removed to avoid hurting gameplay by either confusing the player or muddling a clean, tight story.

Character Behaviors

Once you have defined the basic characteristics of your character, think about how the character will behave. You do not have to design the complete AI for the character, but you need to understand what the character is supposed to do and how it should act. Brainstorm a list of the basic behaviors, which could also be classified as character states or abilities. Possible character behavior classifications include move, flank, work, communicate, fight/attack, block, flee, die, heal, and special actions.

This is only a small number of possible behaviors, and many may be broken down further. Behaviors such as block, flee, or die could even be classified as a subset of the fight behavior. It really depends on how you want to break it down. After developing your character behavior list, look for anything that is particularly different or even unique. Custom behaviors for characters can be good, but having too many of them can be risky. These lists are designed to help you think about what your characters have in common.

Attack Behaviors

It is also important to define possible attack behaviors. NPCs might do any number of things to attack the player character, such as the following:

- staying put when using a weapon
- keeping on the move
- keeping a distance
- trying to get very close
- attempting to move past the player
- attacking relentlessly
- ducking behind cover
- strafing
- running away
- throwing grenades
- attacking alone
- working in groups
- blocking
- jumping around
- becoming invisible
- using fixed weapons in the environment

Reprinted with permission from Microsoft Corporation

Enemies in *Halo 2* may strafe around and even flank the player.

You should consider many different behaviors that characters can perform in combat. Experiment with choosing behaviors that might be unexpected by the player.

Reactions

Physical, emotional, and sensory reactions are essential to creating believable characters. Reacting properly to events in the world makes a character seem more alive. The AI may try to discern these events "intelligently," or the game may have some scripted events that make the characters feel more intelligent than they actually are. *Grand Theft Auto III* (*GTAIII*) is a great example of reactive AI. When the player commits a crime, the cops are called. This is a global response system showing that responses can be individual or widespread. When a character attacks another in *GTAIII*, the other character will fight back. When the player carjacks a vehicle, the vehicle's owner gets angry, and occasionally the owner's friend will chase the player!

Courtesy Rockstar Games and Take-Two Interactive Software, Inc.

Eidos Interactive Ltd.

Carjacking is a core mechanic of *Grand Theft Auto III* that involves reactive artificial intelligence.

It is as important for enemies to die well as to fight well in games such as *Hitman: Blood Money.*

In *Mercenaries,* the AI is also divided into factions that react differently depending on the player's status with them. Each faction can be hostile, friendly, or neutral. If a faction is hostile, it will attack and not help the player. It's a good idea to list a series of actions that the player or NPC can perform that will elicit a response. The more realistic your game looks, the higher the expectations are and the more reactions people expect to see.

Electronic Arts, Inc.

In *Mercenaries 2,* there are many factions to fight or befriend.

Players are used to encountering "unintelligent" NPCs. However, nothing upsets them more than to do something that should elicit a reaction and see the character just stand still or not respond. Characters who do not respond to getting hit in combat are especially confusing and annoying, since players do not know if they are damaging or actually hitting the character.

Part of having the ability to react is having senses. *Splinter Cell* has sophisticated AI that allows the NPCs to see not only the player but conditions in the world such as whether the lights are on or off. They also have the ability to hear and smell. NPCs can react to dead bodies, damage to the environment, smoke and fire, and other problem signs.

What makes a game emergent is allowing the player to interact with an NPC's senses in unpredictable ways. If NPCs can react to something in the world, the player should be able to use this against them. Using noise or other stimuli to affect NPCs is an important part of many games and can be especially useful in stealth games.

Enemies in *Tom Clancy's Splinter Cell: Double Agent* can see and hear the player coming.

Interaction

Even if this interaction is minimal, it can be very nice to have in the game. It is not just about letting the player interact with the world, but about having NPCs who can interact with each other, or allowing the player to force NPCs to react to each other in different ways. In *Mortal Kombat: Shaolin Monks,* there are "hairy ape" creatures called Oni that will fight among themselves if the player kicks one of them into another one. While this is a scripted event, it is still a nice and more believable touch.

There are many different ways for the player to interact with NPCs in the game besides fighting with or against them. The player might choose to interact physically with NPCs—for example, by grabbing them, performing a quick kill or knockout, or torturing them. Having conversations with NPCs is common in many games, especially role-playing and adventure games. In *GTAIII* and other sandbox games, the player and NPCs can have almost limitless kinds of interactions; they can, for example, commit crimes, have sex—and communicate, chase, follow, and protect other characters.

Mortal Kombat: Shaolin Monks contains creatures called Oni that fight each other.

Showing NPCs involved in a robbery adds realism to the world of *Grand Theft Auto III*.

Some games take interaction to the next level, where the NPC's reactions are influenced by the reputation that the player character has earned in the game. *Fable* has a great reputation system that allows the NPCs to address players differently based on actions in the game. Beyond responding differently in conversations, the NPCs could run away from players who gain a reputation as a fearsome fighter, or enemies could attempt to track down players who become dangerous.

Randy Greenback on the Importance of Character Behavior & Personality:::::

Randy Greenback
(Creative Director,
Red Storm
Entertainment/
Ubisoft)

Randy Greenback has worked on 30+ game SKUs on multiple platforms in various roles in the last 11 years. He got his start in the industry in 1996 in the Quality Assurance Department at Westwood Studios, working his way up from there. After leaving Westwood he moved to the East Coast to work at iRock Games as an associate producer and later a game designer on *Savage Skies*, a flying creature action game for the PS2. Randy returned to Westwood Studios and worked there up until the day that Electronic Arts closed the doors. He transferred to Electronic Arts-Los Angeles and worked as a designer there, producing missions and maps for *Command & Conquer Generals: Zero Hour*. After spending a year at EA, Randy went to Red Storm Entertainment—where he has been working since 2004, working on *Rainbow Six: Lockdown* for PS2/PC and producing content for *Ghost Recon: Advanced Warfighter* and *GRAW2*. He is currently a creative director working on the next-gen console iteration of *America's Army*. Randy has two wonderful children, Reece and Madison—and he enjoys sharing his passion for gaming with them and his girlfriend, Mindy.

Players need something to work against or overcome; some games rely on puzzles, some use more strategic plotting against a global AI, and others rely on a mindless onslaught of bullets and drones. Some of the best enemies that players can face are ones that have the ability to surprise them using the game's basic rules in a unique way or combining a series of actions to employ a new tactic. Good AI should evolve and learn from player tactics just as other players would in an online multiplayer battle. Using feedback and observations gathered from playing your game against others can help you find intriguing player behaviors or play-styles that you can carry over into your enemy AI. This approach works very well if you are building a game with adversarial elements.

Taking a more open approach to enemy behaviors and allowing the NPCs to interpret what is going on so they can choose how to react works especially well in squad-based tactical shooters like what I've been working on lately. One AI soldier acting alone can only choose from a small swatch of tactics—but as soon as you have a full team of five AI soldiers, the options they have to counter a player's move increase dramatically. Interesting AI team behaviors that evolve to challenge players and compel them to explore their own options to come up with counter moves, thus becoming a continual game of one-upping their opponents.

Adding personality to your enemies will also help make them more compelling to deal with. Allow your enemy characters to tease and taunt the player when they are putting the pressure on them, and on the flip side you can build up their personas even more by having them express fear and beg for mercy when they are on the run. Building a system that is as dynamic as possible while leveraging your ability to detect a situation and play on its inherent emotional elements will keep the players engaged and on their toes. Really, when it all comes down to it, nothing feels more rewarding to players than knowing they outwitted a realistic and challenging foe.

Mistakes

Game characters seem too perfect and act like robots because of the way we program them. It has been difficult enough to get characters to do what they are supposed to do, let alone anything else. We have always fought the technical limitations on our ability to give characters enough animation, AI, or speed to make them feel natural and more lifelike in a game.

The next generation of games will begin to allow game characters to make purposeful mistakes. Imagine characters that can trip and fall, run into things, slip, misfire, jam their weapons, get hurt, accidentally shoot their friends, or say the wrong thing. Seeing characters become frustrated because they made a mistake would be very interesting in a game.

When a character makes a mistake, it is important that the player realize it was not just something unintelligent that bad AI caused in the game. We have all seen games where characters run into a corner and keep on running, where AI cannot navigate properly, where enemies do not respond to the player or fail to shoot. Bad AI has caused many mistakes—but these are not the kind we need characters to start making. It is probably best to start by having the character make very large, over-the-top mistakes that are scripted and very purposeful; get players used to something like this before including any subtle mistakes.

The key to making mistakes add impact to the game is to be sure they include reactions. If a mistake occurs and the character just keeps on making the same one, it will feel more like a bug. The character that makes the mistake needs to react to the problem, probably in a big way. Even if the mistake is more emergent and not scripted, there should be some kind of reaction.

If a character runs during a fight and slips on some oil, make a big deal about it. Have the character knock over something while falling, get up dripping with oil, and act hurt and upset. The character should do something to react to the mishap, and players will be overcome with joy. In a truly emergent game world, systems that allow the player to manipulate the AI to cause mistakes could create comical situations while also being useful. Other examples would include spraying down oil to make characters slip, taking control of characters to make them shoot their friends, and setting up a tripwire that makes a character fall. No matter how you let characters make mistakes, the important lesson is that reactions are critical if you want your characters to be perceived as intelligent, real, and alive.

Comedy

Adding humor to a game is extremely difficult to pull off, especially for an international market. Many types of humor are possible in a game, whether subtle or over the top. Comedy might focus on only a single character or be part of a routine reminiscent of the classic Abbott & Costello or Laurel & Hardy duos. In most action "buddy films," you will see that one character represents comic relief.

Physical comedy is probably one of the most appropriate uses of comedy in games, although it can be more difficult to do well than humorous dialogue. Regardless of how you use humor in a game, avoid overdoing it and be sure to keep it as universal as possible. It is very easy to add something that the development team finds hilarious, only to discover that players think it offensive. Run it past others first to see if they "get it" and find it funny, and make sure you add a wide variety of humor that will appeal to many.

Deborah Baxtrom on Designing Strong Characters :::::

Deborah has an MFA in screenwriting/directing from Columbia University in NYC. She has written and/or directed two award-winning short films and has optioned several feature length screenplays. She also developed a game story and characters for a course taught at the Art Institute of Pittsburgh—Online Division. She also teaches for AiP-OD and has also worked as a story analyst, entertainment journalist, and script doctor.

Deborah Baxtrom
(Writer & Filmmaker;
Instructor, Art
Institute of Pittsburgh
—Online Division)

Characters should have complex personalities, including flaws and virtues, whether they are 'good' or 'bad.' A variety of different characters is also important. If characters in a story are too similar they will not be compelling or entertaining to the player/audience. I think writers should 'love' their characters, even the evil ones. If the writer is involved with his/her characters, the player will probably be as well.

Character Creation

Many games now use elaborate dynamic character creation systems. Allowing players to create their own characters can be highly rewarding and useful, and creating additional NPCs dynamically increases the variety of characters in a game. Many dynamic creation systems also allow the game to modify characters over time in slightly different ways. Many EA Sports games such as *Fight Night Round 3, Tiger Woods Golf,* or *NFL Street* and other games such as *The Elder Scrolls IV: Oblivion* and *Fable* allow players to customize their characters before they begin playing. The same basic systems that are used to create customized player characters can also be used to create a wide variety of NPCs.

Character customization typically works for human-based characters where most of the body sizes, shapes, and needs are fairly uniform in nature. They are built by being able to swap in several different body parts, pieces of clothing, and accessories and then smoothly blend between the pieces to create a new single character. In the past, these characters looked very rough and were usually of lesser quality than customized characters, but some of the more recent games such as *Fight Night Round 3* for the Xbox 360 have customized characters that look amazing. Relic's *Impossible*

Creatures had technology that was ahead of its time and allowed the player to make different creatures by selecting body parts; the engine would blend between the various pieces to create diverse and impressive-looking characters.

Electronic Arts, Inc.

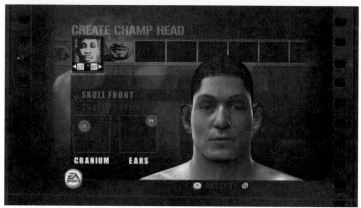

EA's *Fight Night Round 3* can create amazing-looking characters.

Dynamic character creation also allows the player to modify characters. In *Grand Theft Auto: San Andreas,* the player character will become muscular after working out or fat after eating the wrong foods. In *Fable,* the player characters will age over time, age faster if they use magic, and retain any scars they receive in battle. Player characters in *Fable* also begin to change based on how good or how evil they are in the game and can take on more angelic or more demonic features and effects if the player swings too far to one side. These games indirectly change the way the player character looks during the game based on the actions and choices made by the player.

Courtesy Rockstar Games and Take-Two Interactive Software, Inc.

Courtesy Rockstar Games and Take-Two Interactive Software, Inc.

Grand Theft Auto: San Andreas allows the player character's physical appearance to change from fat to buff, depending on what decisions the player makes.

:::::EA's Gameface

EA has an amazing system called Gameface that is used throughout many of their titles, especially sports games such as *Tiger Woods Golf 2006.* Gameface allows players to customize every aspect of their characters. These systems usually let you dynamically alter the geometry of a base model or morph between several different models while creating the desired character. In addition to changing the character's face, body, and clothing, these systems also allow the player to modify vocal characteristics and even change initial stats (as in role-playing games [RPGs] such as *The Elder Scrolls IV: Oblivion*).

Electronic Arts, Inc.

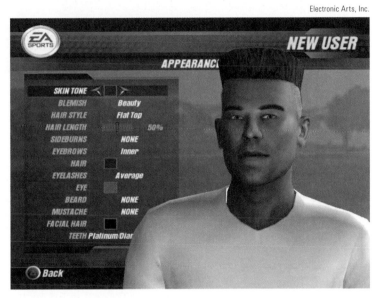

EA's Gameface (shown in *Tiger Woods PGA Tour 06*) can be used to create almost any character the player desires.

Character creation systems are not only used to create player characters; they also allow designers to build many NPCs in the game quickly and easily. This can provide the game with a larger number of different characters much more economically than if the design team had to create all the characters by hand. The downside to most of the custom character creation systems is that the characters usually do not look as good and unique as those created by a real artist who does not have to conform to the standard body types and restrictions of a character customization system.

Grand Theft Auto: San Andreas and *Def Jam: Fight for New York* also let you buy clothing to change the way you look in the game, and the character's appearance slightly affects the way the game plays. At any time in the game, you can buy a wide variety of name brand clothing, accessories, and jewelry to wear that will make the player character stronger. It allows the player character to get a haircut or tattoos as well.

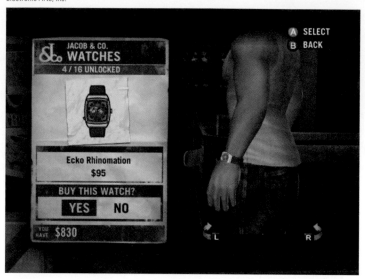

Def Jam: Fight for New York allows the player to purchase all kinds of clothing and jewelry.

Allies

It is possible for characters to help the player in some way. The three main types of allies in a game are those who sell items that you need, fight alongside you, and give you new objectives or things to do. It is important to firmly establish which characters are enemies and which are friends in the game, as well as to provide appropriate feedback to the player. Vendors, merchants, armorers, blacksmiths, trainers, or any other characters that can buy, sell, give, make, and convert items are important to the game. Another type of ally could be a doctor, medic, or healer. Consider how systems in the game will work and how the characters in the game will interact, and determine what actions the characters will need to perform.

Allies who fight along with the player can take several forms. In games such as *Halo* or *Medal of Honor,* there are scripted soldiers who follow the player character around or fight others. These characters are usually not controlled by the player, but they add extra firepower to the player's attacks and make the game feel much more realistic. Some games allow the player to issue a limited number of commands to these ally troops. In some cases, players may even take control or switch between some of the different characters who are accompanying them.

If you decide to create ally characters, decide whether you would like them to be scripted, partially player controlled, or fully AI controlled. The more complicated the characters, the more work that will be required to properly implement them; the more realistic they seem, the higher the players' expectations of what they can do. Make sure you understand the pros and cons of your proposed allies before you commit to creating them. Making characters that help players through their journeys can be an important part of many games. It is possible to drive the player forward using an interface of some kind, but it is far more compelling to have other characters in the game tell the player what to do. Allies should exhibit reactions so that the player does not end up accidentally fighting or killing them. Ally characters that just stand around and allow the player to shoot them without even flinching can also pull the player out of the game experience.

Having troops who help you in a battle in games such as *Call of Duty 2* really adds to the immersion.

Talking to other characters has been around since the earliest video games—and dialogue systems have not changed much. Talking to characters in a game has several functions:

- Gathering information about the world, the situation, goals, or other intelligence
- Discovering new objectives, experiences, and items
- Getting direct help from the NPC, such as repairing an item, teaching you something, or healing you

During gameplay in *Neverwinter Nights 2*, possible player responses in branching dialogue appear as numbered choices.

Dialogue windows, such as those shown in *Neverwinter Nights*, may be used when the camera is zoomed out or when there are multiple responses.

Traditionally, conversations have taken the form of branched trees where players choose from a series of options. Classic examples are the LucasArts games *Day of the Tentacle* and *Indiana Jones & the Fate of Atlantis.* A few games have tried some different approaches to having conversations with AI-controlled NPCs, but there have been no incredible breakthroughs with dialogue systems. The drawback to the traditional dialogue tree is that player choices usually do not mean much, and typical players do not even read the dialogue but just flip through every option in order to trigger any actions that they might need. Some games such as *Star Wars: Knights of the Old Republic* allow the player to be "good" or "evil." This makes players' dialogue choices more interesting, since they are capable of making good or bad choices. These choices might actually be used to make friends or enemies. For most games, characters that are not enemies are very important—and there are many benefits to having them in the game. Allowing the player to talk to characters can be far more interesting than making the player listen to them in cut-scenes.

Enemies

Creating enemy characters in a game can be complex. A game needs good enemies who are fun to play against, entertaining, interesting, and well balanced. The challenge for creating great enemies is different for every game. In a historical game such as *Call of Duty 3,* it is not what the enemies wear, shoot, or look like that makes them interesting but what they do and how they do it. Players should feel they are in the middle of a war zone, where enemies work in squads and utilize appropriate tactics and behaviors.

Activision

It is not about how the enemies look, but what they do (*Call of Duty 3*, shown).

A game such as *Ratchet & Clank* relies more on what characters look like or the cool weapon that they shoot at you to create interest. Characters in *Ratchet & Clank* typically do not live very long, since the player usually has massive firepower and lots of ammunition that kills enemies very quickly, so giving enemies a great deal of artificial intelligence and interesting behaviors is often counterproductive.

In a fighting game such as *Dead or Alive 4*, players can play as every character that they fight, so the characters need to be very interesting and well balanced. However, the AI also must be intelligent, since the player expects the enemy to act and behave as close to a real person as possible. Since the player fights one character at a time for a very long period of time, the AI needs to be exceptionally good but fair to play against.

As you have already learned, there are many different types of possible enemy characters in the world, and they should be classified to ensure they are diverse enough, have specific functions, and get progressively more challenging. Classifying enemies also helps you think about gameplay systems for enemies so that you do not necessarily have to custom create every component of an enemy from scratch but can share pieces of enemies and create a few unique components per enemy.

When you design an enemy, consider which features are important to focus on. It is difficult to create the perfect enemy, so it's best not to try. Keeping your schedule and restrictions in mind at the outset will help you create enough characters that are as detailed as you can make them in the time you have. That being said, you also do not want to stifle your creativity, so you must brainstorm early on and try to push the boundaries a little in order to get the best results possible in the time you have.

Designing an enemy is the second or third step in the overall enemy creation process. You first want to brainstorm enemy ideas, which results in a short description of what makes the enemy interesting or unique. Then you should think about the big picture and create an enemy classification chart, which should help you to understand most of your needs for the types of enemies you want to have in the game. It is good to brainstorm 5–10 times as many ideas for enemies as you will actually need so you can then pick a few and move forward with designing them. Avoid spending a lot of time designing detailed enemies unless you are fairly sure that you want them in the game.

Sony Computer Entertainment America

Ratchet & Clank contains several enemies, but players rarely get up close and personal with them for long.

Tecmo

Fighting games such as *Dead or Alive 4* allow you to get up close and personal.

Do not fall in love with your enemies or be too attached to them. Sometimes it is impossible to throw out an enemy because it is required by the license you are working under, or by the genre, time period, or other requirement or restriction. However, especially while working on paper, you should be willing to walk away from bad enemy designs that are suddenly not interesting. First, create a template using many of the categories or features that you initially created when brainstorming the types, classifications, and roles of the various characters in the game. Figure out what is important to your game and your characters and make sure you include any critical details in your template.

Keep in mind that you should focus on the essentials early in the process and not get too bogged down in unimportant details. After you create a short summary of the character, you should not spend much time filling out the template. Use a shotgun approach that allows you to throw out many ideas, and then pick the best ones. Do not write more than one page per character at this stage. No matter how you design your characters, it is good to look at differentiating them and ensuring they are fun to play.

How the player encounters an enemy in the world has a lot to do with how he perceives the enemy in the game. Traditionally, there have been two main ways for players to encounter enemies. They are either preplaced in the world or "magically" spawned when the player does something. Characters are fairly resource intensive, so having too many characters onscreen at a time is usually difficult, which is why so many games spawn in their enemies.

Introducing new enemies into a scene or having interesting ways for enemies to exist in a scene is very important to the player's perception of most games. The more open-ended the game, the more critical it is to have enemies who live and exist in the world most of the time. In a game such as *Far Cry,* it is necessary to see enemies from afar and plan your approach because you can attack from almost any direction and in different ways. When a game has less freedom of movement and visibility, such as *Doom,* it is less of a concern to see for miles and know where all of the enemies are.

A more linear, story-driven game, especially a horror game, is more likely to script enemies to attack the player in different ways or do something customized when the player enters the scene. In *Quake 4*, the player enters a room and then sees a creature enter on the far side of the room, attack someone, and flee before the player can do anything about it. This attack foreshadows the player character's eventual encounter with the creature and adds a lot of tension to the scene.

Far Cry allows the player to detect enemies from great distances.

Characters in a scene should not be idle and then suddenly "wake up" and attack the player. Allowing characters to exist in the world in a more natural way will make your games more appealing and less jolting. One concept is to have characters perform a "job" while they are idle. Some games rely on a purely scripted system for characters to perform an action in the game. The characters will continue to perform this action until interrupted by the player or some other event. Some games are built more emergently; "jobs" exist in the world and characters are attracted to do a job if they are close to it or it meets their requirements. A "job" could be

Games like *Quake 4* are heavily scripted.

anything in the world that a character can do in the game, such as patrol, work at a desk, move boxes, unload a truck, sell items to other characters, or sweep the street. The goal of a "job" is to provide some kind of action that makes the character feel natural to the world.

Courtesy of Midway Games, Inc.

Spawning is a common technique used to bring more enemies into an area. Sometimes the enemies are predetermined, and sometimes the spawner may select the enemies based on what the player is doing and how strong the player is. Spawners may be off screen or right in front of you. A spawner can be destroyed by the player to keep it from spawning more enemies, or it could be unreachable and always active. The biggest problem with spawners in many games that use them is that they often keep generating the same enemies even after the player kills off everyone.

In *Mortal Kombat: Shaolin Monks,* enemies are respawned often.

There are many ways for new enemies to be introduced into an area. Many games rely on the classic magical teleportation device, while others use the more realistic helicopter, parachute, or other modern device. Some games have enemies come out of doors, rappel down from above, climb up through a manhole, get dropped off by a car, or jump out of a window. Additional units such as transports may be needed in the game. They could have unique characteristics that allow them to enter the scene in surprising ways. Regardless of the era or genre, there should be many ways for you to make interesting character introductions in your game.

Courtesy of id Software, Inc.

Creating the Characters: the game's inhabitants   chapter 4

The concept of calling in reinforcements can add a lot to a game. In a game such as *Mercenaries,* the player must worry about alarms going off. When an alarm is sounded, troops rush out of bunkers to look for the player, making the game more challenging. However, the alarms are destructible objects. In *Far Cry,* the soldiers run for an alarm button when they see you and try to activate it. A good player could keep them from triggering the alarm. In *Ratchet & Clank: Going Commando,* sleeping enemy creatures have "watchdogs" that scream when they see the player waking their sleeping masters. An enemy could call for help on a cell phone, blow a horn, or do anything in the world that would make sense to attract more people. For the player, having a chance to stop the enemy from bringing in reinforcements is a tactical opportunity and is far more interesting than just watching enemies appear.

Electronic Arts, Inc.

In *Mercenaries 2,* a non-player character could call for reinforcements.

Sony Computer Entertainment America

In *Ratchet & Clank: Going Commando*, some enemies watch over others.

Game characters should be integrated into the mechanics—so that working with them in the case of NPC allies, or against them in the case of enemies, feels like an intrinsic part of the gameplay and not a break in the action. Creating truly believable game characters is a challenge I haven't seen entirely mastered yet, but a lot of interesting work is going on in this area. I'm always fascinated with characters that seem to have their own internal motivation and act accordingly.

—*Tracy Fullerton*
(Assistant Professor, Interactive Media Division,
USC School of Cinematic Arts)

Combat

An enemy could not be an enemy without being able to attack the player. Since fighting is at the heart of most electronic games, designing enemies and how they fight is crucial. Making an interesting enemy that does more than just swing a sword or shoot a gun at the player can be very challenging. In games such as *Ratchet & Clank,* enemies tend to live for only a few seconds and do not always have time to appear interesting. Every game has its own environment in which to make its enemies fun, interesting, challenging, diverse, and well balanced—and it is impossible to provide a magic formula. Analyzing what makes your game and the enemy characters fun is challenging and often hard to do on paper. Sometimes you must build some enemies and experiment with what makes them interesting before you will really know.

Movement

Having enemies who can take cover, duck and stay low, stay in the shadows, use a shield, or stay protected in some other way can make things very interesting for players. Enemies should know how to utilize the terrain to their advantage, flank the player, try to destroy the environment and have it fall on the player, or move in the terrain in other more intelligent ways.

Imagine a scenario where enemies recognize that the player is in a room, behind cover, and heavily armed—and there is only one door into the room. Do the enemies just keep trying to come through the door, or is there another way for them to flush the player out? What if the enemies know how to blow a hole through a different wall and enter the room that way? It would not be too hard to set that up and use it throughout the game. Instead of having lots of doors everywhere, have wall pieces that the AI recognizes as doors; instead of playing an open door animation, play a blow-up door animation to penetrate what is actually a wall. It is a little more complicated, but not by much. Players would see this as a huge step forward in the intelligence of the enemies.

In most games, the enemies are fairly static and just react to the player's presence. The player usually triggers the reactions of the enemies by entering an area or doing something that should lead the enemy into action. Having enemies who are just reactive and passive is not terribly exciting in the long run. You want enemies to react to the player without being passive.

Enemies should know how to retreat, flee, or withdraw in a unique manner without having to always fight to the death. An enemy that tries to stay away from the player or move to a safe place could also be more interesting, especially if combined with enemies who retreat and heal, or retreat to call in reinforcements.

Think of a game such as *The Elder Scrolls IV: Oblivion* where the player is walking down a trail in the middle of the woods and sees an Orc or another creature looting a corpse. Imagine that the creature turns, sees the player, screams not in rage but in fear—mumbling something about the player being the Orc killer—and takes off running in the opposite direction, screaming the whole way. The player would get a high sense of satisfaction from this, since the Orc acknowledges the player's status and ability. Just when the player is done laughing at the incident, however, imagine that the Orc suddenly returns with 10 friends—yelling and pointing at the player. This would make for an exhilirating moment!

Orcs are often found looting corpses in the middle of the woods in *The Elder Scrolls IV: Oblivion*.

Enemies can also become more or less aggressive during the game based on the player's actions. The aggressiveness of the enemy should affect how it moves in the game. The more aggressive the enemy is toward the player, the more the enemy should move toward the player character; the more defensive an enemy is, the more the enemy should stay away or hide from the player character.

Death

It can also be very important to think about how your enemy will die. Since many will not live very long, making them die in more interesting ways may be possible. The enemy should die in a way that is appropriate in response to the weapon that did the damage.

© Courtesy of Capcom. Reprinted with permission.

Consider ways to make enemies die in a way that is more strategically interesting. What if a dying enemy blows up, sprays acid, or produces some other interesting effect that could either hurt the player or other enemies, or affect the environment in some way. In *Devil May Cry 3*, there is a giant enemy that explodes when killed—making it dangerous to fight the enemy with a sword, and forcing the player to fight using a gun. However, the player can also damage surrounding enemies if the death of this explosive enemy is timed appropriately.

The large enemies in *Devil May Cry 3* explode after being hit.

What happens to the enemy after death can also affect the player in different ways. Does the enemy's body just disappear after death, or does it remain behind? What if a dead enemy leaves a rib cage and the player uses it like a hazard to damage other enemies? What if the enemy leaves a pool of acid blood that others might fall into? What if the enemy has a canister that may be shot and might explode when the enemy is shot? This could make deciding when, where, and how to kill enemies much more interesting and exciting.

Leaders

A variant of the primary enemy types is the leader—someone who commands others, inspires them, and makes them better. At the most basic level, a leader is an advanced or elite troop type that is found in groups of enemies but does not really affect others or have any special behaviors. A leader should affect the game and cause some change in the gameplay. When leaders are present, there should be others present who are under command. A leader could also have the ability to call in reinforcements. No matter how leaders are used in a game, the concept they bring to players is easy to understand and can add a lot of depth and fun to a game.

Starr Long on Creating Convincing Enemies :::::

Starr Long
(Producer,
NCsoft Corporation)

Starr Long has been in the business of making games for over 12 years. Along with Richard Garriott, he was the original project director for the commercially successful *Ultima Online.* Starr worked his way up through the ranks of Origin Systems, starting in quality assurance on *Wing Commander, Ultima,* and many other titles. He was Producer on *Ultima Online 2.* He also worked with Richard Garriott on *Tabula Rasa* for the Korean online game giant NCsoft, creators of *Lineage,* the world's largest online game.

Make sure that each enemy has some kind of unique behavior. Do not just add another enemy to the game because it looks different. Make the player think about how to fight each enemy differently. For instance, we have a shield drone in *Tabula Rasa* that protects any enemy troops under its shield, making them essentially invulnerable. Players must take out the drone first by using EMP weapons.

Bosses & Massive Enemies

Another subset of character creation involves massive enemies. In the past, enemies that were abnormally large were usually considered bosses. While this may be true for many games, it is now becoming more common to encounter larger enemies that are not bosses. With games such as *Shadow of the Colossus,* we are seeing that it is very possible to interact with large bosses in new and more interesting and direct ways, even if this is still difficult to implement.

A boss does not have to be massive, but it does need to be special and usually fairly tough to beat. In some games, bosses are incredibly hard to defeat and are often next to impossible for many players to get past. At one time, bosses relied on a pattern that players had to recognize and memorize to defeat them. Bosses can be characters, vehicles, props—almost anything. Many bosses also have a custom arena or location in the environment designed just for them and they interact with the game world in interesting ways.

Shadow of the Colossus makes massive enemies really shine.

In *God of War,* the first boss the player fights is a giant three-headed hydra. In this case, the player also can perform special attacks with custom animations that are played when the player fights the hydra, which also has special attacks that create a series of full-screen effects. Having a very large boss can be a memorable moment in a game and well worth while, as long as it does not cost you too much in time and resources.

Large-scale enemies can cause many problems in a game. The player's camera usually does not detect large enemies very well, which makes it difficult to see their bodies and attacks. Massive enemies often have trouble moving in regular environments and may even have to use special scripted movements that allow them to move properly in a world that does not follow the same rules. Unique animations, skeletons, environments, navigation, collision, attacks, and other custom AI make them risky to develop. If your game is going to rely on using massive enemies, it is a good idea to prove your technology ahead of time and make sure you can deliver on it.

In some cases, massive enemies can be faked or alluded to. It is possible to create what looks like a massive enemy by using smoke and mirrors, forced perspective, and other tricks. In some cases, the player might see the giant enemy at a distance, as when the player first sees Ares in *God of War.* Later on, the player might see only a part of the enemy, but because the player knows how big the enemy is, imagination simply fills in the blanks. In *God of War,* the player also climbs on the back of Atlas, a giant character whose back is a massive game level. Having a level *seem* to be taking place on the back of a massive character can be achieved through a few tricks, some crafty level building, and dynamic skybox creation that make it seem like the player is high up and the world is passing by. Making giant enemies the same size as another regular character and then shrinking everything around them is another possibility. Keep in mind that it is often easier and better to fake massive enemies and give the *illusion* that the player is fighting them than to create custom technology that truly supports interactive massive enemies.

Sony Computer Entertainment America

God of War allows the player to fight massive bosses that are unique and interesting.

Sony Computer Entertainment America

God of War allows players to climb onto some enemies and attack them.

Character Cohesion

Characters add interest to a game, help players build an emotional attachment, and drive the story forward. Even a game such as *Command & Conquer,* which is predominantly about a series of vehicles fighting each other, infuses life and characterization into vehicles by giving them unseen pilots or drivers.

Electronic Arts, Inc.

Vehicles in *Command & Conquer 3: Tiberium Wars* have voices that communicate with the player character, helping them appear more as living characters than vehicles.

Whether you are designing the player character, ally, enemy, creature, or other character, it is important to realize that they will need to interact with many of the gameplay systems. Understanding how the various characters will need to use the different gameplay systems is a critical part of determining how the various systems of the game should be designed. It also helps to determine the types of systems that will be needed to support various characters in the game and to make sure that important systems are properly designed and implemented.

In *Oddworld: Munch's Oddysee,* the main character (Munch) is a water-swimming character, and enemies were designed to swim in the water. However, for technical reasons and lack of time, enemies who could swim were never created; this made it extremely difficult to make all of the water levels in the game fun. Core gameplay systems required for the main characters should be completed so that you do not run into long-term problems.

Be aware of what features your enemies will have, even when you are designing your main character. For instance, if many of your enemies can fly and shoot from far away, but the player character has only a sword, the character will be in a lot of trouble. You have to have some inkling of what the various characters in the game will be capable of in order to make sure that the gameplay systems will be balanced, varied, fun, and strategic.

In *Oddworld: Munch's Oddysee,* Munch is a water-swimming character—but he never encounters water-swimming enemies.

No matter how you design the characters for your game, keep in mind that they are almost always challenging and resource intensive to create. Make sure that your character designs are solid and well thought out before you start building them, and you will be thankful in the end. In the next chapter, we will take a look at how to provide players with options in the game.

:::CHAPTER REVIEW:::

1. Play at least three electronic games that feature at least three strong characters. Discuss the roles, movement systems, objects, and behavior patterns associated with each character. What are the relationships between the characters? How do the characters enhance the game experience, and how do they relate to the game's mechanics?

2. Create three character descriptions for your original game idea, including one player character and two non-player characters (one ally and one enemy). The three characters should form some sort of "character triangle" where each of them has a relationship with one of the others.

3. Create a character customization system for the player character so that players may choose physical, personality, and movement/combat characteristics for the character. How will you ensure that the customized character will still work within the character triangle and other structural elements you set up in Exercise 2?

Part II:
Gameplay
Dimensions

CHAPTER

5

Creating
the Options

providing breadth

Key Chapter Questions

■ How does *cinematic* gameplay serve to "hook" the player?

■ How is *pacing* handled in a game?

■ How do you create an *immersive* experience for the player?

■ How do you create *freedom of choice* for the player?

■ What are the advantages of building *emergent* game systems?

A game that contains a lot of breadth can get players hooked and keep them interested by incorporating options and freedom. This chapter is about giving players lots of toys to play with, creating features that put players in control of their own destiny when possible, and making sure they feel empowered while playing the game. If your game is highly interactive and involving throughout, it can immediately capture the players' attention and ensure that they remain engaged in the experience. This may sound obvious—since a game wouldn't be a game without interactivity—but you would be surprised at how many games do not meet this goal. Some games force the player to watch long introductory cut-scenes that can take more than 15 minutes before the game actually begins. This problem doesn't occur just at the beginning of the game; any other part can be tedious and uninteresting to the player. Proper pacing is another technique that will keep the game stimulating for players. Include new and constantly evolving gameplay by allowing the player character abilities to be combined in new and interesting ways. You also can create a more satisfying experience for players by immersing them in a world that is much more than just a static backdrop.

Pacing

Pacing focuses on both the story and level design. There are definitely times in most games where it is good to slow the pace down and let players explore and play at their own pace, but there are also times when it is good to keep players on their toes and moving all the time. You do not want your game to be one long car chase that wears the player out and becomes frustrating because it never lets up.

Diagram by Per Olin

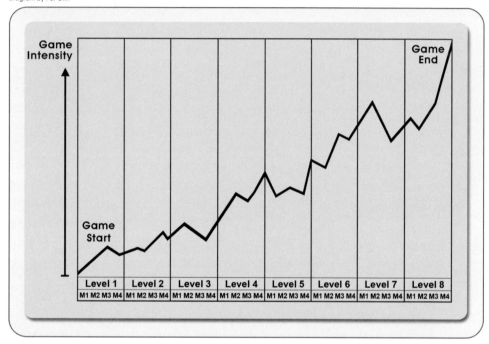

The pacing of most stories includes a series of peaks, valleys, and plateaus. This diagram helps to visualize the high level pacing of a game in comparison to the overall story arc; it illustrates a game that is composed of eight levels, each of which is broken into four missions that are 10 to 15 minutes in length.

More important than a game's high level story pacing is the minute-to-minute gameplay pacing that has to do with what players need to accomplish. The player needs to have several types of goals: immediate, long-term, short-term, and optional. An immediate goal is usually about surviving, getting through a fight, or playing minute-to-minute. Immediate goals are not stated, but they are always present in the game. Long-term goals are generally story-related goals, such as "rescue the princess," "save the world," or "kill everything in the universe." Short-term goals are the most important in the game; players need to have rewards and accomplish something, typically every 10-20 minutes. It is good to divide your game into segments so that the player can accomplish these goals within this time period. It is also good to have optional goals in the game, either implied or explicitly stated. Optional goals, such as discovering a secret, can be just about anything that may or may not affect the rest of the game.

In *Freedom Fighters,* there are helicopter pads somewhere on the map, but each map is broken into 3-5 levels that the player may access in any order. If the player destroys the helicopter pad, the helicopters stop harassing players on all levels in the map. This is a great way to have an optional objective that impacts the game.

Being able to affect the world in games such as *Freedom Fighters* is important to many players.

One way to pace the game is to create what is called a *beat chart*—a flowchart of the level that shows all of the key actions in the level. You can start by putting in the long-term goals and filling in the blanks. The beat chart can become a great way to understand the flow of the game, what the player is going to do, and what key events are going to happen. This chart can also be handed over to a storyboard artist and used to better visualize the game flow.

You need to understand how the features in the game will be used and how players will invest their time at each stage of the game. Identifying the pacing of the game will help you understand whether its features are focused in a single area and if some missing design elements might provide a well-rounded gameplay experience for the player.

I strive to ensure that every decision the player is called upon to make involves trade-offs, so that the player must worry that making one choice will inherently make other things more difficult.

—*Greg Costikyan (Chief Executive Officer, Manifesto Games)*

Hook Them in the First Five Minutes

Players need to be having fun within the first five minutes of booting up your game. That means there's a particular challenge in teaching players how to play, because if the first five minutes of your game sounds like "a tutorial" then you'll fail the five-minute test. Players don't play video games so that they can sit through a boring teaching session first, so we always try to include what we call a "Learn as you Play" option in our games: you get to jump right in and "start killing things," but we're sneaking a little bit of gradual learning in at the same time.

—*Brian Reynolds (Chief Executive Officer, Big Huge Games)*

Diagram by Per Olin

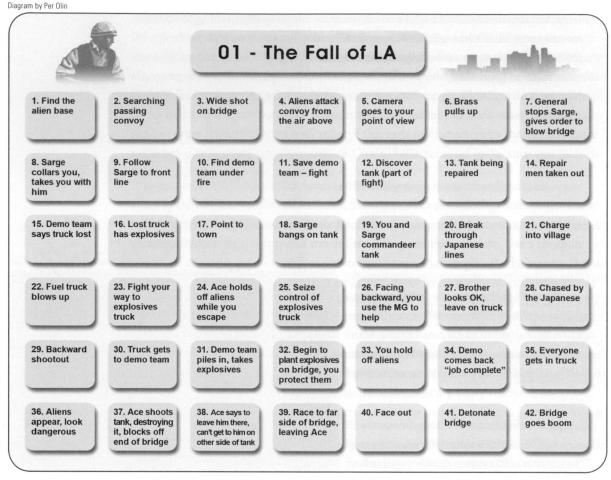

01 - The Fall of LA

1. Find the alien base	2. Searching passing convoy	3. Wide shot on bridge	4. Aliens attack convoy from the air above	5. Camera goes to your point of view	6. Brass pulls up	7. General stops Sarge, gives order to blow bridge
8. Sarge collars you, takes you with him	9. Follow Sarge to front line	10. Find demo team under fire	11. Save demo team – fight	12. Discover tank (part of fight)	13. Tank being repaired	14. Repair men taken out
15. Demo team says truck lost	16. Lost truck has explosives	17. Point to town	18. Sarge bangs on tank	19. You and Sarge commandeer tank	20. Break through Japanese lines	21. Charge into village
22. Fuel truck blows up	23. Fight your way to explosives truck	24. Ace holds off aliens while you escape	25. Seize control of explosives truck	26. Facing backward, you use the MG to help	27. Brother looks OK, leave on truck	28. Chased by the Japanese
29. Backward shootout	30. Truck gets to demo team	31. Demo team piles in, takes explosives	32. Begin to plant explosives on bridge, you protect them	33. You hold off aliens	34. Demo comes back "job complete"	35. Everyone gets in truck
36. Aliens appear, look dangerous	37. Ace shoots tank, destroying it, blocks off end of bridge	38. Ace says to leave him there, can't get to him on other side of tank	39. Race to far side of bridge, leaving Ace	40. Face out	41. Detonate bridge	42. Bridge goes boom

A beat chart provides a way for you to see how the pacing of a mission will take place and highlights the key events in the mission before you begin building it. The chart can also be used by storyboard artists to create some key storyboards or by writers to determine where key cut-scenes will be needed.

Cinematic Gameplay

Cinematic techniques are often used to make games more engaging, visceral, and fun. So what really makes a cinematic game? The most obvious aspect that players notice in a game such as *God of War* and *Prince of Persia* is the camera. With a cinematic camera, the designers allow very limited player control in favor of more dramatic camera angles, rapid camera cuts, and less control. Some players may be frustrated by not being able to control the camera, while other players may find the game easier to use. Before using a cinematic game camera, consider who your players are, what they like, and how they prefer to play.

Having a cinematic camera is critical to some games, such as *God of War* and *Prince of Persia: Warrior Within*, that want players to see exactly what the designer wants them to see—much like a movie.

A truly cinematic experience should be very exciting for the player. It requires a lot of key elements such as these to come together in order to work properly:

- the way characters move
- the types of attacks and weapons available to the player
- where the player can move
- how the cut-scenes are integrated
- how enemies behave
- how enemies die
- what occurs in the environment
- special effects and explosions
- destructible environmental elements

Keep in mind when designing a cinematic gameplay experience that the camera is not the only thing you need to consider. Some highly cinematic games do very well, while others will be rejected by players who feel a cinematic game is too limiting and takes too much control away. What camera you use in a game, however, is a very important decision that must be determined extremely early.

Camera

When you think of something that is characterized as "cinematic," you might imagine a movie with cool camera angles. Does this mean you have to use a cinematic camera in your game to utilize these principles? Absolutely not. A cinematic camera is one that changes to heighten the emotional experience of the player. How many times have you played a platformer, for example, where you were moving to a high and dangerous location but you never realized it? A cinematic camera would

A cinematic camera (*Prince of Persia: The Two Thrones,* shown) might allow players to feel they are very high up and in a very dangerous location; another type of camera may fail to adequately show this.

emphasize the fact that you are up high, in a dangerous location, and that something exciting is happening or other important events are occurring. It is also used to emphasize the artwork and show off the beauty of the levels.

A cinematic camera is only the first of many possibilities when you design a more cinematic gameplay experience for the player. As a designer, you can incorporate any or all of these concepts into your game to make them more enjoyable. Just remember that you are making a game and not an interactive movie, so there are some lines that you don't want to cross, and taking any of this too far can also detract from the overall game experience.

Interactive Cut-Scenes

Another form of cinematic gameplay can be seen in games such as *Tomb Raider: Legend* or *Shenmue,* where the player enters into a cinematic action sequence and must hit a series of buttons within a certain time in order for the character to perform the next move. This is almost like the old arcade game *Dragon's Lair,* where the player is required to press buttons in time to do the next action. While you may not want to create an entire game out of these interactive gameplay sequences, you can consider them *interactive cut-scenes,* which are far more interesting than sitting back and watching a movie, since they keep the player engaged. As such sequences become easier to create, games may use fewer non-interactive cut-scenes.

Eidos Interactive, Inc.

© Sega. All Rights Reserved.

Scripted action sequences in games such as *Tomb Raider: Legend* and *Shenmue II* are fun distractions in some games and provide some variety for the player.

Special Effects

You can achieve a sense of danger with jarring *special effects* sequences that allow the player to experience the environment and story more fully. The goal is to make players truly feel they are a part of the experience and not just spectators, especially in war games and fighting games. If you want players to believe they are fighting in a dangerous war, you must try to recreate the experience as fully as possible for them.

Electronic Arts, Inc.

At the beginning of EA's *Lord of the Rings: The Two Towers,* players are in the middle of a giant war as large catapults are hurling giant fiery objects at them. The players are not really in any danger, but this is difficult to realize when they're surrounded by explosions. Great explosions featuring camera shakes, booming sounds, particles, and other effects can really help sell the experience to the player.

Scripted sequences that involve dramatic explosions, fleeing civilians, and battling armies may make a game feel more exciting, but players must also feel like they are in danger if you are going to properly sell it. You must not only show these elements in cut-scenes but allow the player to experience them during gameplay.

The Lord of the Rings: The Two Towers has a very intense opening sequence that scares some players.

Scale

Elements that are massive in *scale* also add to the cinematic feel of a game. The player really feels empowered, scared, or in awe when taking on large enemies and interacting with huge objects. This contrast in scale can best be seen in *Shadow of the Colossus,* where the player must climb up and defeat 12 gigantic creatures. (The scale of these creatures is so massive that they they dwarf the player—who barely comes up to their ankles!) In the past, giant enemies have been relegated to being bosses, but now it may be possible to have players more frequently take on large enemies as well as more massive structures and objects.

Sony Computer Entertainment America

Giant bosses or enemies in a game can lend a tremendous sense of scale and make players feel like they are really taking on something spectacular. Some games such as *Shadow of the Colossus* have taken this to the extreme; all of its enemies are massive and daunting.

Realism

If you are truly trying to create a more cinematic or exciting experience for the player, you need to look at each feature and constantly evaluate whether it is meeting your requirements. Even the simple act of firing a gun involves many elements working together—such as sound, animation, movement, player control, effects, enemy reactions, and weapon damage. This is especially true for more realistic games such as *Black,* which sets out to fulfill the promise of a highly cinematic action game for players and raises the bar a few notches, elevating player expectations in the process. While it is not critical that you create a cinematic experience, you should consider and understand the topic sooner rather than later when designing your game's features.

Electronic Arts, Inc.

Massive amounts of effects, destruction, and explosions can be important or even the core of a game such as EA's *Black*.

Valve

Characters in *Half-Life 2* exhibit realistic facial features.

Immersion

In order to create a truly satisfying experience, the real key is to *immerse* players in the game so that they forget they are playing a "game" and just enjoy the experience. Many game designers feel that pre-rendered cut-scenes using detailed models, highly complex game interfaces, and other forms of gameplay remind players that they are playing a game. While this is true, it can be distracting and jarring—so designers are looking for more natural ways to make players feel they are part of the experience. Even in games such as EA's *Fight Night Round 3,* interfaces are turned off at the start and players must look for visual clues in the game to determine how well they are doing. The goal of having an immersive experience is not limited to story-based games, even if it is more prevalent there. Immersion comes in many forms—including gameplay features, interface, camera, art, location, story, characters, world interaction, sound, voice-overs, cut-scenes, and much more. Let's focus on how gameplay features greatly affect immersion.

Don't Rely on the "Hook"

A game designer's goal is to have "hooks" in the game, but then build multiple dynamic game systems around them so that players can combine all the base actions with the new "hooks" to use them to define their own individual play style. That is not to say there aren't other tricks that you need to employ to engage players. To design an everlasting game you must weave a bold and colorful tapestry using all of the tools the interactive medium provides. A great game is all about polish and ensuring every component meshes together in a complementary way. When you break down any game, it's a player interacting with your game systems through the use of an input system working towards a goal that is defined by the rule set. To stand out from the crowd you have to use graphics, art style, audio, story, interesting control mechanics, etc… to grab the players and immerse them in the world you are creating to truly hook them. As players' expectations rise, schedules get smaller, and the technical capabilities of consoles increase, this becomes more and more challenging—requiring an experienced team with lots of passion, strong creative vision, intelligent planning, and plenty of luck.

—Randy Greenback
(Creative Director, Red Storm Entertainment/Ubisoft)

Some will argue that the most important result of immersion is for players to forget that they are playing a game. You will find that a game such as *Peter Jackson's King Kong* is arguably very immersive because it does not have a visual interface and includes cut-scenes that are both tightly integrated into the game and use the in-game engine. While these can be important considerations and goals for some games, you risk sacrificing the gameplay experience and fun of the game if you have no interface—since the game itself must then be very simplistic.

Peter Jackson's King Kong immerses players by omitting a visual interface and using other elements such as in-game cut-scenes.

An incredibly immersive game is *Grand Theft Auto* (*GTA*), which happens to be one of the best-selling game franchises of all time. The greatest factor that *GTA* has going for it could very well be its immersive qualities. The features of *GTA: San Andreas* focus on the game's scale, variety of customizable vehicles, cool clothes, customizable characters, and extra mini-games (including the dating game). In the game, the player character is in trouble and must deal with cops and gangs in order to save his family and take control of the streets. The new features work incredibly well with the story and theme to enhance the player's expectation of what street or gang life would be like. Rockstar did not just throw in random features and upgrades to its game engine; it brilliantly chose the best new features to enhance the overall game experience for the player. These features include riding bicycles, getting fat if you eat the wrong foods, getting tattoos, buying "bling," and earning respect. Combine these features with a strong storyline that has the player build a criminal empire, and everything comes into place.

Courtesy Rockstar Games and Take-Two Interactive Software, Inc.

Multi-action genre games such as *Grand Theft Auto: San Andreas* are often top sellers and are popular with players who are immersed in a compelling experience where they can seemingly do almost anything within a living, breathing city.

The *GTA* worlds have always been highly immersive and open-ended in nature, allowing the player to go almost anywhere, navigate vehicles, choose to be good or bad, and interact with almost everyone in the world. The player in *GTA: San Andreas* experiences being a gang member. The locations, music, story, language, characters, and objectives of the world focus on the gangster lifestyle; the gameplay was also enhanced to immerse the player in the culture and lifestyle through character and vehicle customization and thematic mini-games.

The extensive customization in *GTA: San Andreas* can be used to make the player character look the way the player wants him to look, but it also is important for gameplay. The customized clothing, jewelry, tattoos, haircuts, and accessories are not only part of the lifestyle experience of the game but also play an important role in the way it is played. Some characters will help you more or fight you less if they like you, and your overall rating is affected by your player customization. Other games such as *Def Jam: Fight for New York* allow you to customize the player character by buying more items and customizing the character, which will earn the player added points and respect in the game. To take this idea even further, *GTA: San Andreas* even lets players customize their cars, affecting the way they drive and how characters behave toward the player.

GTA: San Andreas is bigger and more open than previous games in the franchise, expanding on the idea that the player can do almost anything in the world. Even the mini-games in *GTA: San Andreas* are there to show some aspect of the urban lifestyle. Rockstar could have easily included random and off-beat mini-games—but it chose to let the player participate in activities appropriate to the character, such as shooting pool and playing basketball.

Grand Theft Auto: San Andreas has improved on the *GTA* formula by immersing players even more into the game and allowing them to customize their characters to a significant extent.

Grand Theft Auto: San Andreas includes many mini-games that help immerse you in the lifestyle.

Another lesson to learn from *GTA* is about reuse of systems. The designers at Rockstar did an incredible job of taking all of the features available to them and reusing them in many different ways in order to make the game fun. Many of the "new" features in *GTA: San Andreas* (such as new vehicles and locations) consist of content added to features that already existed in other games in the franchise. This is part of the advantage of doing a sequel, but it also shows how smart the developers were in designing the features they wanted. For your own game, always keep in mind the cost of the game's features and how you can get the most use out of them.

While not every game needs to be another *GTA*, there is a lot to learn from the success of this franchise. The designers built a set of tools and features that fully supported their vision of the game, and they did everything possible to exceed the player's expectations and fantasies about what it might be like to participate in this world. The developers stayed focused and didn't spend time creating features that made no sense.

Chris Avellone on Techniques for "Hooking" Players :::::

Chris Avellone wanted to develop computer RPGs ever since he saw one of his friends playing *Bard's Tale 2* on a Commodore 64. After receiving a BA in English at the College of William and Mary, Chris started writing several short stories and RPG material—some of which have been published. His writing got him noticed at Interplay, where he worked for seven to eight years before co-founding Obsidian Entertainment, Inc., with other ex-Interplayers. Chris has worked on *Starfleet Academy, Die by the Sword, Conquest of the New World, Red Asphalt, Planescape: Torment, Fallout 2, Icewind Dale 1, Icewind Dale: Heart of Winter, Icewind Dale: Trials of the Luremaster, Icewind Dale 2, Baldur's Gate: Dark Alliance, Lionheart, Champions of Norrath, Knights of the Old Republic II: The Sith Lords, Neverwinter Nights 2*, and *Alien*. He says that his mom still isn't exactly clear on what he does on a day-to-day basis—and neither is he.

Chris Avellone
(Chief Creative Officer
& Lead Designer)

There are a few techniques we use at Obsidian Entertainment, usually revolving on what we've already experienced doing role-playing games here and at Black Isle Studios, and also fueled by our desire to get away from extensive number-crunching systems (at least thrown at the player right at the start). There were systems that we inherited when we did *Knights of the Old Republic II: The Sith Lords* and *Neverwinter Nights 2,* but our home-brewed character generation systems don't use the same mechanics to hook the player.

Our first objective in hooking players is to get them into the game experience early and start letting them interact with the game as soon as possible. In general, throwing a bunch of numbers and panel after panel of character creation options at players is not the best way to go about creating immersion or letting the players do what they've come there to do—play. (The only exception to this rule is visual customization of the character, however. Players seem more than willing to spend considerable amounts of time getting their character look down just right—and *City of Heroes* is perhaps the best example in this regard.) Visual customization systems seem to be a little easier for players to accept.

Our second objective is keeping the player there long enough to experience the game, and this is done through early, frequent positive reinforcement. This is done by including a steady stream of tangible rewards (no matter how minor) for the first hour of gameplay (usually through item and level advancement).

Third, we tailor the challenges and difficulty for the first hour or two so that the game allows the players breathing room to figure out the controls, how to fight, and above all else, allows them to keep playing without reloads if they do something wrong.

Freedom of Choice

Games such as *GTA*, *Mercenaries,* and *Deus Ex* offer a tremendous amount of *freedom* for the player. How much freedom to give the player, as well as the features and the way they are implemented, will affect the overall player experience—and you must think about this early in the design process.

Eidos Interactive Ltd.

Deus Ex: Invisible War offers many choices to players and gives them the freedom to play the game the way they want to and not according to the designer's demands.

Players want to believe that they are in control of their own destinies. They want the illusion of freedom, even if they do not really have it. There are many types of *choices* that you can give the player, but they need to be carefully controlled.

Navigation

Where to go in the game is probably the most obvious choice one could offer the player. It is not always possible or necessary to create a highly open-ended game series such as *The Elder Scrolls IV: Oblivion*. You can provide the player with open-ended worlds, or just worlds with more ways to move around in them. This could imply multiple physical paths for a player to take, or a single path with different ways for the player to get from point A to B in the game.

Take a linear path from your favorite game. Now assume that in the first and most obvious scenario, you walk down the path in a straight line and blast any enemy that comes at you. How might you change the design of the path to allow for multiple player choices? First, you could imagine allowing the player to take an alternate way through the path; on a city street surrounded by tall buildings, the player can now climb up

> We think of the game as being about the interactivity: any time players aren't actively making decisions, they aren't likely to feel very involved in the game. So we try to keep decisions coming constantly, and we try to make all of those decisions important and interesting.
>
> —*Brian Reynolds*
> *(Chief Executive Officer, Big Huge Games)*

and walk along ledges instead of walking down the middle of the street. Now imagine giving the player some kind of gadget or device or even a vehicle to travel down the street, swing above it like Spiderman, skate down it, fly down it, or travel down it in any number of other possible ways. It is possible to create player choices for moving through a level, but that is only the beginning.

© 2006 Bethesda Softworks LLC

Some games, such as *The Elder Scrolls IV: Oblivion* have very open worlds that allow the player to go almost anywhere at any time.

© 2002 Bethesda Softworks LLC

Games such as *The Elder Scrolls III: Morrowind* offer players many gameplay choices that may fit their personal play preferences and personalities.

The way players actually play through a segment of the game can be just as important as how they move through it. Does the player always have to run and gun through a level? What other types of *strategic choices* does your game support? Can the player sneak down the street and silently kill the enemies without raising an alarm? Can the player become invisible? Can the player steal a disguise and stroll unmolested down the street? Can he use a sniper rifle to kill everyone? Does your game support any additional features that allow players to experiment with the game? Does it provide puzzle-solving possibilities and a variety of ways to play? This is another way to give the players some freedom of choice and make the experience more enjoyable.

In a typical strategy game, a designer must allow for the player to make a wide variety of strategic choices, such as which side to be on and what kind of military forces and defenses to build. Tactical choices allow players to choose how they attack, what weapons they use, and much more. These choices are an important part of many games; they provide a puzzle element and give the player a tremendous sense of freedom and ownership.

Moral

Another aspect of providing choices for players is providing *moral* choices. Can the player play as good, bad, or somewhere in between? Is the player rewarded or penalized for performing what are considered good or bad actions in the game world? Games such as *Fable: The Lost Chapters* allow the player to make decisions anywhere along a spectrum between good and evil, and the player is rewarded or penalized accordingly. Players thus choose distinct moral paths throughout the game, resulting in specific outcomes.

Reprinted with permission from Microsoft Corporation

Fable: The Lost Chapters offers the player choices about morality.

Class & Reputation

Traditional RPGs also allow players to choose their character *class*. This can be difficult to balance or fully account for—and it is almost impossible to do with a licensed character—but it can be highly rewarding and provide many choices to players. Offering a variety of character classes allows characters to have different physical attributes, abilities, and other unique elements that set them apart. Character classes were designed not only to allow players to play the game the way they want but also to help represent different factions or races. Some games have predetermined character classes; others allow players to choose or adjust their character classes as they play the game by increasing the abilities of items as they are used or by earning points or items as upgrades. Character classes can be a great way for some games to offer many choices and customization to the experience.

Other games such as *Fable* and *Mercenaries* have a *reputation system* where the player's actions will affect the behavior of NPCs in the game, including how they will react to the player and how helpful they will be. Reputation systems can help in next-generation games to make players realize that their actions mean something without having to build in a system for player choices between good and evil.

While it is not a requirement to provide a broad array of choices for players, games that provide these choices are obviously some of the most successful on the market. An extremely linear and story-driven game is still viable in today's market, but it is still in your best interest to allow the player to make more choices in the game and have the perception of freedom.

Fable allows players' actions to affect their reputations, which will change how characters in the game treat the player.

Feedback

An important part of any system that allows for player freedom is proper *feedback* to the players, who need to know the consequences of their actions. A game must have not only very clear rules for the players but also some system to allow them to determine their progress in the game.

There are many different ways for players to know how they are doing in relation to the overall game and the missions they are on—their scores, their reputations, whether they are being good or evil, and whether they should take some action. Feedback to players must be clear, concise, and relevant. However, if players cannot improve, affect the feedback, or change play patterns based on the feedback, you should decide if such an evaluation is needed or useful.

At some level, a *health bar* is the most obvious feedback system, allowing players to know how well they are doing by how much health they have, or sometimes even how much ammunition they have. This can be a little tough to gauge, but it is important immediate feedback.

In *Star Wars: Knights of the Old Republic,* players can easily determine if they are turning "evil" or staying "good" by looking at an interface screen that is simple and easy to understand. Players also get some additional options or clues to how they are doing by the way NPCs communicate with them. In games like *Fable,* where your reputation will affect the AI, people will address you differently depending on the way you have been playing. Imagine a game where your reputation would affect the AI of enemies at an even higher level, where you could come across a group of enemies who would recognize that you were very powerful and run away instead of fighting you. This would be a great way for your reputation to really affect the game. In *Mercenaries,* for example, players can easily make friends or enemies with other factions. Players' reputations and treatment by NPCs can change as a result of their behavior toward the factions. Players could perform jobs for various factions to be liked by them, but doing other jobs (or killing their people, of course) would make them enemies.

© 2006 Bethesda Softworks LLC

Electronic Arts, Inc.

Both *The Elder Scrolls IV: Oblivion* and *Mercenaries 2* provide feedback on how the player is doing in the game in relation to the other characters. This feedback isn't about winning and losing, but about relationships.

Beyond telling the players whether they are playing as good or evil, or whether different groups like or dislike them, it also may be important to let players know how they are progressing in the game. Some games still use a scoring, grading, or point system on a mission, level, or area of the game. This often gives players the chance to go back and repeat that section to improve their performance. Fighting and other action games that are not mission- or story-based always utilize some kind of ranking system to give players feedback. Many new games (especially with multiplayer mode) are taking this even further and have a ladder ranking system that connects to a central server over the Internet, letting players know how well they are doing compared with other players around the world.

One reason for breaking a story- or mission-based game into smaller 15-30 minute segments is to provide feedback to the player. It does help give players a sense of accomplishment, but it is also there to inform them that they are progressing. This is the biggest problem with larger, more open-ended games such as the *Elder Scrolls* role-playing game (RPG) franchise. Without structured feedback, players sometimes have difficulty knowing whether they are doing the right things at the right time; it is easy to get lost and confused, which is both an appeal and a problem in open-ended games.

For any kind of game, keep in mind that players appreciate both specific, moment-to-moment feedback and a general evaluation of how they're doing in the overall game. This feedback is important to keep the players engaged in the game experience.

Interactivity

Interactivity is by definition what makes a game different from other forms of entertainment. Let's discuss *what* should be interactive in the game to make it even more interesting to the player.

Electronic Arts, Inc.

Valve

Mass destruction is a big trend within the more powerful next-generation games that have been exemplified by *Black* and *Half-Life 2*.

Interactive environments should contain objects that do not just react to players but allow them some form of choice. A switch that triggers a trap and kills an enemy is the most common mechanic, but there are plenty of other possibilities, such as destructible environments that allow a broader range of movement; use of the environment as a weapon; and the ability to destroy bridges and other structures that might actually force a tactical shift in the AI. Games developed for the newest generation of systems change the gameplay based on objects the player destroys and modify the game's AI, events, and behaviors.

Characters in the world are more interactive in games developed for the newest generation of systems, allowing players not only to talk more with them, but to give them more commands and interact with them in new ways. Interaction with NPCs in earlier games was severely limited by many factors, but more players now are able to deal with NPCs as if they are real people.

When you create the rules for an interactive world, remember that you are still designing a game—and that games still have limitations and rules.

> It is critical to make sure that players are always offered interesting choices and are invested in those choices. Also, make sure that there are a range of choices—and that not everything is life or death, because that can become tiring after a while. One of the things I'm interested in as a designer is allowing players the choice to slow down for a bit, relax, and then pick up the pace again when they are ready. Having that kind of 'space' in a game interests me.
>
> —Tracy Fullerton
> (Assistant Professor, Interactive Media Division, USC School of Cinematic Arts)

Just because we can create large free-form worlds in games such as *Grand Theft Auto* does not mean that all games must have them, or that it would be good to have them. Implement interactive environmental objects carefully so that you don't bog the player down.

Emergent Gameplay

Emergence is defined as something new—appearing, arising, occurring, or developing especially for the first time. Therefore, emergent gameplay exists when you have a global set of rules that can interact with each other in many different ways. From a game design perspective, you do not necessarily code every relationship in an emergent game, but you provide a series of abilities and interrelationships among features that the player can exploit in a variety of ways. An example of emergent gameplay would involve designing the following: a flamethrower, objects that burn, the ability to throw items, and NPCs that can be burned by fire. A player might use the flamethrower on an enemy, light an object on fire and throw it at someone or roll it down a hill—or perform some other combination with these available features. Another good example is throwing a rock to make noise to distract an opponent in *Far Cry,* where the ability to distract a guard was not designed explicitly by the designer but came about because a guard investigates noises and the player can pick up and throw items.

The *Grand Theft Auto* franchise is primarily based around emergent gameplay—which is also thought of as building a sandbox, or open-ended game. It follows that if you give the people (players) a group of tools (mechanics) and a big area to play in (the game), they will figure out what they want to build (how they are going to play the game). Emergent gameplay has a lot of benefits, many challenges, and some disadvantages. If you are trying to build a game using this type of system, you must take a close look at what you are building and what types of rules are appropriate. Not every game can benefit from emergence.

Courtesy Rockstar Games and Take-Two Interactive Software, Inc.

Utilizing emergence (*Grand Theft Auto III*, shown) is the latest trend in game design.

Emergent play can be continually rewarding for the player and help minimize repetition because the player is able to do so many different things. In *GTAIII*, players may follow the story and do exactly what they are told, or go off on their own and just play in the world for a while if they become bored or stuck. *GTAIII* is successful because it lets the player live in the world, steal cars, break the law, and get into all kinds of trouble, yet it also allows the player to follow a linear adventure. A good example of emergent gameplay in *GTAIII* can be found in this particular situation: Some thugs jump out of an alley and start mugging another character. The player has the choice of helping the thugs, helping the victim, beating the thugs off and then mugging the victim, or just ignoring the situation and walking on. While none of these solutions directly affects the game, the player is still allowed to do practically anything—and the game reacts accordingly.

Jessica Mulligan on Emergence & MMOGs :::::

Jessica Mulligan
(Executive Producer,
Sunflowers GmbH)

Jessica Mulligan has over 20 years' experience developing in the online gaming sector. Currently Executive Producer for Sunflowers GmbH in Germany, she most recently was Executive Producer and Studio Director for Nevrax SARL in Paris. Before that, Jessica worked for Turbine, Inc., developer of such titles as *Asheron's Call* and *Asheron's Call 2*, as Executive Producer and Creative Director of that company's Los Angeles studio. Prior to joining Turbine, she held a variety of industry positions, including President at the Themis Group, Director of Operations for MM3D, Inc., and Director of *Ultima Online* for Origin Systems. Jessica is also the co-author of the best-selling industry book *Developing Online Games: An Insider's Guide*, published worldwide in Chinese, French, and Korean editions and widely considered the 'bible' of online game development—and she was the author of the industry opinion column "Biting the Hand," now archived at http://www.skotos.net/articles/bth.html.

In the 3D, first-person online RPG *Asheron's Call 2* in 2003, players found a rocky crag at the top of a high mountain that provided beautiful vistas of the scenery. The only problem: it took quite a bit of time to climb down off the mountain. The solution to joining your Guild quickly for a quest? Jump. Your character would probably die, but that was part of the fun. Over time, the players made a game of it, taking screenshots and movies on the way down and judging who had the most elegant deaths. To support this, the developers put a diving board on the crag.

In 1999 in *Ultima Online*, a typical medieval fantasy MMO, several players got together on one server, wrote scripts for stage productions, gathered costumes, scenery, and props from the items in the game and created a road-show theater that featured 30-minute versions of *The Wizard of Oz* and Shakespeare's *Romeo and Juliet*, among other productions. The developers supported this by allowing and assisting the player-actors to move their characters among the 20+ UO servers, so that they were able to take their tour worldwide.

In *Air Warrior* in 1990, players got bored one night of the World War II air battles provided by the MMO and decided to create their own game: Who could fly under a bridge at the fastest speed without crashing into the river? Gun camera recordings of the feat were required. After several players became adept at this, they added a difficulty: Fastest speed while flying under the bridge *upside down*. Within days, players were creating other competitions— my favorite being the 'Full Contact Jeep Races,' which featured racing jeeps from one base to another with .50 machine gun use allowed. The developers didn't have to support this at all; the players handled it themselves.

It is this kind of gameplay that makes MMOs special. Smart developers watch for this kind of play and do whatever they can to support it through game features or new player tools.

Creating Emergence

Emergent technology is also called systemic gameplay because the game is broken down into small systems, and it is these systems that can interact in different and interesting ways. In most cases, players may achieve unpredictable results with systemic gameplay and perform actions never thought of by the designer.

Courtesy Rockstar Games and Take-Two Interactive Software, Inc.

Reprinted with permission from Microsoft Corporation

The *Grand Theft Auto* franchise (*Grand Theft Auto: Vice City*, shown) is the best known of the "sandbox" or emergent games on the market.

In *Oddworld: Munch's Oddysee,* players may do a lot of unpredictable things using the various game systems, which fortunately never breaks the game.

In *Munch's Oddysee* for the Xbox, one of the main characters (Abe) had the ability to pick up bombs, carry them around, and then throw them to cause explosions. The game was not designed to be an emergent game, but it had some emergent qualities. The bombs could explode and do damage to everything, including the other player character (Munch)—causing anything they damaged to go flying with some force or physics recoil from the explosion. Munch could not jump in the game, but players discovered they could make Abe pick up a bomb and throw it at Munch—causing it to explode and launch Munch into the air, catapulting him much higher than he should have been able to go, and allowing him to reach areas he shouldn't have been able to reach.

Eidos Interactive Ltd.

In *Deus Ex,* players could place mines on a wall; they discovered they could jump up onto the mine and stand on it. They could then place another mine, jump up on it, then reach down, grab the first mine, and repeat— climbing the wall and possibly getting out of the world. This was an unpredictable event that hurt the game a little, but players enjoyed the fact that they could do it if they were clever.

In *Deus Ex: Invisible War,* players may climb walls using mines and sometimes escape the level or get to areas they were not supposed to reach.

Developing Emergence

When you develop truly emergent games, the distinct relationships and behaviors between most systems are implicit rather than explicit. If a designer creates fire, then this fire simply has the ability to burn. The designer could define burning to include doing damage, destroying an object, putting out smoke, and so forth. Each object or surface that can burn may be marked as such. If the player then uses fire on an object that can burn, the object will burn correctly. This differs from programming where every relationship is hard-coded or defined, such that how a barrel burns vs. how a person burns would vary tremendously. While these items would burn differently, from a game design perspective you don't have to code all of the implicit details of how each weapon interacts with every object in the world.

Goals of Emergence

The goal of using emergence in a game is to offer the player a lot of freedom and options, without requiring much time to design and build each relationship in a game. Players like emergence because they feel it lets them play a game in their own way, and they feel less driven by the designer. In a linear game, players feel they have to proceed from point A to B to C and so on, while in an emergent game, they feel they can go to A, then play around for a bit, then maybe go to D, back to C, and so forth. There is a perception of freedom.

Electronic Arts, Inc.

Mercenaries 2 allows the player to run around and fight in a fairly large world with few limitations.

In *Mercenaries,* the player is free to run around and fight in a fairly large world with few limitations. The player could explore the world for a long time and just experiment with a large number of different weapons and vehicles to see what would happen, which makes the game fun to play. One highly successful goal of *Mercenaries* is to provide a very open world with many weapons and vehicles with which to destroy everything in sight.

Designing Emergence

Emergent game designs seem to be easiest for games that take place in the real world. Players sometimes have difficulty figuring out the arbitrary rules associated with the artificial game world. An emergent world offers the promise of being more open-ended and free-form and, in theory, it will let players experience a game world as more like reality. However, when players try something that should work in the real world but does not work in the game, they become frustrated. This does not mean that an emergent game can't involve fantasy—but if the result of using different objects together is completely random and chaotic, players will not know how to experiment.

What makes an emergent game so appealing is the sheer number of options available to accomplish a mission. If the player is on a mission to kill an enemy, an emergent game might let the player grab any weapon and try to club or shoot the enemy, kill the enemy from afar with a sniper rifle, or steal a car and use it to run the enemy over. To make it even more interesting, imagine more options:

- The player could hijack the enemy's vehicle, drive it fast toward a cliff or dangerous obstacle, and then bail out at the last second.
- The player could use a helicopter to pick up a car or other heavy object and drop it onto the roof of the building just above the enemy.
- The player could plant a remote bomb on the power transformer for the building and blow it up to turn off all power to the building, which might trap the enemy inside.
- The player could get some poison and secretly give it to the enemy to make the death look like an accident.
- The player could hire someone else to kill the enemy.

These are all examples of how emergent gameplay could be structured in a game. You could provide the player a large number of options with just a few basic gameplay systems that would be inherent to your core game. Emergent players should feel that they have all possible options available to them; the illusion of freedom is very important. Players like to feel they have outsmarted the game!

It is also good to have rewards for certain actions; if players take a more difficult path and succeed, they should be more highly rewarded. Could the player kill the enemy, make it look like an accident, or not alert the cops? Each of these could have different rewards and be easy to monitor. *Hitman: Blood Money* allows the player to kill in a wide variety of ways, which keeps the game interesting. The player may choose from among many tactics and decide whether to take the higher risk and reward, or to play it safe. For emergent games to be successful, designers need to allow players to use a broad spectrum of gameplay options to solve their problems, beyond just different tactics and weapons.

Eidos Interactive Ltd.

Hitman: Blood Money allows the player to kill enemies in a wide variety of entertaining and highly emergent ways.

Designing a Sandbox

It is important to separate the design of a sandbox game and that of an emergent game. A sandbox is an incredibly open-ended game that takes place in a fairly large world with few physical limitations. The player is free to explore all or a large section of the world at any time. The gameplay in the world is inherently diverse, making it fun to experiment and play in the world itself—or the player can choose to follow the game's story and mission structure. A sandbox game is also known as a *multi-action genre* (*MAG*)—encompassing the ability to perform many different actions within a game. It is generally assumed that a player character can run around on foot, drive vehicles, use weapons, and talk to other characters. The layout of the story, levels, and missions is assumed to be non-linear and allows the player perform an assortment of different missions and interact with items in the world at any one time. It is possible, although tricky, for a sandbox game to exist without emergence, but it's very easy for an emergent game to exist without being a sandbox. (For example, *Thief* and *Deus Ex* are two great emergent games that don't take place in a sandbox world.)

Emergent Storytelling

1. Fully Emergent Story (*The Sims, Railroad Tycoon, Battlefield 2*): Players create stories through their actions and events that occur because of what they do in the game. Every game can have fully emergent stories. These games have few or no designer-created stories and rely on players to create their own experiences and turn them into a story.
2. Designer-Created Story with Emergence (*GTA, Oblivion, World of Warcraft, Deus Ex*): These games have designer-created story points that may follow a linear path or several different overlapping or branching paths, but they allow players to play in a very wide, open world in between the key story points.
3. Open-Ended Designer-Created Story (*The Legend of Zelda, Kameo, Oddworld: Strangers Wrath, Prey, Hitman: Blood Money*): These games provide a semi-linear story that allows the players to more openly explore, backtrack, and experiment with where they want to go and how they want to play.
4. Linear Designer-Created Story (*Tomb Raider, ICO, Call of Duty, Final Fantasy, Peter Jackson's King Kong, God of War*): This is the traditional game story where the player follows a very linear path, moving from one story point to the next in a fairly controlled manner.

Construction Mechanics

Some of my favorite mechanics involve construction and creativity, and games like *The Sims* and *Animal Crossing* do a great job providing this type of play. Construction mechanics are difficult, because there is no direct conflict there—only opportunity. To get a player interested and invested, and keep them interested, in constructing a family or a town museum or a theme park or whatever is a tricky thing to do well. These games do it masterfully.

—Tracy Fullerton
(Assistant Professor, Interactive Media Division,
USC School of Cinematic Arts)

Emergent Role Playing

A common mixture of gameplay system ideologies involves emergent gameplay and role-playing systems. The best recent example is seen in *Elder Scrolls IV: Oblivion*. Role-playing games are inherently semi-emergent; players may build custom characters, which gain new abilities, stats, equipment, and weapons as the game progresses. *Deus Ex* is an emergent role-playing game (RPG) in a semilinear world, whereas *Oblivion* is an emergent RPG in a sandbox world. The nature of RPGs makes them prime candidates for utilizing emergent systems and fully capitalizing on them.

© 2006 Bethesda Softworks LLC

The Elder Scrolls IV: Oblivion combines the best of a role-playing game with highly emergent gameplay.

Emergent Attitude

Two different types of emergent or changing attitudes are possible in a game. The first is the way NPCs behave toward the player character. Is it possible for the player character to do things to make NPCs angry or happy? In *Mercenaries,* if civilians or military soldiers are friends of the player character, they will get in the player's car if the player honks the horn and may shoot out of the window, turning a normal vehicle into a lethal weapon. Having NPCs or other players change their attitudes toward the player—reacting to the player's actions, helping the player, or becoming the player's enemy—is an important part of the next generation of emergent games.

Electronic Arts, Inc.

In *Mercenaries 2,* emergent attitude may occur when a non-player character comes to the player's aid by entering the player's vehicle and shooting at the enemy.

A second aspect of many emergent games that players enjoy is the ability to play as good, bad, or somewhere in between. Since players have a variety of options, they are usually offered the ability to accomplish missions in different ways or do things differently than a more linear game would require. In games such as *True Crime,* the player might be able to arrest or kill a criminal. The player can choose how to play this out, and each path has a different set of possibilities. This goes hand in hand with the other possible choices and tactics. In *Hitman: Blood Money,* players can carry out missions in various ways—which will ultimately affect their reputations and make the game either easier or harder. While emergent attitude systems sound complex to design and program, they are not extremely difficult and are very rewarding to players as long as you clearly understand how to influence or affect the various relationships in the game.

The most difficult thing to design in games is making it fun to be the good guy, since it is almost always more rewarding and far easier to shoot first and ask questions later. Using stealth or non-lethal weapons to keep the player character on the good side is not the most rewarding tactic for most players, so designers need to come up with some tactics for our more heroic characters that are more fun and equally interesting to use.

John Comes on Supporting Emergence :::::

John Comes
(Lead Designer,
Gas Powered Games)

John Comes was born in Reading, Pennsylvania and grew up near Cleveland, Ohio. He received a Bachelor of Science in Mechanical Engineering from the University of Akron. After college, John and his older brother wrote *Wolfshade MUD* from scratch – which led to a position for John as Senior Content Designer on *Earth & Beyond* at Westwood Studios. At Electronic Arts-Los Angeles, he shipped *Command & Conquer: Generals – Zero Hour* and *The Lord of the Rings: The Battle for Middle-Earth*. John's most recent title, at Gas Powered Games, is *Supreme Commander*.

The book/movie writing [advice is always] 'show, don't tell.' In games, it's 'do, don't show or tell.' Have your player play out how you want to move the story. Don't rely on cut-scenes to tell your story, but put players in the middle of the action where they belong. Emergence is very important but you need good game systems to support it. The worst thing you can do is get the player into a situation I call 'Guess what the designer was thinking.' Give players enough feedback and information to win the game, but allow them to take multiple courses to get there.

Emergent Gameplay Systems

An emergent system is a series of features that work together to create some sort of underlying theme or set of abilities, which combine to create a much bigger set of emergent gameplay possibilities. The most obvious systems deal with sight, sound, and the elements—but there are many other possible emergent systems for a game. When you design any emergent system, it is important to determine how to make it as cohesive as possible. You can utilize many different types of emergent systems in a game.

Emergent Visual Systems

Emergent visual systems affect how players see things. The most obvious way to accomplish this is by using light and dark. Hiding in shadows and manipulating the light is a key component to any stealth game. Being able to turn lights on and off, shoot out lights—and use flashlights, night vision goggles, and infrared goggles—has been made popular in games such as *Tom Clancy's Splinter Cell.*

Although these systems have been used in many games, they can be taken further still—especially in a fantasy or science fiction setting. Imagine a world like the

© 2006 Ubisoft Entertainment. All Rights Reserved.

one in the movie *Pitch Black* where creatures come out at night, and the game has a day/night cycle that the player has to worry about. Imagine creatures that cannot tolerate the bright sun, like vampires, that hide and lurk in the shadows all around the player: What would happen as the shadows grew closer to the player? What if the player is slowly damaged by the intensity of the sun and is forced to constantly try to stay in the shade, running from shadow to shadow? How about a player who has dynamic light-casting ability, using either a flashlight or mirrors that could bounce light around? Emergent visual systems may be used in numerous ways to create gameplay.

Emergent visual systems are common in stealth games such as *Tom Clancy's Splinter Cell: Double Agent.*

Emergent Sound Systems

Emergent sound systems have also been used in games such as *Splinter Cell* and *Far Cry.* Making the AI react to different noises is nothing new in games, but there are still many ways to use sound in games for new gameplay possibilities. In *Far Cry* and *Mercenaries,* there are alarm towers that sound when you are detected; players must decide whether to take out the enemy who will sound the alarm, destroy the alarm tower, or do something else before being detected. Sound can be used to lure enemies to a specific location as they investigate suspicious noises. Many games also give the player ways to avoid making sound—either by moving slowly, moving over certain "quieter" surfaces, or wearing shoes that are noiseless.

Sound can be used as a weapon to deafen enemies and drive them away. In the movie *The Cave,* the creatures used echolocation to hunt their prey in the darkness—but the explorers had a sonic mapping gun that produced a sound pulse that drove the creatures away for a short time. Stun grenades emit a supersonic sound, along with a concussion that disorients humans.

Players will also need many ways to control how much sound they make. If players are supposed to play quietly, they also need to be able to hide, take cover, and avoid enemies; this requires special moves and ways to effectively hide. In *Splinter Cell*, players can do the splits and hide high above enemies to drop down on them—while in *Metal Gear Solid 3,* players may hang off an edge or below a walkway and let an enemy walk past them.

Emergent sound systems have been used in action games such as *Far Cry*.

In *Tom Clancy's Splinter Cell: Chaos Theory*, the player may hide from enemies, which is an important part of staying silent in the game and avoiding detection.

Knife attacks, choke holds, shooting weapons with sound suppressors, and other silent ways of killing enemies are also needed to make the most of an emergent sound system, unless the game will involve little or no combat. There are many ways to use sound in a more emergent way, even if not as a weapon. Sound could be used in a more musical manner, such as in the old LucasArts classic *Loom* or in *The Legend of Zelda: Windwaker,* which used sound as a musical theme throughout the game. In both, the player had to play music and perform actions using sound as a form of magic.

Emergent Physical Systems

Emergent physical systems can take several different forms. There are plenty of ways you might use water and make it a core theme in the game. Obviously, a player might be able to swim in water, swim under water, or ride on the water, either alone or with help from various vehicles or devices. Water may also be used as a weapon as a puzzle device; it can move objects around, put out fire, and create mud. Water might be frozen or vaporized, and it can also be moved from one place to another, possibly allowing the player to raise and lower its level. The concept of water could be expanded to include all kinds of liquids, such as acids, poison, oil, holy water, and much more. Each of these can also be used to do a wide variety of things. What if the player had a device that could be used to suck up any kind of liquid and shoot it out like a giant squirt gun? There are many ways to make liquids emergent in a game, and most of them require only a few small changes in their properties to utilize the same systems and technologies.

Nintendo

Water is used as an emergent physical system in *Super Mario Sunshine*.

Fire is another emergent physical system that could be used in a variety of ways. You can use fire to damage an enemy, to burn items, to see in the dark, and more. Some animals are afraid of fire, while others might be attracted to the light or heat. Fire can create smoke and intense heat that could be used in different ways for all kinds of puzzles. The concept of fire can also be expanded to include lava, napalm, and other material that burns in different ways.

Air is another emergent physical system. Players can not only fly in different ways but also use air a bit like water as a non-lethal weapon. They may cloud the air with smoke, poisons, and other gases. You can design games that have areas without air, or too much air or wind.

Electronic Arts Inc.

Fire is used as an emergent physical system in *Medal of Honor: Rising Sun*.

Gravity may be another emergent gameplay system. Levels may contain all sorts of gravity systems, including devices that manipulate gravity or allow the player to move in different gravity states.

A single element and theme could become an entire emergent system and hook for a game, but trying to make everything in the world emergent can be tricky. Just find a few core systems and play off of them as much as possible so that players have more than one tool in their belts to use at any one time. This allows players to create a free-form gameplay experience.

Emergent Equipment

Emergence will depend on the various objects in the game that the player can use. The different types of weapons, items, gadgets, and devices will have abilities that lend themselves to emergent gameplay. A piece of emergent equipment could be as primitive as a club, spear, or torch—magical, modern, or high tech. There is no limit to what the player can use; in *Far Cry*, even a stone could be thrown to distract a guard, used as a weapon, or used to trigger a trap.

Weapons and vehicles may be used as emergent equipment in games such as *Far Cry*.

The challenge with emergent equipment is ensuring that each object is good for something different, yet similar enough to work together in interesting ways. For instance, if you emphasize emergent visual systems in your game, you would want a series of objects that could interact with light. In a modern game, they might include night vision goggles (to see in the dark), a flashlight (also to see in the dark, using less energy), a flashbang grenade (to blind enemies), a concussion grenade (to destroy lights), camouflage clothing (to make it more difficult to be seen), a mirror (to bounce light), a flare or flare gun (to illuminate an area)—and many other items that might generate, utilize, or disable lights and areas of a game.

Emergent Skills

Emergent systems do not have to utilize only objects, devices, equipment, vehicles, or other created objects to work. The skills a character has in the game should also lead to some type of emergent gameplay. Granted, some skills, such as being able to see in the dark, could either be inherent abilities of the player or devices. Lock-picking could be an inherent skill that a thief must know how to use and master, or it could be seen as an emergent object. Being able to pick locks may lead to several possibilities and opportunities in a game, even beyond theft.

Emergent Immersion

It can be argued that the main reason for the success of the *GTA* franchise is not its emergent gameplay or sandbox world (even though this is a major part of it) but its amazing ability to immerse the player into the world. This is really about the emergent abilities that were chosen for the player, and how all of those abilities also line up with other elements such as art and audio to give players the sense that they *belong* in the world.

Courtesy Rockstar Games and Take-Two Interactive Software, Inc.

Grand Theft Auto: San Andreas effectively immerses the player into the hip-hop gangster lifestyle.

It is very easy to get caught up in designing an emergent sandbox game and to try to do everything. Obviously, you should not bite off more than you can chew; the hard question is what features should be kept. The best advice is to keep as many as possible of the features that can be interrelated. A group of emergent features that can't interact with each other will be useless. However, you also want to focus on which features will truly contribute to player immersion in the experience and to the overall vision of the game.

Challenges to Emergence

Emergent games still have limitations. They are extremely difficult to develop in many ways, including both design risks and technological challenges.

Streaming

The biggest technical challenge for most teams is to get streaming to work properly. This is a huge task and should not be underestimated. It is critical to be able to stream the world, characters, missions, and everything else into the game. Most sandbox games have few if any load screens to help keep the player immersed in the game. Streaming is critical, because of the large size of the worlds and the complexity inherent in them.

Scale

The immense size of the world in *GTA* set an incredibly high bar for the games that followed. That much art is very time-consuming and difficult to create—and getting it into and out of memory is technically challenging. There is also the design problem of how to allow players to easily navigate a huge world, rapidly move around it, locate objectives, and do much more. Just putting the player in a large world doesn't make it more interesting or fun.

Living World

Making the world feel alive is one of the best tricks of all in a sandbox game. The world feels full of people, cars, and life; everywhere players go in the city, there is ambient life surrounding them. On top of this, random events are happening as you travel through the world. These could take the form of random fights, muggings, or many other possibilities. A console does not have enough memory to keep all of the events of an entire city in memory, so games such as *GTA* use some incredible smoke and mirrors to maintain the illusion that the world is alive all around the player.

Persistence

Since games rely on a living world around the player, it is often hard to find enough memory to keep track of all the persistent data in the game. It is especially tricky for games such as *Mercenaries* to account for all the buildings that are blown up, but they need to keep the players' actions in memory to make the world feel more alive. A lack of resources for keeping persistent data in memory is a tremendous design or technical challenge.

Mercenaries 2 allows the player to blow up many structures, which requires the game to keep track of a great deal of persistent data.

Ramping the Player

An emergent sandbox game, like any RPG, has the challenge of ramping the player (discussed in more detail in Chapter 7). If players can go anywhere and do anything along with building themselves up, this poses a potential problem. How do you keep the game fun, challenging, and interesting for players who can go anywhere and do anything, and thus can build themselves up before accomplishing many of the story goals? *Oblivion* solves this problem by ramping up the enemies as the player gains strength. This can work in some circumstances, but it does not give the player a great sense of accomplishment overall. It is important to keep the game interesting but still allow the players the freedom to play any way they prefer. This is a tricky design dilemma that you will need to address.

The Elder Scrolls IV: Oblivion ramps up the enemies as the player gains strength.

You also have to be careful that nothing players can do will ruin their ability to go forward in the game. For example, if players can get money only by doing certain things, it would be unfortunate if they have spent all their money just when they need to buy something in order to progress. Make sure that as players ramp through the game, the resources they will need to advance are not tied directly to limited resources they can acquire only in another limited way.

Storytelling

Telling a great and compelling story in a semilinear game can also be problematic. It can be difficult to always let players know where they are supposed to go next, what they can do, and what matters in the game. You have to ensure that players know what is currently driving the story forward. Designing a fully emergent game can provide a lot of breadth and options. Even if you do not design a fully emergent game, you can still learn many lessons from the types of systems a fully emergent game can create and what it can offer to a player.

Once you understand how much breadth you are going to have, it will be important to determine how much depth you will incorporate into the game and which types of depth will be redundant or too time-consuming to build. The next chapter focuses on how to create and implement deep gameplay.

:::CHAPTER REVIEW:::

1. Play at least three electronic games that are currently on the market. Identify at least three areas in each game in which your character is given a breadth of choices (preferably where more than two options are clearly available). If possible, play those sections of the game several times so that you can find out what happens if you make different choices. (You can often do this by saving the game before you make a choice.) How is the outcome of the game affected by your choices?

2. Play a game that is emergent or that contains emergent elements (such as *Grand Theft Auto* or *The Sims*) and play around with ways of creating your own personal experience in the game. What might you do to create a "sandbox" for your original game?

3. Create a set of at least three challenges in your game that can be addressed by three strategies each (for a total of three challenges and nine strategies). Discuss each challenge and its three accompanying strategies (choices). How will each strategy affect the course of the game, including its outcome?

CHAPTER

Creating the Connection

providing depth

Key Chapter Questions

■ What systems might you include in a game to create *depth*?

■ Why are *rewards* effective in gameplay mechanics?

■ Why is it important to create *attachment* for the player?

■ How do you create *diversity* in gameplay using combat and equipment?

■ What role does *strategy* play in keeping players addicted to a game?

Once players are hooked and playing the game, it is important for them to have the desire to keep playing once the novelty wears off. A "deep game" is one that contains a variety of features and options that hold the players' interest. Gameplay depth is created through many elements—including detail, rewards, role-play, attachment, diversity, and strategy.

Creating Detail

A deep game is one that contains a lot of detail within the same areas (such as equipment, skills, and abilities). It sometimes offers hundreds of variants on a theme, which players will learn how to use very quickly but then must learn how to master. For instance, casual players may not care that there are 50 different swords in a game, but hardcore players will care that they have the "+5 Silver Broadsword of Redemption and Might."

While it is not critical to design a game that is deep, you do need to understand what is important in a game that is to be played for a very long time. These features are most commonly found in role-playing games, strategy games, massively multiplayer games, and some others.

Ratchet & Clank, which is designed to be completed in only 10–20 hours, may be replayed many times because it uses a variety of techniques to keep the player engaged, such as collectables, secrets, and unlockables. Other games such as *World of Warcraft* were designed to keep players engaged almost indefinitely and provide a deep gameplay experience that is extremely difficult to master (not to mention time consuming).

Sony Computer Entertainment America

Some platformers such as *Ratchet & Clank* are designed to be finished in a relatively short time (10–20 hours), but they may be replayed numerous times.

The beauty of a deep game is that typically a casual player does not need to master all of the variety in the game or become addicted to have fun. A casual player will pick up and use a sword because it looks cool and might occasionally bother to see if another sword is better than the current one. A casual gamer should be able to just play the game and enjoy it for what it is, while a hardcore player appreciates being able to decide what object is best to use on every occasion.

The "Min-Maxer" Player

"Min-maxers" enjoy figuring out all the advantages of everything in the game. They will determine which weapon is best for each circumstance, which spell to use when, and exactly how many seconds it will take to do almost anything in the game. These players see games as a giant action puzzle of sorts and try to calculate the best strategy for every circumstance in the game. At some level, you must understand what the min-maxer likes and why.

Creating Rewards

It is critical to reward the player often. Players need large rewards for completing major tasks, objectives, or goals in the game, as well as small rewards for completing small tasks. A large reward for the completion of a mission could consist of money, points, equipment, praise, and more. A small reward could include ammunition, increased score, health kits, power-ups, or information that the player might need.

Sony Computer Entertainment America

Rewards are common enticements in games such as *Ratchet: Deadlocked*.

Studies by major publishers such as Electronic Arts and Ubisoft have found that players should not go more than around 15-30 minutes without some type of large reward. This is one of the reasons that games are still broken down into levels, missions, objectives, and plot points. This short segment is called a gameplay loop by some designers. Not only do these gameplay loops give the player something to work toward in a manageable chunk, but they also tend to hold the player's attention. Even larger rewards may be earned for bigger chunks—which might be chapters, worlds, or other segments that take longer to complete but still have common story, environmental, or thematic cohesiveness.

Rewards & Positive Feedback

Positive feedback is the key to keeping players' attention for long periods of time. Defining your reward loops and crafting them to chain together to give the player incentives again and again is the first step. That can be something as simple as giving players a power-up once they have shot a target so they can shoot more targets to collect more power-ups, or something more complex such as in a game of chess where every piece taken leads up to a more empowering victory. The more simplistic the reward loop, the more likely a player is to get bored with it. You will want to define multiple levels of rewards within multiple different reward loops and allow players to go after the ones that mean the most to them. You really cannot have a reward without some form of risk, so ensure that the rewards mirror the amount of risk a player is putting in to earn it. In squad-based tactical shooters, some players enjoy a game of cat and mouse leading up to a tense moment that decides the outcome of an entire match (large risk/large reward), others might like taking head-shots on a distant enemy and going for an end reward of having the highest level of accuracy (low risk/low reward), while still others may find joy in blowing up enemy vehicles to see the explosion effects (medium risk/medium reward). Layer in a variety of rewards, tune the pacing of them for the many types of players that there are, and then you will be well on the way to providing a fun play experience.

—Randy Greenback
(Creative Director, Red Storm Entertainment/Ubisoft)

To keep the players involved for long periods of time, we try to introduce a variety of advancement systems so that the player is getting a constant stream of rewards, whether skill advances, perk advances, town reputation, faction reputation, harvesting for crafting materials, gold, level ups, stat advancements, journal advancements, fog of war removal, and so on, so that no matter what the player is doing in the environment, there's *something* they are doing to make some sort of tangible progress. To reinforce that, we try to make sure there is a way of tracking and displaying all these advancements so that the progress is visible to the player—if players see a status bar, they want to fill it. If they see a number on their character sheet, they want to increase it. If there is an icon beside their character portrait for a spell buff or special power, then they want more and more of them. One of the best ways we've found in role-playing games is to provide the player with a variety of options to pursue while adventuring, and they can choose the one that best suits their mood at the time—whether they want to simply go on a killing spree in the local mines, do courier missions, or pursue a side quest without necessarily following the main "plot." I've found that introducing quests with a number of goals that can be accomplished step by step in 10-15 minutes is often the best hook for keeping people playing, and it certainly works well in *World of Warcraft* to keep the player constantly on.

—Chris Avellone
(Chief Creative Officer & Lead Designer, Obsidian Entertainment)

Shorter rewards are equally important to the player. Players should be rewarded as often as possible; even every 15 minutes is too infrequent. Rewards should be given for killing enemies, accomplishing short goals, exploring, and much more. Having enemies drop items for the player or having "loot" available on their dead bodies is probably the most common form of short reward for players. Arcade games usually have a score and give the players points for every kill or important accomplishment in the game—along with special bonuses for doing things in special ways such as killing a group of enemies, using a special attack, and so forth. Even text that appears on the screen indicating "Good Job" is a form of reward.

Without rewards, you cannot truly build addiction in games. Designers often take for granted that many gameplay elements such as rewarding the player were pioneered by psychologists and are not by any means specific to game design. It can be fascinating and helpful to study psychology and its relation to video games.

It does not matter how you reward the player, but the rewards must be often enough and compelling enough to satisfy the player. Players must feel that the risk/reward ratio is worthwhile or they will probably stop playing or stop doing certain things in the game. If players risk their lives, use up $1,000 worth of ammunition, and spend a lot of time on an optional mission—only to get a "thanks and here's $20"—they will often feel cheated and be unwilling to play another optional or side mission and only begrudgingly go on the main missions because they have to in order to advance in the game.

Creating Role-Play

Role-playing games by their nature are some of the most addictive games on the market. Massively multiplayer online role-playing games (MMORPGs) such as *World of Warcraft* may keep some players busy for 50-100 hours a week, month in and month out. Even console role-playing games (RPGs) such as *Kingdom Hearts II* may take around 100 hours to finish, while *Jade Empire* may take 50 hours to finish the first time through. Compared to some first-person shooters (FPSs), action-adventures, and other games that may typically be finished in 5-10 hours, role-playing games fill a much greater amount of the player's time. This means that many of the systems you create for a great epic RPG should be different than for another game that you plan to make 5-10 hours in length.

You do not have to build a full-blown RPG in order to need RPG systems in the game. Even action games such as *Grand Theft Auto: San Andreas* use statistics to keep track of the player's stamina, weapons proficiency, driving, player character appearance, character lung capacity, and muscularity.

Console role-playing games such as *Kingdom Hearts II* may take around 100 hours to finish.

Even strategy games such as *Warcraft III* utilize role-playing systems to add heroes and quests and to allow players to obtain new equipment for their heroes.

An RPG typically consists of the following features:

- character statistics and classes
- character development and progression
- story-driven plot
- quest system
- conversation system
- combat
- boss monsters
- mini-games

A wide variety of different systems are involved in the design of an RPG. Even when designing a full-blown RPG such as *The Elder Scrolls IV: Oblivion,* you do not necessarily need to incorporate every feature. No matter what RPG systems you choose to utilize in your game, you should first ensure they are systems that players will enjoy repeatedly.

Creating Attachment

A player's attachment to a game is not about caring whether characters live or die because they seem interesting; it is about players feeling that their characters and other elements of the game are their own, which will often make them care more about these elements and sometimes go to great lengths to improve them.

Allowing players to customize things can go a long way toward creating attachment. You may allow the player to change anything in the game—the player character, weapons, even vehicles; the only hurdle is the difficulty in creating the ability to do so. If you are creating a basic tool that allows players to customize their characters, find a way to leverage this ability for much more customization in the game.

Midway has a sophisticated character creation tool originally called "Create a Person," which was primarily designed to create a really wide variety of NPCs in the background. This system was then expanded to include the ability to create custom player characters, called "Create a Player" or CAP. Eventually the designers understood that the system used to drive CAP had no real limitations and could be used to easily create anything that needed customization and

Courtesy of Blizzard Entertainment Inc.

World of Warcraft allows players to create and customize new characters before they begin playing.

variety—expanding it to include any static mesh objects, such as vehicles. Midway's "Create a Thing" system may be used to create any type of custom object in a game—whether it is a person, place, or thing. This tool will ultimately be widely used in applications on most of Midway's games.

> Involving story and characters combined with meaningful actions a player can successfully take to advance the game combine to [keep them playing]. Make sure these exist throughout your game.
>
> —Frank T. Gilson
> (Senior Producer, Wizards of the Coast)

Pacing Management

You have to keep the pacing moving the game ahead in just the right way. If the players find themselves doing something for long periods of time, even something arguably fun, they'll start losing interest. Baseball pitchers cannot throw the same pitch every time; they have to change it up, and keep surprising the batter. Pacing can be a function of the environments and monsters, and/or include the weapons used, or the challenges presented... or all of the above. It is about continually making the player believe that something exciting is right around the next corner, and the next corner, etc.

—Chris Taylor
(Creative Director & Owner, Gas Powered Games)

Creating Diversity

To keep a player engaged for a long time, you need both breadth (discussed in Chapter 5) and a lot of feature depth. For instance, if you are designing a fantasy RPG—and you give the player a sword, axe, club, knife, flail, staff, bow, blowgun, and the ability to cast spells—the game would be considered to have a lot of breadth. Each of the weapons is of a different class, with a different base functionality. However, if the player's choice included only 10 swords, 10 bows, and 10 axes—each with slightly different attributes—the game would have depth, but not a lot of breadth. You need to make sure that your game has as much breadth as possible before adding more depth to it.

Creating depth in a game is usually by far the easiest thing to do because you are typically just using statistical variance. However, creating a lot of variety may be difficult because it takes not only producing more artwork but often designing and programming a whole new system as well. Creating an M-16 and then an AK-47 rifle requires basically an art and stats change, whereas creating an M-16 and then a flamethrower would require a great deal of additional programming, effects, and design. Do not underestimate the cost of designing an extremely broad set of features.

Keep in mind that there are many different kinds of players in the world. Casual players who do not play many games will probably be initially turned off to anything that requires too much skill or is too difficult or confusing. Hardcore players will be frustrated by anything that is different or out of their control. "Completionist" players enjoy lots of secrets, hidden objects, and goals, but they also want to get everything perfect.

Diversity in games such as *Ratchet & Clank: Up Your Arsenal* contribute to depth.

Combat

Creating diverse gameplay is about giving players goals and options that allow them to play using their preferred style. Not every gamer likes to snipe, use stealth, or always go in with guns blazing. This does not mean that your game has to be emergent to support different styles of play. The types of weapons, equipment, skills, and abilities the player has—and the way the levels are designed—will determine how the player must play. Even in a fairly linear game, you might still design the levels or the player's abilities to allow doing things in different ways. Could the player take an alternate route to reach the goal? Could the player use stealth or invisibility to reach the goal? Does the player have access to lots of armor and healing along the way? Does the player have a sniper rifle? Where are the enemies placed? May the player use a vehicle, heavy weapon, or teammate to help him? Many different variables may be tweaked to make a level more interesting.

Sony Computer Entertainment America

Far Cry contains diverse combat—but will non-player characters always respond when the player throws a rock?

Even in a non-emergent game, the artificial intelligence (AI) must be reactive to the player and responsive when the player tries something new. If players diversify their tactics, but the AI does not respond correctly, then the players will eventually learn that trying new tactics is pointless and will stop experimenting. There are many ways to make combat more diverse in any game, but the important thing is to evaluate what players like and don't like in a game and try to understand why.

Direct Attack

The most obvious form of attack is direct. The player could largely ignore tactics or perhaps utilize a take-cover system such as the one found in *Perfect Dark Zero* or *Tom Clancy's Rainbow Six: Vegas*. While there may not be a lot of diversity in a direct attack, providing many different enemies and enemy positions can drastically change the way the player makes an assault. Also, small things such as grenades, weapon rate of fire, available ammunition, clip reload time, and other weapons can greatly affect how a player fights directly against enemies.

Reprinted with permission from Microsoft Corporation

Cover systems are found in games such as *Perfect Dark Zero*.

Stealth

Games such as *Tom Clancy's Splinter Cell: Chaos Theory* and *Metal Gear Solid* have revolutionized the stealth game genre, introducing innovative mechanics and controls to allow the player, a lone operative, to take on an army and succeed. These games use a variety of systems revolving around sound and vision, along with sophisticated AI, to make them interesting. Players may use silenced weapons, distractions, camouflage, and other sneaky devices to reach their goals. Stealth players enjoy puzzles, high-tech devices, and the feeling that they have outsmarted the enemy.

Games such as *Tom Clancy's Splinter Cell: Chaos Theory* have revolutionized the stealth genre by providing innovative mechnics and controls to the player.

Non-Lethal

Non-lethal or less-than-lethal weapons are not used to much in games. However, when considering what options to give players, do not overlook the ability to give them non-lethal weapons. Many very real weapons that the United States is already developing, both experimental and in current use, could add a lot to a game. You just need to make sure that the risk/reward for using the non-lethal weapons is appropriate, especially if lethal weapons are also available for use. Non-lethal tactics could be seen as not only less violent, but also necessary because players could possibly capture characters for interrogation or other purposes. When designing a nonlethal combat option, think about what other reasons the player might have for sparing an enemy.

Melee

Melee players like to get up close and personal. Some games have no weapons at all and expect players to use just their hands and feet, while others offer basic melee weapons such as knives and swords. Melee combat may be another way to allow for more stealthy combat, a way for players to save ammunition, or just the only option that is available to the player. However, if you're going to mix melee combat with modern weapons, make sure there are strong reasons for the player to use melee attacks if guns are available: "You should never bring a knife to a gunfight."

Jade Empire is the first martial arts role-playing game with a dynamic fighting system that allows players to use martial arts moves, weapons, or magic during combat.

Team Players

Some players are dedicated team players, while others are inherently lone wolves and like to go it alone. Not all games support having multiple player characters or friendly NPCs that can fight, but these options may be highly rewarding for a player, even in a purely single-player experience. *Halo* has a great sense of team play with its helpful AI soldiers, and *Mercenaries* supports helpful troops and civilians, while games such as *Kane & Lynch* not only have two main characters but allow the player to build an entire team of allies. Even the *Medal of Honor* game series has evolved from being more about a player fighting alone to having the player fight with a large group of soldiers who might help in ways other than providing more firepower (such as even healing the player).

A game such as *Tom Clancy's Rainbow Six: Vegas* takes team-based play to the next level. The player is always accompanied by a team of three special forces soldiers. These soldiers may fight alone or be commanded to perform a wide variety of functions. The team can assault rooms in ways that include non-lethal (to avoid killing hostages), explosive (for quick entry), silent, and more. The team may also rappel down the side of a building and enter from the outside, go through doors and windows, and blow through weak points in walls. Players even have access to a door scope that allows them to look under a door and see the enemies on the other side. While looking under a door, the player has the ability to issue orders and specify targets for team members to kill, allowing for precision timing and attacks from multiple directions simultaneously. This level of team play and interaction gives the player diverse options when assaulting an enemy position.

Games such as *Kane & Lynch: Dead Men* have two main characters, but the player may also build an entire team of allies.

In *Tom Clancy's Rainbow Six: Vegas*, players have access to a door scope that allows them to look under a door and see the enemies on the other side.

Defensive

Defensive players are those who like to stay put, wear lots of armor, and make enemies come to them. They will often be the snipers in a game as well. They are the guys who like to hold down the fort to keep it safe. These players like fortifications, fixed heavy weapons, mines, and other defensive weapons that allow them to set up traps or other lethal defenses. In an RTS, defensive players may also be called "turtles" because they like to build walls and huge bases, fortifying everything and making the enemy come to them.

Defensive tactics are not available in every kind of game and every situation, but you could set up a situation in which the player could choose to play more defensively or to go on the offensive. Imagine a scenario where the player is supposed to protect someone on a rooftop. The player might choose to stay there, run from side to side, and keep enemies from getting onto the roof—or choose to climb down off the roof and take it down to the street level. Giving the player these types of choices will help keep the game more diverse.

Games such as *Lineage II* exhibit defensive play.

Long-Range

Many players enjoy sniping or shooting enemies from afar. There is less risk in doing so, and the player usually feels more skillful when making a long-range shot. Many players may be frustrated because they perceive sniping to be cheating. In games such as *Medal of Honor*, the enemy snipers might kill the player in one shot and with deadly accuracy. Figuring out the snipers' locations and the patterns necessary to avoid them is an extremely tedious puzzle for players. If your game involves other players with sniper rifles, or NPCs with sniper rifles, balance their use against the player with the player's use against them.

Players will often be frustrated by the lack of response from an NPC, even if it works in their favor. Some players may like to find ways to exploit the game and use them—but most prefer the satisfaction of winning because of their own skill and aptitude. If the player shoots a character with a sniper rifle, and a nearby character continues to stand there until he also dies, the player will feel cheated. The player would expect the second character to react and take cover, or at least to become alarmed or try to help his friend.

In many games such as *Resident Evil 4, Ratchet: Deadlocked, Halo,* and *Medal of Honor,* sniper rifles really are almost a cheat. When the player has the ability to snipe opponents, the AI may react in some way but usually will not be smart enough to counter the player's sniping. Most game designers thus tend to severely limit the ammunition of the sniper rifle and allow it to be used only in some areas. While this is a very valid control method, it may still be difficult to prevent the player from exploiting the power of sniping.

Electronic Arts, Inc.

Reprinted with permission from Microsoft Corporation

Long-range combat such as sniping is used in many military and action games such as *Medal of Honor: Pacific Assault* and *Halo.*

You could also require more skill in order to use the sniper rifle effectively. Do players have to compensate for high wind, hold their breath, or experience low light conditions or other factors? In video games, sniping is always so easy to do, but in the real world it takes a highly trained marksman. Maybe the act of sniping itself might be made more difficult and interesting.

Another approach to making the sniper rifle more fun for players, besides limitations, is to make the game more reactive to it. One improvement would be giving NPCs the ability to take cover and hide so the player cannot easily shoot more than one of them. It could be interesting to have enemies send out search parties to hunt you—or call in helicopters, tanks, or something more challenging and immune to a sniper rifle.

Combat Support

Many games such as *Dungeon Siege II* and *World of Warcraft* contain characters that specialize in combat support—such as medics who heal members of the player's party. Support characters could also include spell casters or others who shield players from harm, weaken enemies, or strengthen the player's team. Such a character could also be a commander or someone who is coordinating the fight, telling others more of what to do, such as in an RTS. There are many possibilities for giving players or characters they control the ability to play a supporting role in combat.

Many characters in *Dungeon Siege II* offer combat support.

Equipment

For most games it is not enough to think about the weapons you will give the player. It might be just as important to consider other equipment players will need to have fun and achieve their goals. Some equipment may be standard and readily available, such as armor, torches, health kits, and pouches to hold items. Other things may be highly specialized for some specific needs, like a grapple and rope to climb up and down at certain places or rappel. Equipment may be used to protect players, heal them, get them to new locations, and call for help or support from others.

In *Ratchet & Clank,* the players may collect a series of gadgets that help them do all sorts of things. These gadgets are often "keys" to unlock new areas or solve puzzles. For example, the hydrodisplacer raises and lowers the level of the water in some rooms; the hoverboard: allows the player to compete in races; the rail boots allow the player to slide on grind rails; and the bolt detector helps locate buried bolts and make more money; There are many gadgets and pieces of equipment in *Ratchet & Clank* that the player is able to use in a variety of situations.

Tom Clancy's Splinter Cell: Chaos Theory also contains a variety of equipment such as nonlethal sticky shockers, a remote camera, lockpicks, night vision goggles, gas grenades, an EMP gun that disables electronic devices, and computer hacking equipment. All of these devices along with weapons allow for a very stealthy and nonlethal game. The player would not be able to play the game without them.

Sony Computer Entertainment America

© 2005 Ubisoft Entertainment. All Rights Reserved.

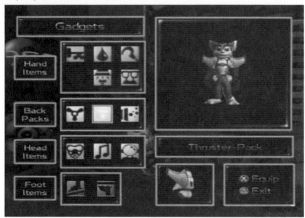

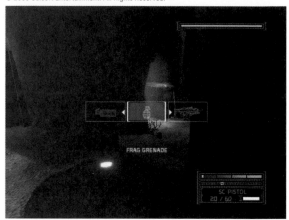

Inventory screen from *Ratchet & Clank,* in which players collect a series of gadgets that may help them unlock areas or solve puzzles.

Tom Clancy's Splinter Cell: Chaos Theory contains a variety of equipment that is available to the player.

While there is no way to say how many gadgets or pieces of equipment will be needed to keep the game interesting, the best thing is to identify which equipment would make sense to have in your game. Then figure out which complements the game in a major way and will not be too difficult to implement and will not risk breaking the game.

Upgrades are a great way to keep players addicted to games. When designing a new article for a game, whether it is a new weapon, piece of equipment, vehicle, clothing, or something else, you might opt to either create a whole series of new items or find a way to upgrade objects. The advantages of creating upgrades instead of new items may be severalfold. First, all of the new art pieces need not be created from scratch. If you properly design your objects from the start, modular design may allow you to upgrade most pieces and create at most a few new ones—thereby saving time.

An upgradeable object need not have a different set of rules; the fewer new concepts a player must learn, especially early in the game, the easier it will be to play. Upgradeable objects also provide some small sense of ownership, since players tend to keep their favorite pieces and improve them over time. Players are also collectors by nature, so having upgrades gives them something else to collect and work toward.

There are three main ways in which an item may be upgraded:

1. It may become stronger over time, with some increased stats. This may be accomplished by an art change or may happen automatically.
2. It may upgrade only along a predetermined path such that it gains new abilities, but in a fixed order and configuration.
3. It may be able to take a variety of upgrades of the player's choice. This forces players to make difficult decisions about the type of functionality they may want their objects to have.

Weapons and Mods

Weapons are the most obvious objects to benefit from upgrades. It does not matter whether you are making a fantasy game, a science fiction game, or a realistic modern-day game. Weapon upgrades are relatively easy to justify and design.

In *Diablo II,* players may upgrade their swords with gems, which give them new abilities. Fantasy weapons may be imbued with all kinds of magical abilities. Even if the game is realistic and set in ancient times, players might still find a few ways to upgrade or modify their weapons to improve them (e.g., by adding poison to a blade or adding a much sharper blade that cuts through most anything). A simple bow could be used with normal arrows, fire arrows, and other configurations that could be relatively realistic.

In *Ratchet: Deadlocked,* players may upgrade any of their 12 weapons in several different ways. Each weapon has one Omega Mod slot that might hold any one of 10 different functional mods if the weapon supports it. These functional mods change the way the weapon works by giving it new abilities, such as shocking anyone near the target spewing lava when it explodes, or even making an enemy become a friend. Each weapon also has the ability to gain levels as it is used and to gain experience.

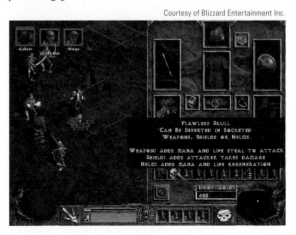

Courtesy of Blizzard Entertainment Inc.

In *Diablo II*, players may upgrade their swords with gems, which give them new abilities.

Each time a weapon gains a level, it gains an Alpha Mod slot. Alpha Mods can then be placed in these slots—affecting the statistics of the weapon and allowing the player to change the weapon's rate of fire, ammunition capacity, knockback, and damage. The player can either try to keep a weapon balanced or stack it with several of the same type of mod and make it stronger.

In *Tom Clancy's Rainbow Six: Vegas,* players may modify modern guns by adding or removing parts. Modern guns may have various sights and scopes to change their accuracy, clip size, rate of fire, triggers to increase sensitivity and help with accuracy, heavier and longer barrels to increase accuracy, sound suppressors, and folding stocks to make them more portable. A grenade launcher might even be mounted underneath them. For instance, the Heckler & Koch XM8 Prototype Assault Rifle was a modular weapons platform that allowed users to reconfigure the same base weapon into many different arrangements. It also had an super advanced grenade launching system that could explode grenades that flew through a window. If we know about such inventions that really exist, imagine what secret equipment the government may be developing to take its place. Players may also experiment with ammunition; for example, a modern shotgun can fire shot, slugs, flechettes, rubber balls, bean bags, fireballs, flares, gas, and much more. Each type of ammunition could be considered an upgrade, since they could potentially be used for different purposes.

In *Ratchet: Deadlocked,* players may upgrade their 12 weapons in several different ways.

In *Tom Clancy's Rainbow Six: Vegas,* players may modify modern guns by adding or removing parts from them.

In some fighting games such as THQ's *WWE Smackdown! vs. Raw 2007* and Midway's *Mortal Kombat: Armageddon,* players not only get to create custom fighters, but they may also customize many of their fighter's moves. This allows players to assemble any assortment of different moves and try to create the ultimate fighter. Players in *Mortal Kombat: Armageddon* can design their own custom finishing moves known as "fatalities," while *WWE Smackdown! vs. Raw 2007* also lets them put together custom moves for wrestlers and even create custom wrestler entrances that play before each match.

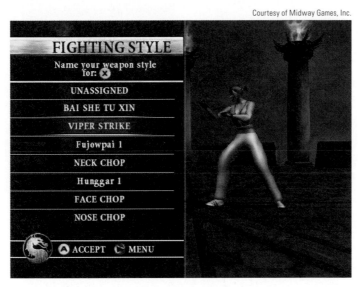

Mortal Kombat: Armageddon allows players to customize many of their fighters' moves.

Customizing vehicles may also be exciting, especially if the game is more vehicle based. Racing games allow you to repaint vehicles, put on new decals, and even change around parts of the car to improve performance. Allowing the players in open-ended games such as *Grand Theft Auto* (*GTA*) to keep their vehicles, upgrade them, and customize them gives them something else to work toward and enjoy doing. Every game has the potential to use upgraded weapons and equipment that give players all sorts of additional abilities or features.

Power-Ups

A *power-up* is a temporary upgrade that instantly benefits the player. Usually power-ups provide a boost in power, skills, abilities, or something special. Power-ups traditionally take the form of a small item that the player touches once in a game to activate, which instantly affects the player before wearing off. One of the classic power-ups in video games is the "power pill" in *Pac-Man* that, when eaten, allows Pac-Man to also eat the enemies on screen for a short time instead of having to run from them.

Players could consider an item in their inventory a type of power-up if it may be used once to boost them up for a short time before being exhausted. The only difference is that it may stay in the player's inventory, where it can be used at any time instead of just where it was placed in the world. Some power-ups will also respawn in the level after a time, becoming occasionally available to a player, while others are a one-use-only item. Sometimes they are random—and they could be fake or even harmful or dangerous to the player. Power-ups are an easy way to control where players use special abilities. Designers usually place them in the world, often as glow-ing objects that float in the air—or sometimes arrange for enemies to drop them as a reward for killing the enemy. Some power-ups are also hidden inside an object such as a crate, or they are hidden somewhere in the world.

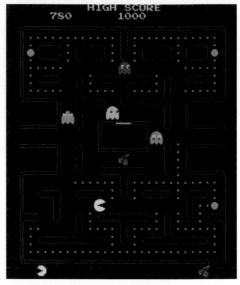

Early "power-ups" were introduced in *Pac-Man* in the form of "power pills."

Power-ups can also help you balance the game, since you can place them at key loca-tions that players may find too difficult or challenging for some reason. Power-ups may also be a significant component in action-based puzzles—giving players an ability to solve a puzzle or challenge that is not available to them at other times. Power-ups may take many different forms. They may be offensive and give players a special attack such as fire or increase the amount of damage done during an attack. They might be defensive and give players a shield, resistance to some type of attack, or even temporary invulnerability. Power-ups may be used to alter time, allow for higher jumps, or even make players invisible; they might also affect player health, refilling it, providing extra health for a time, and much more. Power-ups are a great way to add a lot of variety to a game.

Sony Computer Entertainment America

In *Jak Combat Racing*, power-ups float in the air.

Advancement and Technology Trees

Technology trees became prevalent in real-time strategy games as a visual way
to show what you could research, and how research would lead to your goal.
Technology or advancement trees are branching upgrade paths that can add much
potential interest and variety for players. *Age of Empires* and *Civilization* are probably the best-known games that feature an elaborate technology tree. In it, the player
must progress through four technological "ages" to gain more advanced units, abilities, buildings, and technology.

Firaxis Games Inc.

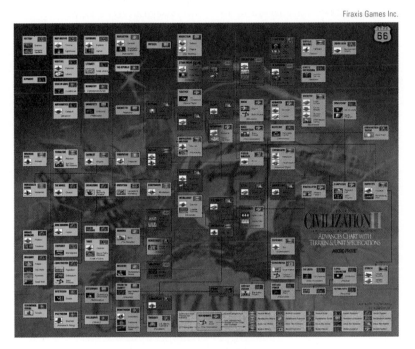

The *Civilization II* technology tree is large and elaborate.

In some games, a player may move down a path to its end, building almost anything along the way. Sometimes a player may then be able to travel down a different branch. Other games offer branching paths; once a branch is taken, the other
path becomes unreachable, forcing players to make difficult decisions. These trees
may allow the player to unlock new abilities—to buy new units and items or use
new weapons, equipment, or skills. Players should have to make hard choices about
where and when to spend their resources or whether to save them. It is usually helpful if a player knows what is farther down the tree—which should include not only
some inexpensive but not terribly powerful items that a player may quickly purchase,
but also some strong and expensive items or upgrades.

Advancement and technology trees are not just for strategy games. They can be used even if the player need not do any research in the game. Sometimes these trees are readily shown and apparent to the player, while sometimes they are hidden behind the scenes. An advancement tree is purely a way for the player to unlock things in the game and for you as a designer to control the conditions for unlocking things. For instance, if players are going to have access to some accessories for a sniper rifle, it would make sense that they cannot buy the accessories or possibly even see them until they own the sniper rifle. Other conditions may also apply: Maybe players must be at Level 12 in an RPG before they can buy an item, or maybe their bartering skills must be at a certain level. Many different factors may determine access to resources; a player should not be able to buy all of the good items in the game and use them in the first level.

Electronic Arts Inc.

Even in a fighting game such as *Def Jam: Fight for New York* the player may unlock, earn, and acquire new moves throughout the game. These moves require a certain amount of skill, money, and other conditions to unlock. Choices that players make in the game will determine when or if they acquire desired moves. Some moves have to be unlocked by winning specific fights or doing other things in the game. This is not unlike a strategy game where the player has to make tough decisions about when and where to spend resources and time in researching or buying new technologies faster. The same sort of dilemma in a sports or fighting game might involve buying new moves, clothing, or even a teammate.

Def Jam: Fight for New York allows the player to acquire new moves through skills training upgrades.

Besides controlling how players advance through the game, technology trees can also enhance the addiction to a game because there is always something else to strive for just around the corner. In the same way that players will keep playing an RPG "just a little longer" in order to gain the next level or desired item, a technology tree provides a series of short-term goals for a player to continually pursue.

Farhad Javidi on "Farming" Opportunities :::::

Farhad Javidi serves as Chair of the Simulation, Modeling & Visualization Center and of the Simulation & Game Development Program at Central Piedmont Community College (CPCC), North Carolina's largest community college and the fourth largest in the nation. Farhad developed the first state-approved associate degree program in Simulation & Game Development in the nation. He is a recipient of the 2007 National Institute for Staff and Organizational Development Excellence Award and was CPCC's Faculty of the Year in 2006. In 2005, he was named Outstanding Faculty Advisor by the National Academic Advising Association and an Unsung Hero by the Charlotte, North Carolina, Chamber of Commerce. He serves on the advisory board of GarageGames and The Enterprise Developers Guild. Farhad is also Chair of CPCC's Senate Technology Committee. He has been an adjunct faculty member in the Computer Science department at the University of North Carolina - Charlotte and has taught various courses in the Computer Science department at the University of South Florida. From 1997 to 2002, he served as director of information technology for Epley Associates Inc., one of the largest communications firms in the southeastern United States. In 1998, he co-founded Digiton Corporation, a North Carolina consulting firm.

Farhad Javidi
(Chair, Simulation, Modeling & Visualization Center / Simulation & Game Development Program, Central Piedmont Community College)

Among many techniques [that promote addictive behavior is] the creation of 'farming' opportunities. The action of players who play for hours repeating the same basic behavior, in order to be rewarded, is called farming. Because 'farmers' will often have to repeat a behavior many times, the length of time spent playing the game is extended. The eventual acquisition of the sought-after accomplishment may cause reinforcement of the general behavior of farming. This theory coincides with the sunk cost fallacy to a high degree. The threat of not accomplishing the goal, combined with the feeling of accomplishment when meeting such a goal, may drive players to exhibit symptoms of addictive behavior.

Creating Strategy

You do not have to design a strategy game in order to use strategic elements within it. Strategic elements add a lot of depth to the game. Using emergent systems might help with the problem of giving the player these choices in the game, but it is not required. Recall in Chapter 5 that we discussed the importance of making the game very broad, with numerous choices to hook players and keep them interested. Strategy allows a much deeper set of possibilities for a player.

Even fighting games have a massive amount of strategy, besides the twitch and memorization needed to play them. Players must not only know what each move is, but they must understand how it is supposed to be used, when it should be used, how it may be countered, what is good to combine with it, and much more. A fighting game might be picked up and played by just mashing buttons, offering lots of cool visceral excitement right from the start. To play fighting games competitively requires a great deal of strategy. Not only must players learn how to play a single character, but they also may have to learn how to play with and against many additional characters, which have a lot of different nuances that make them very different to play.

Courtesy of Midway Games, Inc.

Mortal Kombat: Armageddon contains special moves known as "fatalities."

In a fighting game, players must learn how to play offensively and defensively. They may even have to learn how to perform special moves, such as "fatalities" in *Mortal Kombat: Armageddon* or other in-match moves that give the player character unique abilities that set it apart. Fighting games are all about risk and reward. Do you play it safe by sticking with short, fast moves but become predictable, or do you branch out and use heavier, slower moves that do more damage but leave you vulnerable for a longer period of time or are more susceptible to being countered? There are many choices and strategies available to players in fighting games.

Any action game in which a player controls more than a single character contains some level of strategy. Games such as *Tom Clancy's Rainbow Six 3, Baldur's Gate,* or *Dungeon Siege* allow players to choose to construct their teams with a wide variety of different characters and equipment. The type of team they choose will highly influence the strategies they use when playing the game, and in many cases they may find that they need to use different strategies in order to succeed. This allows players to experiment with many different team configurations in order to see what works well for them.

The strategic components in *Munch's Oddysee* include the ability for the player to take control of any enemy in the game and use it in many ways as well as recruit an entire horde of friends, each of whom could be upgraded to use better weapons. Furthermore, most of the levels may be completed in different ways, which gives the players numerous opportunities to utilize their strategies.

Even in an online game such as *Battlefield 2142*, players may adopt various strategies. The player may choose from different character types, weapons, equipment, and vehicles. Then, depending on how the player and team choose to play, they might utilize a really broad range of tactics. Does the team play more defensively and guard their base, rush the opponents' base and try to capture their flag as a group, or split up and try to be sneaky? The team might also choose to capture key points such as a missile silo that may give them additional special abilities in the game. Players and teams may also try to go it alone, on foot or in vehicles, either on the ground or in the air. These types of choices call for a large amount of strategy and might exist in either a single-player or multiplayer game. Incorporating strategic elements in your game is a good way to help make it deep and enjoyable for a long period of time as players strive to master the game.

Reprinted with permission from Microsoft Corporation

Oddworld: Munch's Oddysee is an action platform game with strategic elements.

Electronic Arts, Inc.

In *Battlefield 2142*, players may choose from a variety of different character types, weapons, equipment, and vehicles.

I'm not interested in having players become 'addicted' to a game. I think that being involved, having a great experience, and taking something interesting and enjoyable with you when you leave the game is much more pleasing.

—*Tracy Fullerton*
(Assistant Professor, Interactive Media Division,
USC School of Cinematic Arts)

Creating Puzzles

Puzzles are another great way to keep players interested in your game. They can take many different forms and may not appear as explicit puzzles to a player but might be disguised as something else in the game. Puzzles may exist within the storyline and take much of the game to uncover, or they may be very small and persist throughout the game. For instance, just figuring out how to kill an enemy in *Kameo* may be a challenge, since the player must often first spray enemies with water or knock off their armor using a special punch to make them vulnerable. In *Kameo*, the player may play as one of 12 different characters, each of which has different abilities.

Puzzles in games may involve logic, strategy, pattern recognition, sequence solving, word completion, timing, and many other attributes. Puzzles might be part of the regular game or a diversion offered by a mini-game.

There are many ways for players to interact with puzzles, either through a custom interface or through the regular game interface. Games such as *Perfect Dark Zero* use puzzles controlled by devices players carry to unlock doors and open items. Many platformers such as *Ratchet & Clank* are full of puzzles. The player must constantly figure out how to get to something, go somewhere, kill an enemy, or get past a mini-game.

> **P**layers should always work toward something. This is very easy to do in RPGs because players are often trying to reach their next level or next set of gear. With other game genres, you can use unlockables, player look changes, or even the promise of more story/action.
>
> —*John Comes*
> *(Lead Game Designer, Gas Powered Games)*

Combat in *Kameo: Elements of Power* involves spraying enemies with water or knocking off their armor using a special punch to make them vulnerable.

Perfect Dark Zero uses a puzzle mini-game that helps players unlock doors in the game.

Puzzles might also be used in conjunction with the plot to hide secrets and then slowly reveal them to the player. High-level puzzles may be used to help add some mystery and intrigue to a game, and players will want to keep playing just to solve them.

Brain Age uses puzzles as a foundation for its gameplay mechanics.

Puzzles can add a lot of depth to a game, as well as a lot of needed diversion. You do not need the next version of *Tetris*, *The 7th Guest*, or *Monkey Island* to include puzzles in your game, but there are many ways to use puzzles to keep players interested for a longer period of time.

Creating Extensions

Another way to add some long-term play using your online components is to offer downloads to extend the game on Xbox Live or through other sources. Games such as *The Elder Scrolls IV: Oblivion* have added additional features that players may pay to download for new abilities, story elements, and missions. More games offer free or inexpensive upgrades to expand their content, for either better online play or an enhanced single-player experience.

The Elder Scrolls IV: Oblivion allows players to buy and download the horse armor after the game shipped on the PC and on Xbox Live.

Far Cry Instincts Predator for the 360 contains an editor that allows players to create multiplayer maps and share them with friends.

Player-created mods have been extremely popular for PC games and are starting to become more prevalent on consoles. Games such as *Far Cry Instincts Predator* for the 360 allow players to use an editor to create multiplayer maps and share them with friends. *Shadowrun* was the first game to offer players the ability to play on the Xbox 360 against PC players running Microsoft Windows Vista OS. Once PC-to-console connections become more prevalent, we may see the expansion of player-created mods being created on a PC and uploaded to a console.

The last few chapters have covered numerous systems that may be incorporated into a game. Although not every game includes all of these aspects, many such as *GTAIII* and *Oblivion* do incorporate a large number of features. The challenge in game design is to incorporate and combine many different features and still maintain a cohesive experience for the player, while keeping the scope and scale of the project manageable enough to produce it in a reasonable amount of time. Remember that games such as *GTA* and *Oblivion* did not reach their full potential until after several sequels, and designers had time to perfect them in their current form. When you create depth, focus on adding content and new abilities that may work well together and enhance the game without making it too complicated or obtuse for players to grasp and enjoy.

:::CHAPTER REVIEW:::

1. Play at least three electronic games that are currently on the market and identify at least three ways in which each game keeps you playing. (If one or more games do not keep you playing, see if you can identify why not.)

2. How will you best ensure that your game incorporates deep gameplay? Will you focus on strategy, puzzles, combat, rewards, role-play, attachment, or another element? Will you create advancement with the use of equipment or weapons? If so, create either a technology tree or equipment list with power-ups for your original game.

3. Play a game that features combat and analyze its elements, including types of combat and how it is used. Did the combat system have an "addictive" effect on you as a player? Why or why not? What would you do to improve the combat system so that it is more diverse?

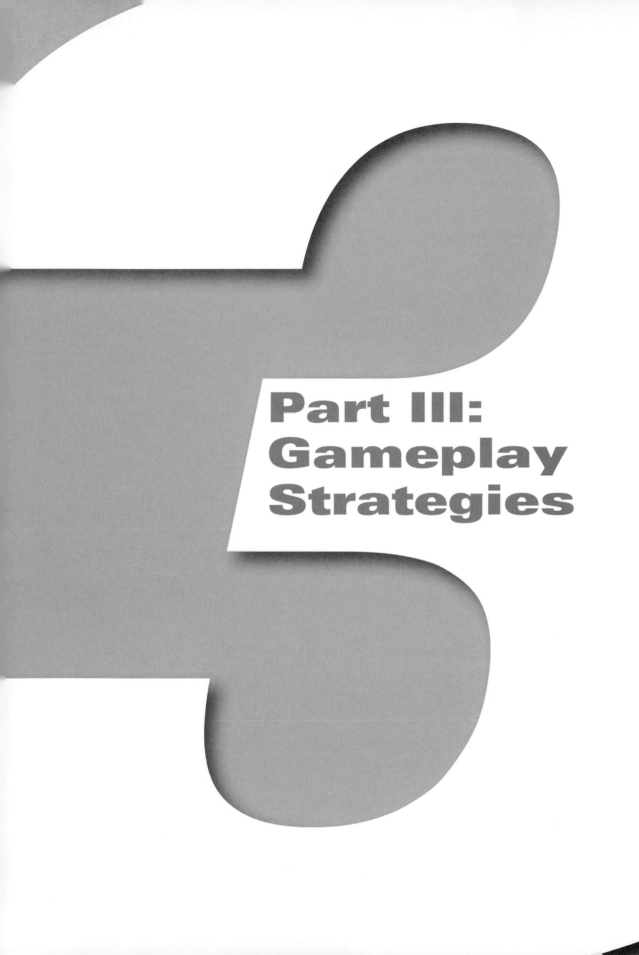

Part III:
Gameplay
Strategies

Creating Progression

ramping the player

Key Chapter Questions

- Why is it important to *ramp* the player through the game?

- What are the possible *load and save* systems, and what are their benefits and disadvantages?

- What is a *dynamic difficulty adjustment* system, and how can it be used to help ramp the player?

- How can *blockade* systems be used to maintain immersion?

- How can *navigation* systems be used to inform the player?

Players want a game that changes and adapts to their needs, and part of your job is to determine how to help the player through the game. You can't just throw together features and expect them to be fun. Planning and adjustments are required in any game to facilitate the player's progress through it. You must give the player the proper tools to learn how to progress and to become better at the game over time. This involves making several design decisions—including how players will learn new skills, save the game, encounter enemies, and keep from getting lost.

Creating Progression Systems

An important part of most game designs has to do with how the player will progress through the game. Everything from the difficulty level of the game to ways of saving the game and progression from level to level contribute to the long-term enjoyment of the game. Players need to be able to get from the start of the game to the end while continuing to have fun and avoiding any major problems that might stop their progression. These problems may easily exist in your game if you balance it incorrectly, confuse the player about what to do next, cause the player to continually get lost, make a section of the game too hard to navigate, or create a puzzle that is too difficult or obscure to get past.

Keeping players happy in a game is a challenge. Few players finish any game; even fewer ever replay a game. Casual players want a game experience that is lighter and easier to get through and never horribly difficult; many hardcore players want a challenge and also want to know that they are "better" than their friends because they got farther in the game, achieved a higher score, or got past a formidable boss.

Devil May Cry 3 was so notoriously difficult to complete that it was re-released as a special edition with decreased difficulty for the less hard-core players.

Many video game designers and players come from a different school of thought when it comes to game design. They believe that games must be extremely difficult to be enjoyable. This mentality seems to come from the days of making arcade games, when players were not supposed to play the game for a long time and the game was supposed to ramp up in difficulty very fast to keep players from playing all day on a single quarter. Many old-school console games, especially those from Japanese developers, also tend to be very hard-core in nature and seem to enjoy punishing players. However, games need to be fun and not too difficult to achieve ultimate success.

Progression through Novel Gameplay

Introduce new ways for the player to play your game and then build on them. Allow the players to use what they've learned all the way through the game and have those elements bolster what they learn later in the game. Then, make sure the game doesn't get too difficult. You'll very easily lose the players if they have to redo something several times. No matter how good your story may be, the same level played more than once will lose a lot.

—John Comes
(Lead Game Designer, Gas Powered Games)

Load & Save Systems

Although deciding how to record the player's progress sounds easy, it might be fairly difficult and subject to philosophical arguments. Saving the state of some games might actually be extremely difficult because of the technical challenges, especially on consoles that traditionally have had small save-game files. Trying to record everything players have ever done, where they have gone, and with whom they have interacted is tough for some game engines—which is why some games allow players to save only at the end of a level.

Lives

Some game designers believe that a game should be difficult, which might include giving the player only a few lives. The concept of giving lives to players is another artifact left over from the days of arcade machines where each quarter players put into the machine bought more time or lives to keep them playing. This is necessary when players are not able to save the game and come back to it later.

Platformers such as *Ratchet & Clank* and *Jak & Daxter* give the player unlimited lives. These games are broken down into sections, each having its own objectives, and if players fail while trying to accomplish a goal, they respawn at the beginning of the section. Players may choose to replay a section as often as they want without any

Jak & Daxter purposefully gives the player unlimited lives.

penalty. Many platformers also teleport players back to safety when they fall off certain high ledges. This might keep some platforming segments from becoming too difficult and frustrating.

Games such as *Grand Theft Auto* (*GTA*) limit the number of lives by how much money players have. If players run out of money before being caught by the police or killed, they might not be able to pay to heal themselves or get out of jail, thereby ending the game. However, the cost for both of these is very small, so it is extremely difficult to lose the game.

There are many ways to control and limit the progress of a player without making the game too tedious. Each game will be different in this respect; some solutions will not work because of the type of game it is, while other solutions will work well in any situation. In Microsoft's *Shadowrun*, a player may resurrect teammates who have died. The resurrected teammates' lives are then tied to that of the player—and if the player dies, the resurrected teammates slowly begin to die. This works well for the magical sci-fi setting and should provide some new gameplay challenges and interest for players.

Reprinted with permission from Microsoft Corporation

In *Shadowrun,* players may resurrect teammates who have died.

Controlling players' lives and saves (which is connected to the game's healing and damage systems) is directly related to controlling their progress. All of these aspects should be carefully thought out and properly understood before you make too many final decisions.

Limited vs. Unlimited Saves

Many designers feel that we should also limit the number of saves a player gets. This may be accomplished by allowing the player to save only at key predetermined points, such as at the end of a level, or by giving the player only a fixed number of saves. Sometimes players might earn or find more saves as they play. Besides making the game tougher, limiting saves will add tension to the game. If players know they have unlimited saves, they will not be worried about their health because they may reload at any time. Survival-horror games such as *Silent Hill* and *Resident Evil 4* are designed to inspire the fear of death to add more tension.

© Courtesy of Capcom. Reprinted with permission.

Survival-horror games such as *Resident Evil 4* are designed to inspire the fear of death to add more tension.

Saves can be limited by allowing the player to save only at key predetermined points, such as the end of a level, or to use only a fixed number of saves. You can give players the opportunity to earn or find more saves as they play.

Many game designers dislike to giving players unlimited saves for several reasons:

- It removes the tension provided by limited saves.
- It decreases the game's immersion and continually reminds players that they are playing a game.
- It makes the game too easy because a player may save and load at any point— even during combat or right before difficult challenges.

Although some designers disagree if players want to get through difficult parts of a game by constantly saving and loading, why stop them? The player has already paid for the game and is still playing it, so the game must be a success at some level. It is not a good idea to limit players artificially and keep them from playing a certain way, unless it severely breaks the game. There is no right or wrong answer to whether you should limit saves, but you should be aware that limiting the saves in a game may increase frustration and put pressure on many players.

Checkpoint Saves

Some games contain only checkpoint saves for all of the preceding reasons, but also because they make the game much more immersive. Checkpoints are also an advantage because they happen behind the scenes and players do not have to remember to save; this avoids irritation when players forget to save manually, suddenly die, and must replay a large amount of the game. Checkpoint saves may be triggered when the player enters a certain part of a game or by an event, such as the completion of a mission or goal. They are easiest to use in a linear game where the player may logically go from one checkpoint to the next. Checkpoint saves are harder in games such as *Oblivion* or *GTA* that are more open ended. Checkpoint saves might also be dangerous, because it is sometimes possible for players to do something wrong, get stuck, and be unable to reload—especially if the game keeps only the last save.

Progression & Ramping in Real-Time Strategy Games

With an RTS, you can create a 'progression' and 'ramping' in the solo play part of the game by unlocking portions as the player progresses from mission to mission. This gives the player new units, structures, and even super weapons to play with as they progress—and, if those are fun to play with, your player stays engaged. Related to giving the player new toys to play with across the missions, the way the missions take advantage of the new toys and present new challenges to the player is also important. I like the progression of missions to alternately give the player a challenge that is best solved by the new unit they have available and then in the next mission, challenge the player to become an expert at using the unit, structure, or super weapon they received in the last mission. When you overlay this structure of challenges with giving the player new toys every mission, you can create multiple types of challenges within each single mission and it can be very engaging.

—*Mark Skaggs*
(CEO & Executive Producer, Funstar Ventures, LLC)

Statistics Systems

Once you have figured out how to keep track of the progress of the player by using a save system, you need to look at how the player's progress will be tracked throughout the game. Are the players going to know how well they are doing by using any kind of score, statistics, or information to track their overall progress?

Stats Tracking

There are several different ways to use tracking stats in a game. In an RPG, it is critical to track the various stats of a player and how they improve over time based on the player's actions. In sports or action games, players may track their shots, kills, and other elements caused by their actions. Players may even track what weapons they use, what game modes they use regularly, and other factors to improve the game experience. It is also possible to track stats such as players' deaths in order to help determine the difficulty of the game. Sometimes these stats may be shown to players to encourage their efforts toward self-improvement; other times the stats are hidden and the designer uses them to tweak aspects of the game behind the scenes.

Score

Many games use some kind of player score to determine how well the player is doing. However, the problem with a score is that it is relevant only in comparison with others. Using scores in an online game could is valuable because players may compare scores with each other. Scores in a single-player game are not useful for comparison unless players like to use them to drive themselves. Sometimes the game gives players a rating or ranking based on comparing their scores with what the designer feels is a representative scoring index.

Scoring helps players understand how they are doing minute-to-minute or even second-to-second in the game. If players perform one punch and earn 100 points but throw another one and earn 500 points, they instantly assume that the second punch is much better and that they should attempt to do it again. If a player kills one enemy and earns 100 points (versus 500 points for another), the player will also get some sense of enemy difficulty and know which enemies are better to kill. However, the same result may also be achieved by rewarding the player with money for killing enemies; the more the player gets for killing an enemy, the stronger the enemy. In *Ratchet: Deadlocked*, enemies drop bolts when the player kills them. The player may pick up bolts (which usually attach themselves automatically to the player anyway), which could be used to buy new weapons and equipment; players thus have some additional incentives to do better in the game in order to get more bolts. The downside to using a score in some games is that it is one more mechanic that reminds players that they are playing a game, which some designers now like to avoid when trying to immerse the player.

Sony Computer Entertainment America

The scoring system in *Ratchet: Deadlocked* involves bolts that are dropped by enemies the player kills.

Message Indicators

Many games such as *Mortal Kombat* and *NBA Jam* use onscreen messages to inform players how they are doing. Special messages are flashed on the screen when the player performs a special attack or combo. The screen may flash text such as "perfect" if the player finishes an enemy without taking any damage. There are an unlimited number of ways to reward the player's actions with messages in the game. The trick for designers is in knowing the frequency of the messages and making sure they do not overwhelm the player.

Courtesy of Midway Games, Inc.

Mortal Kombat uses onscreen messages to inform players how they are doing.

Difficulty Systems

Most games contain some form of difficulty level that the player may adjust. There are many ways for you to affect the game based on what difficulty choice the player makes at the start of the game. You might easily increase or decrease the stats of enemies or players to make the game easier or harder, depending on the difficulty level chosen by the player. However, sometimes this is perceived as a bit cheap, since the enemies just become tougher and thus either more challenging or impossible to kill, which may make the game a lot more tedious to play.

Non-player characters in *Halo* become more intelligent as the game progresses. On Legendary Mode in *Halo*, the enemies will know how to flank the player from behind. They will leave one or a few units in front of the player as a distraction and keep the player pinned down; then everyone else will attempt to sneak around behind the player. Modifying the artificial intelligence (AI) to be better when the game is put on a higher difficulty level is one of the best techniques to use, but it is probably the most time consuming and most difficult to implement.

Non-player characters in *Halo 2* become more intelligent as the game progresses.

You may also adjust the method by which the player heals and how often, along with other features related to health or lives, to make the game more or less challenging. Some games also alter the number of enemies or enemy spawn rates to change how many enemies in the entire game and at one time the player has to face. There are many ways to adjust the difficulty of the game, but you need to determine what is right for your game and makes the most sense.

Most games contain three to four different difficulty levels, but there is no limit. Some games such as *Ratchet: Deadlocked* contain a "super" difficulty option reserved for the most extreme players that is available after the game is won.

The egos of many players do not allow them to play an easy level, so it is usually best to call levels something such as "Normal, Challenging, and Maniac" rather than "Easy, Medium, and Difficult." It really depends on the primary difficulty level.

Sony Computer Entertainment America

Some games such as *Ratchet: Deadlocked* contain a "super" difficulty option reserved for the most extreme players that is available after the game is won.

Ramping Systems

A game must change over time to stay interesting. Even a game such as *Tetris* gradually becomes more difficult the longer it is played. There should be systems in the game that allow it to scale to the skill of the players and remain challenging for them. It is okay for the game to be very easy for a short time—but if it stays too simple for too long (to the point where there is no challenge), it will become boring.

Dynamic Ramping

Dynamic enemy ramping or scaling is found in games such as *Oblivion*, which automatically scales the difficulty of the game based on the player's level and abilities. Some players hate this because the game does not really get any easier or harder over time. The player may work very hard to get to a higher level, only to find that it is still just as hard to kill a creature. This can be a little confusing for some players who realize what is happening in the game.

© 2006 Bethesda Softworks LLC

The Elder Scrolls IV: Oblivion scales the difficulty of the game based on the player's level and abilities.

Discreet Ramping

Discreet ramping is slightly different than dynamic ramping in that enemies are spawned into the game based on how good the player is. The designer may want an "enemy of type X" doing something at a certain level. However, when the player enters the level and it is time to generate the character, the game actually determines what needs to go there in order to make the encounter challenging for the player. The game may look at the player's level and spawn in an equivalent-leveled character, or some combination of characters the designers deem appropriate. This approach may also help keep the game unpredictable and interesting, since players will encounter different enemies even if they come back to the same area.

In some games such as *World of Warcraft,* the player character must be of a certain level to enter an area because all of the challenges in that level will require the player to have certain abilities in order to accomplish anything there. Each level may contain its own required or perceived level of difficulty that you might assume players have achieved by the time they reach it, or a requirement may be available to keep the player in check.

Courtesy of Blizzard Entertainment, Inc.

In *World of Warcraft,* the player character must be of a certain level to enter an area.

Rubberbanding

Human nature dictates that close contests will be more interesting. If one team in a football game or one player in a boxing match is far ahead of the other, the event quickly becomes boring. However, if the competition is close, spectators might be on the edge of their seats in anticipation. If first place is able to lap second place 20 times during the Indy 500, most would probably stop watching. However, in video games we are able to cheat to make sure there is always pressure on the player and the game will remain close. This is best seen in games such as *Mario Kart,* which always has one opponent either right on the player's tail or just ahead of the player, no matter how poorly the player is driving. Players do better if they are being pushed or pulled through the game.

In a wrestling game, such as THQ's *Smackdown! vs. Raw 2007,* who is winning and who is losing is a bit more ambiguous, partially because of the nature of professional wrestling itself. It is easy for the player to seemingly get ahead, but then the computer suddenly starts winning. In professional wrestling, one wrestler will attempt to pin the other down repeatedly before finally succeeding. This helps to greatly increase the tension of the match, especially since most of the counts reach two and almost get to three before the other wrestler suddenly and seemingly miraculously breaks free. This back-and-forth action makes a game far more exciting than if a player or non-player character (NPC) is allowed to suddenly move far ahead—which could cause the player to lose interest and stop playing the game.

Nintendo

In *Mario Kart: Double Dash!!,* there is always one opponent right on the player's tail or just ahead of the player, no matter how poorly the player is driving.

Finding a Balance

There are plenty of solutions and compromises available to a designer who is willing to think outside of the box. Some ramping solutions may be difficult or at least challenging to implement and balance, while others will not be too hard to do. For instance, enemies that the player has not yet encountered could ramp up dynamically with the player and thus would be challenging the first time they're encountered. Then the enemies could stop changing so that if the player becomes a bit stronger and still must face the enemy, the player will feel more powerful because the enemy can be easily dispatched—at least for a short time.

However, one reason games such as *Oblivion* ramp enemy characters is because it is difficult to create enough content to fill up these massive games. This will be a major challenge for all next-gen games when art creation times increase dramatically because of the added complexities. Even if you have resource problems as a designer and might not create nearly enough content, there are ways to add diversity and still make the ramping of the game obvious to the player. If there is a "create-a-character" system in your game, creating new variants to enemies should be easy; however, without it you could use color, weapon, and effects variants to create more enemies. This might be important when trying to keep ramping the players, since you do not necessarily want them to encounter the same enemies throughout the game.

@ 2006 Bethesda Softworks LLC

Massive role-playing games such as *The Elder Scrolls IV: Oblivion* ramp enemy characters because it's difficult to create enough content.

Instead of just dynamically increasing enemy stats as the game progresses, consider ways to make new enemy variants that are obviously, even if subtly, different for the player. For instance, if there is a basic swordsman in the game, give him a sword and shield, followed by a heavy two-handed sword, a magical sword, a pike or halberd, and so on. Just changing a weapon will make the enemy seem different to the player, especially with some small color and accoutrement changes.

Keep in mind that it is not just different enemies that give the game more depth over the long haul, but the tools that the player receives as well. If the player faces a basic swordsman but has only a club, the swordsman will probably be tough. Each time you give the player a new weapon, skill, or ability, even the same old enemy might become new and exciting once again if done properly. This is especially true if the enemies have the proper AI to react to the new weapons and player's abilities as well.

Combinations of enemies are also important for keeping the game interesting in the long term. You must utilize the concept of combined arms to make the player really feel challenged. Start the player off facing one of something, then start adding more of the same kind. Watch how a player takes on a single enemy, versus a group of enemies. Then start adding different types of enemies, especially ones with different functions. In almost any war movie, you will notice that not every soldier in an army uses the same weapon. Obviously, different weapons have different uses. Think about how soldiers would behave in real life if possible. Swordsmen with shields would protect archers, pikemen would protect the shield holders from horses, and cavalry would flank enemies and rapidly strike at them. The same goes for a modern army with soldiers, tanks, missiles, boats, and airplanes.

Figure out how to use a combination of simple systems to form a wider variety of elements for the player to experience. Think about how things might be combined in new and interesting ways so that the player first learns how to deal with one thing and then must deal with it in combination with something else. This will help make your game easier to learn and far more interesting throughout.

New Enemy Introduction

Another aspect to the difficulty of the game is how and when new enemies are introduced to the game. If a new enemy that is impossible or close to impossible for the player to currently handle is introduced too early, it may ruin the game. Enemies should come into the game at the right frequency and difficulty, not only to keep the game interesting to the player, but also to ensure that enemy difficulty and abilities are kept in line with the player's abilities and skills.

Dynamic Difficulty Adjustment System

More and more games are beginning to use what is called *dynamic difficulty adjustment* (*DDA*), in which the game constantly monitors or regularly checks the player's progression and determines how well the player is doing, then adjusts the difficulty of the game to compensate. DDA was first used heavily in the *Crash Bandicoot* series by Naughty Dog and a few others, and then in the *Ratchet & Clank* series by Insomniac. The game would do a variety of checks to see how often the player had died and then adjust the game. If the player died more than seven times on a level, the game would start compensating by giving the player more health and reducing the stats of the enemies. DDA may be used in a wide variety of ways.

Sony Computer Entertainment America

Dynamic difficulty adjustment was first used heavily in the *Crash Bandicoot* series.

In *Crash Bandicoot*, it is easier to compensate players without their realizing it because all of the pickups in the game are inside of crates and hidden until players open them. This allows the designers to change the contents of the crates dynamically to provide players with health, shields, or other needed items. In *Ratchet: Deadlocked*, when the player fights a boss, the HP of the boss is reduced by approximately 10% each time the player dies, down to a minimum level. The effect is very subtle, and most players probably don't realize they are being helped. While a full-blown DDA system is a little time consuming to build and properly balance, it may be well worth the effort.

Tracy Fullerton on Self-Motivated Progression :::::

Tracy Fullerton is a game designer, writer, and educator, with 15 years of professional experience. She is currently Assistant Professor in the Interactive Media Division of the USC School of Cinematic Arts, where she also serves as Co-Director of the Electronic Arts Game Innovation Lab. Recent credits include faculty advisor for the award-winning student games *Cloud* and *flOw*, and game designer for *The Night Journey*—a unique game/art project with media artist Bill Viola. She is also the author of *Game Design Workshop: Designing, Prototyping, and Playtesting Games*. She was one of the founders of iTV game developer Spiderdance and also served as a creative director and producer at the New York design firm R/GA Interactive for several years. Her work has received numerous industry honors, including best Family/Board Game from the Academy of Interactive Arts & Sciences, *ID Magazine*'s Interactive Design Review, Communication Arts Interactive Design Annual, several New Media Invision awards, iMix Best of Show, the Digital Coast Innovation Award, IBC's Nombre D'Or, and *Time Magazine*'s Best of the Web. In December 2001, she was featured in the *Hollywood Reporter*'s "Women in Entertainment Power 100" issue. She holds an MFA from the USC School of Cinema-Television, and is a founding member of the Interactive Peer Group in the Academy of Television Arts and Sciences. She is also an active member of the Academy of Interactive Arts and Sciences and the International Game Developers Association, and she serves as a mentor for the AFI Intel Enhanced Television workshop.

Tracy Fullerton
(Assistant Professor, Interactive Media Division, USC School of Cinematic Arts)

Most games create progression by steadily ramping up the challenge, with some dips to keep players feeling confident. I'm interested in experimenting with a different approach—one that allows players the choice to advance in difficulty when they feel they are ready. If you think about how you learn to play a musical instrument, for example, you'll see what I mean. There is no automated system ramping up the difficulty of the music; instead, you choose the piece you want to play, and you push yourself when you're ready. Games could learn from this kind of self-motivated progression.

Blockade Systems

It is usually important to control the player's progress through the game. Even games such as *GTA* do not let players access the entire game from the beginning. There are missions the player must complete in order to progress and gain access to more areas and features. Some of this control allows the player time to learn how to play the game, but most of it helps the designers to properly ramp the player through the game and provide a cohesive experience. You might control the player's access into any area in many different ways.

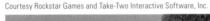
Courtesy Rockstar Games and Take-Two Interactive Software, Inc.

A police blockade in *Grand Theft Auto: Vice City* may control the player's progress through the game.

Locks & Keys

Making the player find, earn, or uncover keys to open the door to the next area is an age-old practice of game developers. Games such as *Doom* use this technique almost exclusively to control movement through a level. A key could take many different forms, but it is basically any object that is needed to go from one location to another. A map to know how to go somewhere, a key code to open a mechanical lock, a special object, a light to see by, a gas mask to breathe with, or someone to tell the player how or where to proceed might all be considered keys; they could be used to open up the necessary door or supply something else that would hold the secret, skill, or ability to get there. Unfortunately, this technique has also become a little old and may seem tiresome very quickly, so be careful not to rely only on traditional locks and key hunting for progression.

Mission Accomplished

The other common method is to unlock an area in the game for the player after a mission, level, quest, or goal is completed. The new area may be accessible because players have simply reached it, or a character may grant them access to the area as a reward. There are many ways that completing missions might easily unlock new areas of the game for the player.

Player Abilities

You can regulate where players may go by controlling what they are able to do. In *Mortal Kombat: Shaolin Monks*, players will not reach gates that allow them to travel to other worlds until they gain certain platforming abilities. These gates require the player to learn how to perform acrobatic moves that allow them to reach a new area in the game hub and get to the gate. The downside to using this kind of player limitation is that many cool acrobatic moves are not available in the game until much later, which feels forced and a little too convenient. The acrobatic skills players learn could feel like those a master martial artist should already know.

Courtesy of Midway Games, Inc.

In *Mortal Kombat: Shaolin Monks,* players won't reach gates that allow them to travel to other worlds until they gain certain platforming abilities.

Player Skill

The player may also require some special skills to progress through the game. To unlock doors, the player might need a lock pick and instruction in how to use it. Or maybe the player needs to get through a door that contains a computer lock and must learn how to hack it. In *Jade Empire,* there is a magical teleporter that can transport players to other realms, but players must first earn the right to use it and be taught how to use it before they may travel to faraway places. There are many ways to use the players' lack of skill to keep them from going somewhere.

Bosses

Having a tough enemy that players must defeat to progress is a very common part of games and is expected in many genres such as platformers. In *God of War,* the player must face the Hydra, the Hades Minotaur, and Ares the God of War. Most games require beating the bosses before the player may progress. Bosses are notoriously tough in most games and may lead to lots of frustration for casual gamers. In some games such as *Shadow of the Colossus,* the player must face 12 giant monsters who are all basically bosses. Bosses are also usually very difficult to create, since they are often close to unique—requiring a custom design and extra work from everyone on the team. However, bosses are expected and often required in many game genres.

Sony Computer Entertainment America

In *God of War,* the player must face several bosses (such as the Hydra) that must be defeated before the player may progress further.

Navigation Systems

When you design progression systems, ensure that players are able to easily navigate through the world, find needed locations and characters, and accomplish their objectives with a minimal amount of frustration. These navigational systems may take many shapes and forms, but they share essentially the same goal. Whether you use many navigational systems or none at all, you must understand where navigational issues may arise and compensate for them.

Courtesy Rockstar Games and Take-Two Interactive Software, Inc.

The heads-up display for *Grand Theft Auto: San Andreas* contains a map component that serves as a navigational system for the player.

Maps

The most obvious navigational system in a game is the inclusion of any number of map systems. This could include in-game maps, a full-screen map, or in-game navigational aids to help players get around in a 3D world.

In-Game Maps

A variety of in-game map systems can be used in a game. *GTA* and *Mercenaries* use an innovative circular map, which has small icons on it that show the location and direction of key things in the world, including the player's current objective, stores, and characters who might give the player more jobs (objectives).

Dungeon Siege and *Diablo* use a small semitransparent on-screen map that may be enlarged several times and made to overlay most of the screen but is transparent enough to let the player play the game with the map fully enlarged. This type of map may be useful, but it is generally confusing for most players to try to watch a map and the game at the same time.

Courtesy Rockstar Games and Take-Two Interactive Software, Inc.

Grand Theft Auto: Vice City uses an innovative circular map that contains small icons showing the location and direction of key elements of the world, such as current objective, stores, and helpful non-player characters.

Courtesy of Blizzard Entertainment, Inc.

Diablo II contains a map that may be turned on to overlay the game world to help the player navigate.

Pause Screen Maps

Whenever the player pauses the game, there is a chance for many games to display a full-screen map of the game world. These maps help show players where they've been, where they need to go, the location of key items, and possibly much more. They might also offer ways for the player to travel somewhere quickly or exist only for educational information. Some of these maps show only the level the player is on (*Ghost Recon: Advanced Warfighter*), while other maps show players the entire game world (*Oblivion*).

Full-screen maps are an important part of many games and should not be overlooked in most cases. The bigger and more complicated your world is, the more you must help the player navigate through it.

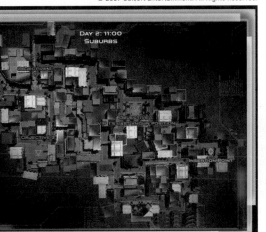 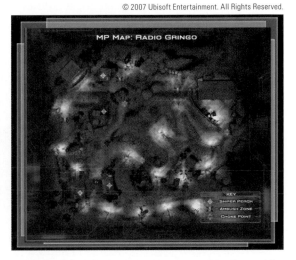

Tom Clancy's Ghost Recon: Advanced Warfighter single-player in-game map (left) shows all of the player's mission objectives, while the multiplayer in-game map (right) shows not only the level—but tactical positions for sniping, ambushes, and choke points.

Objectives

Players should always know what they need to do in the game. Even if they decide to explore the world and not continue on a quest immediately, they should always be able to identify the quest and where it might be found. The challenge for players should not be about figuring out what and where, but how.

If the full game map does not list objectives, or if the in-game map does not show them, another alternative is to use icons or in-game art to show where key objectives lie in the world. This lets players more easily navigate in a 3D space and find their objectives, and it also keeps players from constantly having to reference a small 2D map and navigate a 3D world at the same time. Of course, for many games, a large floating icon or other piece of art in a 3D world will feel very out of place.

Ratchet: Deadlocked uses giant beams of light in the distance to help players find objectives.

Rapid Transportation

Another aspect to navigational systems is the use of and need for rapid transportation, which you can design in many ways. In *World of Warcraft*, the player may pay to take flights to new areas very quickly instead of running there; in *GTA*, the player may take the subway to far parts of the city; and in *Oblivion*, the player may use the world map to quickly go to places we've been all over the world. While rapid transportation is not necessary in all games, it is important to allow players to quickly move around the game world.

Courtesy of Blizzard Entertainment, Inc.

World of Warcraft allows the player to rapidly transport to different parts of the game world.

Determining Progression

Many different systems in the game work together to ramp the players' experience and ensure that players do not get stuck because the game becomes too difficult or because they do not know what to do or may not figure out where to go. This requires game designers to look at a wide variety of different systems and how they operate alone or in conjunction with other systems.

Very often, designers are unable to play through their games until very late in the development cycle, which usually means there are systems in the game that interact in unexpected ways. This may lead to exploits or other problems for players that can halt their progression and cause other difficulties. It is important to determine on paper how to safely ramp the player.

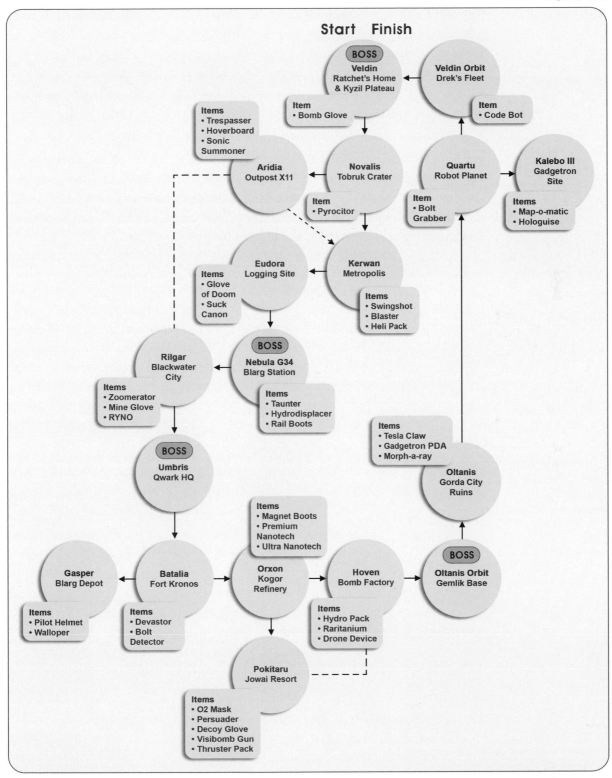

The game macro flowchart for *Ratchet & Clank* shows all of the different planets in the game and where new items in the game may be acquired.

The best thing to do is to create a game timeline of sorts, or what could be called the game macro or game flowchart overview, that allows you outline all of the key progression moments in the game. Here you can lay out—level by level, chapter by chapter, or scene by scene—the game's possible items, enemies, skills, key story events, and rewards. The game macro will be updated constantly throughout the game as things change, but it should be clearly understood before moving into production.

Having a plan for the progression of the game will help the level designers and character designers tremendously. Considering in detail what needs to happen in the game will go a long way toward ensuring that your characters, levels, and gameplay systems are designed cohesively and will not have to be redone.

:::CHAPTER REVIEW:::

1. Play at least three electronic games that are currently on the market and identify how each game handles progression. Discuss load and save, statistics, ramping, blockade, and navigational systems. Are each of these systems effective, or do you feel they need improvement? If applicable, what improvements would you suggest?

2. Which load and save system would you choose to implement in your original game? Why would this system be preferable to others? How will you balance immersion with player control?

3. Choose a ramping system discussed in this chapter and incorporate it into your original game. How does the ramping system you chose conform to your core mechanics?

CHAPTER

8

Creating Variety

involving the player

Key Chapter Questions

- What are some techniques for *reducing* repetitive gameplay?

- What are the *benefits* to having repetition in a game?

- How do you provide *variety* in a game's storylines, levels, and characters?

- How do you create an *immersive* experience for the player through realism, detail, and drama?

- How do you create an *exciting* experience for the player through action, movement, and choices?

Games must often contain a wide variety of mechanics to keep players involved. One of the biggest problems in games, even if they contain many interesting features, is repetition—which also can be difficult to avoid and can even sometimes be desirable. Some people may play *Tetris* or solitaire for months on end, while others become bored with these games in a very short time. Some players gladly replay a particular level many times, while others stop playing after the second or third time they feel forced to perform a specific action. It is essential to understand your audience. Players today are more discriminating—with short attention spans and many more games to choose from. Since next-generation games are so much more difficult to build, it is becoming increasingly difficult for us to create enough content to keep a game lasting 10 or more hours interesting. Repetition is becoming more of a problem, and gameplay design should incorporate techniques to minimize it.

Avoiding Repetition

One of the most common problems in many action games today is how to make them fun for a long time. A majority of the action games on the market have a tendency to become very *repetitive* or boring after only a few hours of gameplay, and most suffer from the same problems. For a game to be rewarding for a long period of time, a lot must come together. A game with overall high production values will be more widely accepted than a game that is strong in some areas but weak in others. Trying to minimize repetition is pointless if the overall game is bad. Glaring problems such as bad camera, controls, graphics, or frame rate will keep any game from reaching its full potential.

Keeping a game rewarding for a long period requires more than just adding some replay incentives or ability. If the game is not extremely rewarding the first time around, most players will not bother to play it again. Results of playtests at major publishers have shown that most players rarely finish a game, so replayability might not have any effect. (Players of multiplayer games, sports games, and arcade style games usually fall into a different category.) Research how many players are really going to replay your game before you invest a lot of time trying to make it so open-ended that players will want to replay the game's story over and over again. Keeping your game from being repetitive and adding replayability are two different elements that are often lumped together. Ensure that the game is first and foremost *not* repetitive. If you toss in some replayability, it's the icing on the cake!

There are two main types of games when it comes to their ease of use—simple and complex. Making a game simple has many advantages; "simple" does not mean "simplistic." A simplistic game might be an old Atari game remake or a puzzle game such as *Tetris*. A simple game will help the player pick it up and figure it out quickly; it is intuitive and easy to play, does not require a lot of time to play, and may be enjoyed by a wide range of players. *Devil May Cry IV* is a good example of a fairly simple action game to learn, since all the player really needs to know to play it effectively is how to press the jump, use the sword, and use gun buttons.

A game that requires players to read a manual or go through a long tutorial, or that constantly challenges players to figure out new things, may be considered a complex game. Many games have some complexity, but they are often missing what is known as *deep gameplay*.

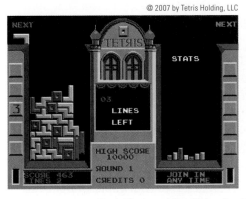

Both *Tetris* and *Devil May Cry 4* contain simple movement rules.

A deep game does not have to be complex. Deep gameplay relies on the use of *rules* that allow players to know what they are supposed to do in a game. These rules are often based on real-world rules or laws, such as physics. In a game such as *Super Mario Sunshine,* players may fall from great heights and not hurt themselves; in *Tomb Raider*, players know that if the fall looks too high, they might not survive it. The same rules apply to weapons. A person playing *Medal of Honor* expects all of the weapons to function realistically and may predict their behavior—whereas in a game such as *Halo* that uses science fiction weapons, the player must learn a new set of rules.

Super Mario Sunshine and *Tomb Raider* are both moderately difficult to play, and they contain complex puzzles and controls that require some level of mastery.

How does knowing the rules of a game minimize repetitive gameplay? Very simple rules may be combined to form more complex or deeper gameplay rules or mechanics. For instance, if the player has a gun, the player would know that it shoots. The player then figures out that shooting at barrels makes them explode, so it is logical for players to kill enemies by shooting at barrels next to them. Later, there may be some barrels next to a door that the player cannot open—so the player finds that shooting the barrels will blow open the door. Still later, the player may acquire a force field that protects against explosions and find that exploding a barrel while protected by the force field will reveal a previously unreachable location. Although this is also a kind of puzzle, there are several rules the player knows—guns shoot and barrels explode when shot—that are combined in different ways to add some new twists to the gameplay. The player still has learned only two rules.

The best way to understand rules is to look at some games and see how their rules help create either a fun experience for players or problems that make the game lack fulfillment. Therefore, every rule or mechanic in the game has relationships with other rules, and these relationships can add great depth to your game without adding a lot of additional complexity.

Genre-Specific Variety

With massively multiplayer online games, variety is easy. Regardless of the lack or fullness of your feature set, the players provide large amounts of variety through their own emergent gameplay. In a very real sense, the players *are* the variety. You just have to pay attention and support that play—when possible and when appropriate.

—*Jessica Mulligan (Executive Producer, Sunflowers GmbH)*

Civilization was a strategy game with a lot of emergent behavior—each individual part of the game (combat, food, production, terrain, happiness, buildings, movement) was pretty simple, but the interactions between them made for endless variety and replayability.

—*Brian Reynolds (Chief Executive Officer, Big Huge Games)*

We recognize there are a number of different play styles that role-playing gamers fall into. One is the hack-and-slash marauder who wants to chop through a game quickly; others are the obsessive mini-maxer, role-player, and explorer archetypes. We try to make sure that the players have options in how they complete the game to complement their style. For example, in *Fallout 2* (as in *Fallout 1*), the character creation process supported three main ways to make progress through the game—stealth, combat, and diplomacy—and we built areas and objectives so that each of these styles would give the players a viable option for success, a tangible reward, and also an ego-stroking experience based on how they constructed their character. It's not simply providing a variety of options, but creating reactivity to the players' actions (and their character creation choices) that can provide the best hooks to keep players going. The more the game reacts to things the player has done ("Hey, you're the guy who allied himself with the City Watch and cleared Neverwinter of the thieves' guild," "You're a Made Man with the Salvatore family; let me give you a discount") or character creation options ("You look strong enough to tackle those orcs in the hills"), the more it fuels the player to keep going in the world.

—*Chris Avellone (Chief Creative Officer & Lead Designer, Obsidian Entertainment)*

Repetitive Travel

Continually traveling across a barren and open world may become very repetitive. Some worlds are very pretty and just fun to explore, but others are painful to cross.

An additional gameplay system, such as the subway in *Grand Theft Auto: San Andreas*, is sometimes needed in order to allow the player to move quickly through an open-ended world, especially when a mission requires the player to travel long distances.

Courtesy of Rockstar Games and Take-Two Interactive Software, Inc.

The subway in *Grand Theft Auto: San Andreas* (map shown) helps the player travel quickly through the game world.

Repetitive Tasks

Requiring the player to perform the same task over and over again in the story may also become boring. Many games incorporate "fetch quests" that make the player go from point A to point B to pick up someone or something and then return it to the starting point or some other location. *World of Warcraft* utilizes fetch quests and provides a huge world in which to perform them. While a game might be successful when built around a highly repetitive model, you still need to be aware of what you are doing and decide if it is an appropriate design technique for you to use.

Besides repetitive quests, you might also make the player do something in the game far too many times. Toward the end of *Munch's Oddysee*, the player must use a crane to move a series of objects in the world; this is horribly repetitive, but the story and cut-scenes were completed long before the level, and it is necessary for the player go through this repetitive step in order to make it cohesive. This is the danger of working on story and level designs independently and not having enough crossover between the two.

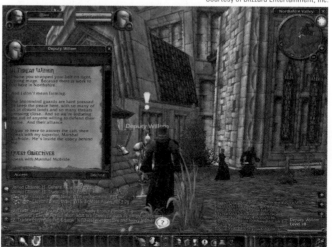

Courtesy of Blizzard Entertainment, Inc.

World of Warcraft utilizes fetch quests and provides a huge world in which to perform them.

> ## Balancing Repetition & Variety
>
> Players should not be doing entirely identical things throughout a game. The other side of the coin, however, is that players should not be doing radically different things from moment to moment. Add sensible small chunks of the new along the way while you phase out non-core elements of early gameplay.
>
> —*Frank T. Gilson*
> *(Senior Producer, Wizards of the Coast)*

Repetitive Storylines

Many action games contain storylines, but very few action games contain *great* storylines. Only a handful of games have exceptional storylines. Many games such as the *Final Fantasy* series tend to forsake gameplay in favor of story. While this may sound like a harsh statement, especially for the die-hard *Final Fantasy* fans, what really makes the series great year in and year out for most players is the storyline.

While this book is not about writing stories for games, it is important to understand how the story for the game, or the structure of the story, may greatly affect the amount of repetition in a game by affecting the way levels must be designed. The story might dictate how the player must move through the levels; the size, content, and style of the levels; and what characters, creatures, objects, vehicles, and structures populate the world to make it interesting. Since the story has a lot to do with how much repetition the player will face in the game, you need to examine it for problems that will make the game become tedious or boring over time.

Repetitive Storytelling

Pre-rendered movies or in-engine movies that take away player control during a cut-scene are still the most common game storytelling tools. If players are constantly being forced to watch long movies and are unable to skip through them—especially if this pattern continues throughout the game—many will find it annoying. Some games such as *Final Fantasy, Metal Gear Solid,* and *The Bouncer* are similar to large interactive movies, but players of these games come to expect this structure and often look forward to it.

Cut-scenes are not the only way to tell stories in games; there are many other techniques that are far more interactive. However, most game designers are still struggling with how to tell stories in games as an interactive medium. Cut-scenes allow games to try to cross between interactivity and non-interactivity—attempting to make a game similar to a movie. The problem is that cut-scenes are often the only technique that a game uses to tell a story, when there are many more possibilities such as non-player characters (NPCs) who talk in the game and provide information and objects in the world for the player to read.

God of War II contains long, beautiful noninteractive sequences.

Remember the old adage that a picture is worth a thousand words? This is very true in games in that the levels and locations in which you place the players and the events that are going on all around them—along with the objectives they must accomplish—will contribute a large portion of the story. Imagine walking into a giant field that is reputed to be ancient but contains few or no remains of a long-ago war, compared to walking into the battlefield and seeing destroyed machines and ancient remnants everywhere. You would immediately know that a war had occurred there, without having to be told. The visuals of the levels are an important aspect of a game.

> Fun, entertaining characters and an intriguing storyline will hook most players, in addition to great gameplay.
>
> —Deborah Baxtrom
> (Writer/Filmmaker; Instructor, Art Institute of Pittsburgh - Online Division)

Scripted Events

Having scripted events in the world that the player may watch, but not necessarily interact with, might also be a good technique to use. In the beginning of *Quake IV*, a giant creature enters on the far side of the room, violently attacks a soldier standing there, and drags him out of the room screaming. The player cannot do anything about it, but the sequence does a good job of foreshadowing the power of some of the creatures and makes the player hesitate before walking through the door.

Stories are not necessarily linear (in fact, nonlinear storytelling is often much more compelling) and they may be affected by the player's actions. When you think about the overall story for a game, consider that several levels of storytelling may be given to players throughout the game—including cut-scenes and other interactive scenes as well as the minute-to-minute story that players create through their actions and choices. If you listen to players talk about the "story" in a game, you will see that sometimes they retell the overall master story plotline, and sometimes they recount their play experience as a story, using their actions to complete a new story that is *unique* to their experience.

Used by permission from id Software, Inc.

The initial cut-scene in *Quake 4* foreshadows the power of some creatures.

Adding a "Twist"

Surprise and variation on expectations are classic dramatic techniques for keeping people involved in an experience. Taking a known mechanic and adding a variation or a twist can be a great way to increase challenge and reinvest players in a game. One nice example of this is the way that a lot of casual games will ramp their levels by adding simple twists—appetizers and drinks, the line, etc. in *Diner Dash* are a good example of this.

—*Tracy Fullerton*
(Assistant Professor, Interactive Media Division, USC School of Cinematic Arts)

Consequences

In some cases, stories may even be directly affected by the player's actions, either through an actual branch in the storyline or through other short interactive sequences that do not really affect the overall plot of the game but allow some event to play out differently. For example, in *Splinter Cell Chaos Theory* there is a moment where the player is told to kill another character but actually has the option to let her live. The player may be reprimanded for letting her live, but there is not a major consequence for the player's actions. The player also learns that someone else then kills the character, thereby keeping the overall plot intact. This player choice does not really matter, but the player feels that it has some meaning.

In some games, such as *Half-Life 2*, players cannot hear their own voices and conversations are one-sided. This may allow players to inject their own personas more deeply into the game characters and be more immersed in the game. Designers are split on this technique; some feel that it is more important that the character's personality be a major part of how the story is told, as well as the events within it.

Half-Life 2 does not allow the player character's voice to be heard.

If you include a lot of story throughout your game, try to spread it out and keep the length of any one sequence to a minimum. It is also critical to let the player bypass the cut-scenes. Just be sure not to include essential information in the story sequences that would keep players from progressing in the game if they are skipped.

Vary Everything

Vary everything you can. You can vary the number of foes, the speed of the game, the lighting, the audio, the setting, the use of game mechanics, and anything else that comes to mind. You should change something up as often as possible to keep things interesting.

—*John Comes*
(Lead Game Designer, Gas Powered Games)

Repetitive Levels

Most games are broken into levels that are designed to be distinct in some way. In a game such as *Medal of Honor: Pacific Assault,* each level has its own objective such that the story defines the level. Sandbox games such as *Grand Theft Auto* are not broken into levels, but they take place in one big open world that is full of different objectives to keep the player busy. In most cases, each game level takes place in a different location. In a game such as *Half-Life 2*, each location is a different part of the city—whether it is the underground, a base, or somewhere in between.

Electronic Arts, Inc.

In a game such as *Medal of Honor: Pacific Assault,* each level has its own objective such that the story defines the level.

There are many reasons to break games into levels; this used to be done because each part of the game had to be loaded into memory separately. From a game design perspective, breaking the game into discrete chunks makes it easier to design the game and to determine who is going to build what. It also helps the designers determine how to ramp the player throughout the game and assess the game's difficulty. From a player's perspective, discrete levels offer the player opportunities to feel a sense of accomplishment and to digest the game and story more easily.

Levels in a game may be boring for a variety of reasons. It is very hard to make levels that are well-balanced, fun, challenging, and interesting. Try to ensure that the objectives, goals, look, feel, and gameplay associated with each level are as distinct as possible, especially if you're reusing art or levels. Make players want to keep going from one level to the next.

Levels may become very repetitive. For example, in *Super Mario Sunshine*, players may play through each level in many different ways, but they are often expected to perform similar tasks from one level to the next. While the levels are interesting, they also often require the player to do the same thing over and over again. This is also compounded by the fact that the player might climb up a hill for a long time, miss the final jump, and have to start again. The irritating episode with the crane in *Munch's Oddysee*, mentioned earlier, is another example of repetition that must be carefully monitored and controlled.

You may need to develop tools so that the game can minimize repetition. It is extremely important to ensure that the game identifies when the player is having too much difficulty. The *Ratchet & Clank* series utilizes act balancing, which determines key points where the player must always have full health (e.g., before a boss fight) so that the experience can be properly tuned and balanced. The games also utilize dynamic difficulty adjustment or DDA. The game tracks how often the player dies in a level, or within a section of a level, and then adjusts the stats in order to subtly and quietly make the game easier so that the player does not need to replay levels too many times.

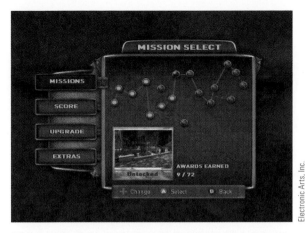

Electronic Arts, Inc.

Nintendo

Games such as *James Bond: From Russia With Love* allow players to go back and replay any level at any time in order to achieve a better score.

In *Super Mario Sunshine*, players may play through each level in many different ways but they are often expected to perform similar tasks from one level to the next.

As discussed in Chapter 7, the *Crash Bandicoot* series is a great example of a game that uses DDA to enhance the player experience. Since all of the rewards and health in the game are distributed in boxes, the game can minimize repetition by choosing what is in the boxes to help the player get through the level. Ensuring that your levels are not too difficult is only one aspect of avoiding repetition.

Dead Space

Many games have large amounts of empty, dead space. This is really common in games where players must travel through the same area many times. Some games simply leave the areas open—while others respawn the same enemies at the same locations, as in *Soul Reaver 2*. While this is often unavoidable, keep in mind that it is not fun to have the player simply run through a level for five minutes—especially for the third or fourth time.

While a game is not one solid battle, try to minimize large areas in which there is nothing for players to do. Every level does not need to be action-packed—but exploration, discovery, puzzle solving, socialization, negotiation, and other activities should be used to spice things up in areas where no enemies are present.

Respawning Enemies

Try to avoid having enemies reappear in the same places; this will make it less obvious that the player is traversing that place again. If players must go through the same area twice, you could add a script that triggers a whole new set of characters or enemies once the players accomplish a goal, but before they have to go back through the area. This will keep the players thinking that the world has responded to them.

For example, if a player kills several enemies in one area (and if there is enough memory to keep the dead bodies around), consider running a script with another group of soldiers and doctors trying to figure out what happened. This might even become a gameplay device, since players may want to then hide bodies or ensure that everyone is dead before they move on. Otherwise, if they return, they may have to deal with the consequences—such as another group of soldiers seeing those dead soldiers and attempting to hunt the culprit (the player) who killed them. However, if the player hides the bodies of the dead soldiers, any additional characters that show up might be just moving through that area—and the player could either bypass, sneak around, hide from, or kill them.

A simple mechanic such as being able to hide the bodies in an area could result in several different gameplay possibilities. The action of dragging a body could also be used to move other things in the game. Players could pick up branches and cover the bodies, but picking up those same branches and placing them over a hole could create a pitfall trap!

Having new areas to explore is not necessarily the only solution to dead space. It is important to be familiar with the needs of the game's target audience; players expecting a fast-paced action game may not want to do lots of exploring. Any exploration should be kept as interesting as possible by providing new areas to look at, objects to interact with, and enemies to fight. Most importantly, the process of exploring should be rewarded with something such as items, skills, points, and information leading to the resolution of plot points or puzzles. If players explore during strategy games, they often find random valuable items or information leading to the capture of the enemy or the location of essential resources. Rewards such as these keep exploration interesting on each level. Exploration early in strategy games also fills dead time when players are waiting to build bases and armies, so it fills a secondary need.

Movement

In games such as *Dynasty Warriors,* players often must run around a level for a while in search of an enemy. If they are low on health—which is provided to them randomly after defeating enemies and may be found in sparsely placed boxes—they face problems. Players cannot afford to fight enemies when their health is low, so they must look for health—which may take forever (especially when players are avoiding a fight).

In *Dynasty Warriors,* the player must find and kill every enemy, which may become tedious without the right feedback mechanics and interface.

Other games suffer from a similar problem when players must obtain health or healing from a faraway place. *Diablo 2* and *Neverwinter Nights* solve this by giving players teleport spells, which allow them to return and heal whenever necessary. This may seem too easy, but there is a small cost, since the player must buy the spells and needs to know when to use them. However, the game keeps moving forward with only a short pause for healing before a return to battle or exploration. This teleportation at least keeps the player from having to backtrack excessively.

Greg Costikyan on Randomness and Variety :::::

Greg Costikyan
(Chief Executive Officer,
Manifesto Games)

Greg Costikyan is CEO of Manifesto Games, an online retailer of independently created computer games. He has designed more than 30 commercially published board, role-playing, computer, online, and mobile games—including five Origin Award–winning titles. Among his best-known titles are *Creature That Ate Sheboygan* (board game), *Paranoia* (tabletop RPG), *MadMaze* (first online game to attract more than one million players), and *Alien Rush* (mobile game). His games have been selected on more than a dozen occasions for inclusion in the Games 100, *Games Magazine*'s annual round-up of the best 100 games in print. He is an inductee into the Adventure Gaming Hall of Fame for a lifetime of accomplishment in the field, and won the Maverick Award in 2007 for his tireless promotion of independent games. He also writes one of the most widely read blogs about games, game development, and the game industry (*www.costik.com/weblog*).

In order to have variety, it's necessary to have an underlying system of mechanics that permits tweaking of a large number of variables to pose different strategic challenges. The use of randomness—generally thought of as a negative—is actually highly useful in this regard; techniques such as random events and variable outcomes (with predictable limits) can greatly increase the variability of the game.

Repetitive Enemies

Having too many enemies in a game who act the same, look the same, or fail to react or learn over time will be very noticeable to the player. Repetitive enemies can be seen very easily and will be a major problem for some players; they should be avoided if at all possible.

Static Enemies

Moving through a level and seeing static enemies that come to life and charge only when players get close is becoming very old in games. Enemies that are immobile or animated in a rudimentary way look bad visually, and fighting them repeatedly gets boring very quickly—just like enemies that keep teleporting into the level or appearing randomly. Why can't players enter an area and face enemies that come at them from different places? If you want the player to fight a dozen enemies, don't have the enemies stand at the end of the street looking as if they have nothing to do until they are approached. Perhaps a lookout might sound an alarm if the player gets close, or a group standing around a fire warming their hands could jump the player first. Other enemies could then stream out of a doorway, jump out of a van, rappel down from a helicopter, jump in off the roofs, come up through a sewer, or break through a window and hop out of it. Constantly introducing new enemies in new ways will keep the players guessing and on their toes.

Consider ways to use entry or exit points as an enemy spawner. This point may continue to generate a certain number of enemies unless it is stopped or blocked. Perhaps players could blow up a car that lands against the wall and blocks the door or use a flamethrower on a manhole cover to melt it shut. Players can then use their skills and the few rules they know to do different things that affect how the game plays and how difficult it is. Whichever way you choose to do it, a little attention to detail in this area will keep the players much more interested in the game.

Most of the enemies in *Ratchet & Clank* do not wake up until players get close to them.

Enemy Variety

Having a wide enough variety of enemies is a problem that most games face. It is still very difficult to create good enemy characters. There are a lot of *gating* factors in design—art and programming problems that stop developers from creating as many enemies as they would like in the game. Enemy creation is extremely time-consuming for all disciplines. In the past a character could be modeled and textured in a few days; now it takes months. A character could be animated in days, and now that also takes months. Characters have far more complicated artificial intelligence (AI) and behaviors. All of this adds up to making character creation more expensive and harder for us to do than ever before, which means setting a limit on the number of characters. Games that try to be historically accurate may also suffer from a lack of diversity in enemies.

Some games create a variety of similar enemies that have only a few minor differences in either look, attacks, weapons, accoutrements, AI, or other abilities. Games need more than enemies that are identical except for their clothing and weapons. A character variant is one that uses some aspects of another character, or most of the aspects of another character. Variants could be as simple as two different characters who use distinct weapons. Some games are even using what is called a "create-a-player" system that may actually create many different characters dynamically by combining a wide selection of body parts, clothing, and accessories in order to create a new character. Some "create-a-player" systems, such as the one found in *Smackdown! vs. RAW* 2007, are so advanced that almost any type of character may be created using them.

Courtesy NCsoft

City of Villains contains a wide variety of non-player character enemies.

THQ

Electronic Arts, Inc.

"Create-a-player" systems are used by some games to help the designers create a wide variety of different visual looks with a smaller amount of art resources by combining pieces (*WWE Smackdown! vs. RAW 2007* and *Tiger Woods: PGA Tour 07,* shown).

If you have only a limited number of enemies, there are some important things you should do to ensure sufficiently diverse characters in the game. These include using graphical diversity (many enemy shapes and sizes); functional diversity (allowing enemies to do everything needed in the game); and reuse and repurposing of characters. A variety of enemies should be delivered throughout the game, with new enemies appearing at least halfway to three quarters of the way through.

Smart Enemies

How do you implement enemies that keep the game from getting repetitive? You first need to make the enemies fit the game. They need to look, act, and be as authentic to the game as possible; this goes for nonhistorical games as well. If the enemies are interesting, the player will enjoy fighting them. This means that you must script out effective custom AI behaviors and events for them to follow or create more intelligent AI so that they learn and adapt to the player's actions.

Making smart and relatively realistic characters can really help propel your game forward. Players are always moaning about how "dumb" the enemies are in games. It is important to make better, smarter enemies that seem more realistic to players. They needn't be more challenging or tougher to kill; they just need to be more visually interesting to the player and have more compelling behaviors or abilities that set them apart.

Half-Life 2 contains smart non-player character enemies.

Creating Interesting Enemies

Interesting enemies behave more like real people or react in ways that seem natural or expected. Players notice how enemies move, how they work in groups, which weapons they choose to use, how they respond to what the player does, how they react to stimuli in the world such as noises, and what tactics they choose to utilize against the player. Interesting enemies are also fairly unpredictable. Keep in mind that players need to win and know that their tactics are going to work, but they also do not want to see the enemies react in the same way over and over again and ultimately become easy to kill due to their predictability. If you talk to players who play predominantly multiplayer games, especially first-person shooters such as EA's *Battlefield 2*, you will find that hardcore players enjoy the challenge of playing against other humans because they are much more unpredictable in nature. Players must learn to be on their toes and think quickly when facing another human in combat, which is often not the case when players play computer AI opponents.

Players notice many subtle nuances when they fight enemies, so any small inconsistency may make them believe that the entire AI system is flawed. This makes writing intelligent enemy AI extremely difficult. For instance, players may notice that the AI enemies are trying to flank them and get behind them, which is an advanced technique—but if these same enemies just run straight to the position and do not take cover or follow a path to the location, the illusion is broken. Another case where AI often looks bad is when NPCs repeatedly try to come through a door or choke point while the player kills

Tom Clancy's Rainbow Six: Vegas has incredibly intelligent enemies that react to the player's actions.

the others in front of them. In *Tom Clancy's Rainbow Six: Vegas*, the enemies will detect that the players have killed a comrade in a doorway and then mark the door as off-limits and not try to use it unless there is no other option. You do not need to program truly intelligent AI systems to make AIs that seem intelligent, but you do need to set up some simple and obvious rules for AIs to follow when attacking or being attacked to make them more humanlike and hopefully more interesting.

Groups and Teams

In the real world, soldiers usually do not work alone and usually are found in groups or teams. A lone soldier is usually a scout or guard, but even loners such as snipers work in two-person teams in the real world. When was the last time you saw a group of five enemies in a game really working well together, covering each other, fighting side by side? *Metal Gear Solid 2* has some intelligent soldiers who like to cover each other. On the tougher difficulty levels in *Halo 2*, the enemies work well in a team; a single enemy will distract the player, while the rest of the group tries to flank the player.

Although it might be tough for players as individual soldiers to fight against a well-armed and disciplined group of soldiers working together, there are ways to compensate. Generally, the increased skill of players—along with their ability to use a variety of weapons, tactics, and healing—is enough to allow them to face a larger group of opponents, but there are many different ways you can make players "tough" and able to withstand a larger onslaught of enemies and feel like Rambo.

Enemy Tactics

Other relatively easy-to-implement AI behaviors that are not seen very often in games include: heal themselves or others; retreat and take cover, switch weapons when needed; take hostages or utilize them; and call in reinforcements and air strikes. These behaviors are not that difficult to design into the game or program and may add a lot of perceived value for the player.

Do not introduce impossible situations for the player; this is where the rules come in. Instead of relying on high-level AI, much of this behavior may be scripted to give the player the illusion of enemy intelligence.

Reprinted with permission from Microsoft Corporation

Halo 2 contains some very intelligent enemies who are tough to get around.

New AI and enemy tactics and behaviors should be slowly introduced throughout the game. The player may start off fighting only a few enemies at a time and then slowly fight more and more enemies that gradually become smarter and smarter. This gets increasingly interesting when you factor in combined arms, and the fact that multiple enemies may be combined to create many new situations. For instance, soldiers may get together and fight in a group—shield-carriers in the front (blocking the player), a commander with a sword, and an archer in the rear. The player then has the choice of how to fight the group, which might involve taking out the archer, the commander, or one of the shield-carrying soldiers first. If the player takes out the archer, the shield-carrying soldiers may pull their swords and attack— but if the player takes out the commander first, the others might flee. These simple choices would not only look better but would be more interesting to the player. The choices may also subtly change with the types of units that are in the mix; however, they will not require that players learn any new rules, but rather adapt the ones they already know how to use.

Later on in the game, the AI could make things more interesting for the player. Imagine that same group of four soldiers. Now when the player takes out the commander and two of the soldiers flee—but the remaining soldier hollers and keeps them together, taking command; the player realizes that he is a corporal (not a private)—and the rules change slightly, causing the players to adapt. This would keep players on their toes and more observant about their opponents.

Some of the changes in AI could also come from adaptive learning or pattern recognition. You do not need high-level AI to do this, and it is very simple for the AI to track how many kills the player has made and even categorize them. Imagine that the player has killed 50 orcs and is now known as "the great orc killer." If the player encounters a few orcs in the game, the orcs will flee from the player's sight. This is fun for a while, until the player realizes that now the orcs are coming back and bringing help in the way of reinforcements. The player will feel that the AI is adapting or learning when it is really just changing. This might also be used by enemies during combat to detect when the player is using the same moves repeatedly, and then providing a block to the moves and forcing players to adapt and change their play patterns. Players need reasons to do new things, and it starts with the use of an effective and more interesting AI.

Solutions for Repetition

There are many elements of gameplay that can be repetitive, tedious, frustrating, annoying, and boring. Most of the problems listed in this section might seem obvious, but it is surprising how often they are still seen in games. A good usability test or playtest should help you find and solve many of these problems before shipping your game. Always perform deep gameplay tests to ensure that the game stays fun for everyone after the first few hours of play. Many games pass the first hour or two of testing with flying colors, only to hit a sharp dropoff after the first few hours of play.

Moves & Actions

Every character has a certain number of possible moves. Sometimes all of the moves are taught to the player at the beginning of the game, while these moves are spread out in other games. Most first-person shooters (FPSs) contain movement—primarily forward, backward, strafe, jump, and duck moves. Platformers typically contain the most moves, allowing the player to run, jump, and attack in many different ways. Fighting games are almost nothing but a series of moves.

The moves are complicated by the need to keep the game simple and easy to play, and the difficulty of actually controlling a character in 3D space through a variety of moves. When fighting games transitioned from 2D to 3D, there were a lot of problems. It was difficult enough for players to memorize 50-100 different moves and try to fit them all onto a console controller—but when the need for 3D movement and often camera control was added, things got a lot trickier. Fighting games had an easier transition to 3D, since they take place in smaller arenas and are less complex than action-adventure games.

In an action-adventure game, it is possible for players to need a ridiculously high number of different moves and abilities. If you take away any type of move (e.g., jumping), players may become very frustrated. On the other hand, if you offer too many moves, players cannot control their characters very well—especially if they are fighting a bad camera and other quirks in the controls.

Super Mario Sunshine is a good example of a game that has many different moves, but these moves may be used in only a few ways. However, since many of the moves are so difficult, players must repeat the same move over and over again because they just cannot physically make the move happen—even though they know what they are supposed to do. This issue is complicated further by a manual camera that hinders players as much as it helps them. Pulling off the move may be a challenge, since players cannot see what they are doing. *Devil May Cry* also suffers from a similar problem occasionally because of its fixed cameras; for example, when trying to attack enemies off camera, it is impossible to know which moves are needed.

Nintendo

© Courtesy of Capcom. Reprinted with permission.

Both *Super Mario Sunshine* and *Devil May Cry 4* contain control schemes that are fairly easy to learn.

The best overall solution is to allow players to learn, discover, or buy new moves for at least the first half of the game. If you combine this with the introduction of new weapons, abilities, and items throughout the game, you can provide the player with a lot of depth.

Weapons & Abilities

In the majority of action games, the player is bound to possess some kind of weapon, magic, or another ability. Whether the weapon shoots projectiles, launches missiles, fires a laser, drops a bomb, or any one of a number of different possible forms of attack, the problem is often the same. Many games contain weapons that are too scarce, limited, similar, or realistic to add a lot of depth to the game. If you are making a realistic game such as *Medal of Honor*, there may not be too many choices in your selection of weapons and your job will be a lot more difficult.

No matter what special items are used by the player—such as night vision goggles, a jet pack, or some other gadget—they often will get old after awhile. If the player must keep solving the same puzzle, or doing the same thing in the same way with the same item, it will become boring. The idea here is to limit repetition and add depth to the game.

However, just adding more weapons, items, and abilities is not always the right choice. Some games such as *Diablo* contain a tremendous number of weapons and items that players may collect. Granted, this is part of the addiction factor of the game, but there is also a point at which the players

Electronic Arts, Inc.

Medal of Honor uses many very realistic weapons that are closely modeled after the real weapons from WWII.

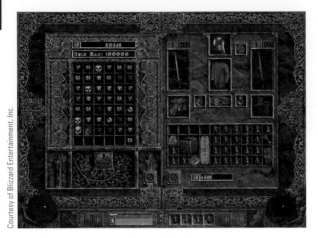

Courtesy of Blizzard Entertainment, Inc.

Diablo contains a tremendous amount of different weapons and equipment that players may find, buy, and even upgrade.

might stop caring. A player might find a favorite weapon and just stick with it, only occasionally acquiring enough money or becoming lucky enough to get a super powerful spell or new sword that is much better than the current one. If the new items stop having a perceived increase in value, the player will stop caring. A more casual player usually does not know the difference between M-16, AK-47, or G36 assault rifles, but they usually understand the difference between an assault rifle, a flamethrower, a bazooka, and a grenade. While having a variety of weapons in a game is important, it is more essential to introduce new features or items that add gameplay value and variety to the game,

not just different art and a few stat changes. Ensure that the majority of weapons, equipment items, and upgrades are noticeably different so that players can make easier and better choices.

Every weapon and ability in a game should be carefully chosen, and something new should be added to it. What is achieved by having several different weapons if they all function in the same way? Would the average player know the difference between an M-16 and an AK-47, or between a long sword and a bastard sword? If you can choose the kinds of weapons you are giving the player, it is most useful if you think about adding *classes* of weapons. Each class of weapon should serve a different purpose. There are many possible types of weapons classes: Handguns contain plenty of ammunition but are good only at close range; rifles shoot long range; bazookas and rocket launchers blow things up; and grenades are thrown by hand. You could create a list that resembles the accompanying table.

Diagram by Per Olsen

Weapon	Type	Amount of Damage	Rate of Fire	Range	Ammunition	Area	Special Feature
Pistol	Gun	Low	Slow	Short	Common	None	Single Shot
Assault Rifle	Gun	Medium	Medium	Long	Common	None	Burst
Machine Gun	Gun	High	High	Medium	Rare	None	Full Auto
Sniper Rifle	Gun	High	Slow	Very long	Rare	None	Scope
Frag Grenade	Grenade	Medium	Single	Short	Uncommon	Medium	Indirect
Flamethrower	Particle	High	Stream	Short	Rare	Medium	Fire Damage
Bazooka	Missile	High	Slow	Long	Rare	Large	Anti-Armor

Weapon balance chart showing the type, amount of damage, rate of fire, range, ammunition, area, and special features associated with each.

The accompanying chart shows only some of the factors that you might have to take into account when balancing your weapons. Consider armor penetration, clip size, reload speed, accuracy when moving, burst rate, scopes, and customizability as well. This is even more difficult when dealing with science fiction weapons that have few limitations. There might also be certain additional disadvantages when using some weapons, such as inability to move when shooting, slow movement, and amount of noise made when firing.

A "Catch-22" of game weapon design is that it is often hard to separate the weapons from the enemies and the weapons from the characters. If you were to design a WWII real-time strategy (RTS) game, you would not separate the weapons from the units—since all of the units (such as rockets) are also weapons, and they rarely change. In order to know what weapons players will need, you will often need to understand what weapons they will have to be effective against. Do the enemies have strengths and weaknesses? Are some enemies immune to some attacks? You must carefully understand the balance of the game when designing the weapons.

Variety in Real-Time Strategy Games

Variety can be accomplished in an RTS by unlocking the tech tree and giving the player new toys to play with. If your armies are designed well, they have a variety of unit types and styles available within each one. You could for example have a side built with mobs of infantry, a number of heavy armored vehicles, tanks that shoot flames, jets and then a huge giant mega tank that can have individual upgrades placed on its back. If you mix up the way these units are introduced to the player, you engage the player in different play styles using these different 'toys' and there is plenty of variety. For example, in the first mission you have the player master using infantry. In Missions 2 and 3, they work with the first set of armored vehicles and the infantry. If Mission 4 is about the flame tanks and a type of super weapon, you can see that there is plenty of variety to keep things interesting.

Mark Skaggs
(CEO & Executive Producer, Funstar Ventures, LLC)

Weapon Power-Ups

Something else to consider when creating more interesting weapons that do not add a lot of complexity to the game is to include new weapon power-ups or modifications. In *Diablo II,* players may add gems to some weapons to make them more powerful. In a game such as *Tom Clancy's Rainbow Six: Vegas,* a player might be able to add a grenade launcher to the machine gun. Players might learn early that there are two ways to attack with each weapon, and then when they get a modification and choose to equip it, they do not need to learn anything new.

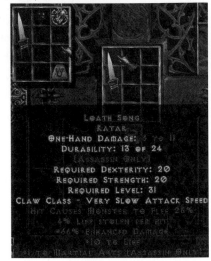

Courtesy of Blizzard Entertainment, Inc.

Diablo II allows players to upgrade their weapons.

Ensure that the new weapon, item, ability, or power-up you make available to players is rewarding. If players do not see an obvious improvement in the way they might fight or get some other kind of reward, it may lead to a lack of satisfaction. In *Devil May Cry,* each weapon and move is visually more interesting than the last and each new weapon might do different and flashier things. Getting new items in the game feels rewarding and satisfying to players, who are motivated to improve so that they may buy the next cool thing.

Repetitive Audio

A small annoyance that is sometimes easy to solve is the repetitive audio in games. This may sometimes be the music, but it is often the voice acting. If a player character says the same thing after every kill, and the player plans on killing many enemies, players will often stop playing the game just because the audio has become too annoying. Ensure that you offer a variety of sounds that don't frustrate the player due to repetition.

Animation

Looking at the same *animation* over and over again might be boring as well. While this is a minor complaint, consider ways to add lots of random animation to the game. In a fighting game, for example, it would not be good for players to continually press high punch, just so that the player characters could do the same moves. A good design team would know what the players' intentions are; a high punch could translate into a jab, a hook, a spinning backfist, a chop, an elbow, or any number of different moves — and yet still accomplish the same results without requiring additional learning or thought from the players. It is important for developers to truly understand what players need to accomplish during a game.

::::: *The Mark of Kri*: Variety in Animation

The Mark of Kri does a wonderful job of providing characters with over 20 different ways to stealth kill enemies. Not only is this great to watch, but players never get bored with it since there is a lot of variety. Think about ways to add some variety to your animation sequences to keep players interested.

Sony Computer Entertainment America

The Mark of Kri has a complex animation system that plays a wide variety of different animations each time the player kills an enemy, which keeps combat fun and interesting.

The Player Experience

Creating an incredible player (or user) experience is very challenging; it requires that you think through a large portion of the game before getting too deep into the design. You must truly understand several aspects of your game and be able to fully discern what it is about. While this is usually the job of the creative director, all game designers on the project should always ask themselves the important questions such as whether the features they are incorporating into the game are the best possible. Some features are needed to make the game fun, others are needed because of the type of game it is, and still others are needed in order to make the game experience the best it can be. It is extremely difficult to figure out what features are important and reinforce the user experience.

You've seen that for many games it is important to be exciting, to keep the player interested, and to be immersive and compelling. For other games, the challenge is more about the experience. It is tricky to successfully determine what the minute-to-minute and long-term gameplay loop experiences are for the player and what features are needed to make the experience both complete and compelling.

Tom Clancy's Rainbow Six: Vegas has an open structure that is designed to reward the player every 10 to 15 minutes.

Call of Duty contains a very immersive game experience that sucks players into what it is like to be a soldier in WWII.

Try to imagine what the player *wants to do* in the game, and then consider what the player *should be doing* in the game. It is not necessary to develop a highly realistic game such as *Tom Clancy's Rainbow Six* or *Call of Duty* in order to worry about the player experience. Put yourself in the player's shoes. If the player is supposed to be an adventurer, soldier, rogue, trader, race car driver, mechanic, or explorer, then make sure that the features you provide the player character help to maximize this fantasy. You then need to ensure that the features also take into account the story of the game, its theme, and the grand experience that the player is supposed to encounter; this will go a long way to making the game experience far from ordinary and closer to extraordinary.

:::CHAPTER REVIEW:::

1. Play at least three electronic games that are currently on the market and identify any repetition—whether it involves the storyline, levels, characters, navigation, or tasks. Does this repetition cause you to be less interested in continuing to play? If so, what techniques would you use to reduce repetition?

2. Discuss any games that you played in Exercise 1 that successfully provided you with an immersive and exciting experience. Identify the techniques used to accomplish this. How might you use these techniques in your original game?

3. How will you avoid unnecessary repetition in your original game? Where might you expect to see repetition? Create a list of at least three solutions you might use that relate specifically to your game's storyline, characters, and environment.

CHAPTER

9

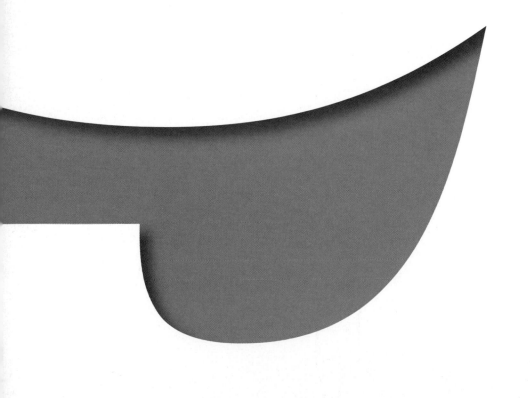

Creating Cohesion

putting it all together

Key Chapter Questions

- What types of gameplay structures are possible?
- How should you teach the player about new mechanics?
- What are the steps you should take when designing gameplay mechanics?
- Where are game mechanics going in the future?
- How do you become a game designer?

The action players of today expect great things from an AAA game—but because next-generation games are so much harder to build, it is becoming increasingly difficult for us to create enough content to keep a game of 10+ hours interesting. Trying to understand everything about game design is extremely difficult. This chapter is all about how to take everything you know about game design and use it to make terrific games. You will follow a case study that focuses on creating gameplay systems for a new intellectual property (IP) concept. However, just reading about game design isn't enough; you will ultimately learn only by doing.

Applying Gameplay Design

Now that you have a good understanding of how to create compelling gameplay mechanics, you must understand how to apply it all. It is very easy to get caught up in the theory of how mechanics are fun, but much harder to understand how to actually apply the mechanics in a real-world situation. It is even harder yet to create great game mechanics when you are faced with time crunches, technical limitations, executives or team members who pressure you to change your beliefs, and pressure from licensors and marketing to change certain aspects of the game. As a game designer, you must be able to come up with great new mechanics not only in a vacuum, when there is no pressure—but on the fly, during a meeting, while everyone is pressuring you. That is the reality of being a great game designer.

The only way to learn how to put it all together is to practice. Come up with an idea for a game and practice designing game systems and writing design documents. Fortunately, you may do this on your own without a development team, a game engine, and everything else needed to make a full game. Early on, you could design the game genre that you like the most and are interested in developing, as well as a game design that is modest in size and complexity and not overly ambitious.

You must also keep in mind that we have only discussed how to design gameplay mechanics and not entire games. If you are not familiar with the other aspects of writing a game design document, writing stories, designing interfaces, or the many other aspects of game design, you should think about also studying up on those topics and reading some of the other books in this series.

Process

How you design games may be just as important as what you design. Spending a lot of much time designing certain features too early on may be bad for several reasons. First, if you are working with a team, especially one that is waiting for you to design the game, and you spend time designing features that are not needed yet, you could be wasting their time. Second, if you design certain systems before you fully understand your game or its key features, you will inevitably need to redo things later. Last, if you design some systems too early in the process, they may have to change because they do not fit the license, story, or ultimate vision for the game. There are complex design docs from experienced game development studios that show every character fully designed—with every stat, feature, and ability; however, the design document does not mention the gameplay, controls, or interface.

Usually, when beginning the design of the gameplay systems for a new idea, you need to have a solid vision for the game in place. However, sometimes you must put the cart before the horse to come up with some great new mechanics and turn them into a game.

Structure

Structuring a game is good for a variety of reasons. First, you need to determine how the game will play out to the player. Second, you need to decide how the missions and stories will be structured. Third, you need to plan how you will ramp the player and where you will introduce new features. However, beyond all this, it is important to understand from a logistical standpoint how the game will be structured.

Figuring out how the game will play is an important early step for the player. You must decide if the game will have very discrete levels or offer an open-ended world. You also must decide whether players will play through missions or objectives in a straight line, or whether the game will be non-linear with backtracking, branching paths, alternate routes, optional missions, and side quests. Determining this structure is important because it could have a huge impact on the technology, the way the story is created, and the way the game is built.

Once you know how players will play through the game, it is time to look at how to get them through the game. This may be complicated in a role-playing game (RPG) or other types of games that are more open and allow the player to roam around or perform actions in any order. Balancing a game and keeping it fun over time is a challenging problem that needs to be addressed early in the design process. If players engage in many fights that are too easy, they will often become bored and even stop playing the game, just as they would if the game is too difficult.

Elder Scrolls IV: Oblivion ramps up the difficulty of all enemies in the game along with the player's ability. As the player becomes more powerful, so do all the enemies; if a small animal such as a wolf is hard to fight in the beginning, it will still be hard to kill halfway through the game when the player is much more powerful. This takes away much of players' incentive to upgrade their characters because they will never feel really powerful.

The Elder Scrolls IV: Oblivion ramps up the difficulty of all enemies in the game along with the player's ability.

Traditionally in most action game designs, the player starts off with a weapon and faces enemies that are of low to medium difficulty to kill. Then the game will introduce a more difficult opponent that the player really has a hard time with and maybe cannot even kill, causing the player to feel a bit scared. Just as the odds seem hopeless, the player may get a new weapon that slays new enemies, making the player feel powerful for a while, until the next new and tougher enemy comes along and the process repeats itself. While following this pattern is not critical, you do need to decide how and why you will help players progress through the game and provide them with weapons, skills, equipment, enemies, and obstacles.

Before designing the next *Oblivion* or *Grand Theft Auto* (*GTA*) you really need to understand the challenges you face while trying to create a linear or less-than-linear game. A linear game is much more focused, contains a stronger story, and is more visceral. You may control and carefully tune the players' experience because you know basically where they are going to go, what they are going to do, and how they are going to do it; this allows you to carefully script a perfectly crafted game experience.

Diagram by Per Olin

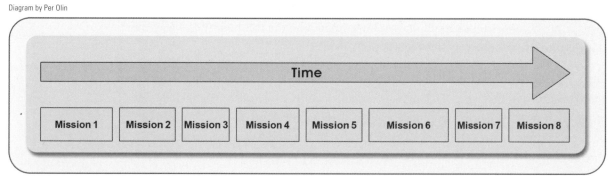

In linear games, missions are played in a particular order.

Very few games are truly non-linear. Most open-ended sandbox games still have semi-linear story structures. Players usually choose to strive for one of several goals at any one time, in addition to "playing" in the world. However, at some point—in order to progress through the game and story—the player will need to complete missions that are often given out by different characters; each character has a finite number of missions to offer, and the player is forced to seek out new characters to make progress in the game. Key story events may then be triggered by the completion of any mission in the game or anything the player does.

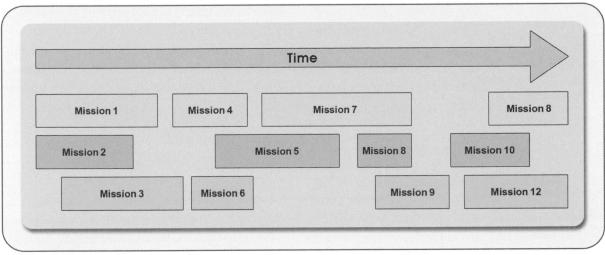

A semi-linear game structure is used in *Grand Theft Auto*.

Some games contain branching paths. The branches are usually based around player choices. In some cases, the player is unable to go back and play through anything on the other branch—but in other games the player may go back and do everything in the branch. A branching game progression may add a lot of replay value but is usually not worth the investment in time and resources, since very few players even finish a game, let alone replay it. It may also be very difficult to keep the story in a branching path cohesive for the player.

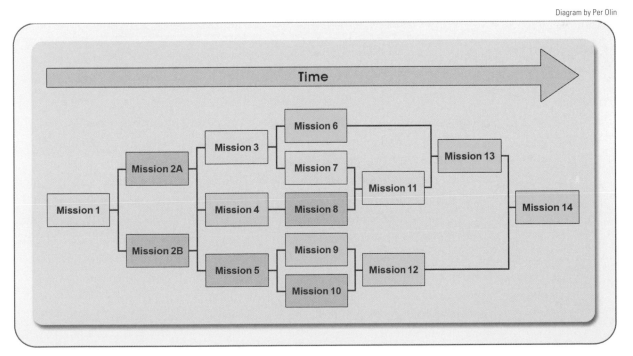

This is just one example of how a branching game path could be set up.

In a non-linear game, you never know what the player is going to do—or when. There are potential problems concerning how players will know what to do next, as well as how you can balance the game so that they do not get into areas that should not be accessed too early in the game. Understand that how you decide to structure your game goals may affect many of the decisions you will make throughout the rest of the game design.

Micro-Play

If you look at an RPG such as *Oblivion* or an action-adventure game such as *Devil May Cry 4,* you will see that at any point in time the player is moving, shooting, solving puzzles, using an item, or interacting with the environment from second to second and from minute to minute. What the player does here for the bulk of the game is called *micro-play* because it happens at the smallest scale possible.

© Courtesy of Capcom. Reprinted with permission.

In *Devil May Cry 4,* the player is moving, shooting, solving puzzles, using an item, or interacting with the environment from second to second and from minute to minute.

A setup is each and every encounter within the game. Usually when you are designing a level, you find a location in an environment for something to happen, such as where combat is to occur. You then decide how many enemies will be in that area and how they will interact with the player. There is no rule about how large or how small a setup might be. Breaking gameplay down into micro-play or setups might help a designer better tune the game experience for the player. Instead of randomly spawning enemies or monsters all around, a setup is much more deliberate and usually will be better tuned; it may even contain an indirect puzzle the player needs to solve in order to survive. Micro-gameplay may also be broken down into gameplay segments or what might be called a gameplay loop. A gameplay loop is a pattern of play that persists throughout the game and is used over and over and in different combinations through the game.

Short-Term: Collecting, Maneuvering, Shooting, Fighting

Short micro-play gameplay loops are what the player experiences every few seconds to every few minutes. In an action game, this could involve the player needing to move, fire, reload, take cover, and heal in different patterns. This is about how the player defeats one enemy, completes one play, or performs some short segment of play. At the lowest level, you must ensure that these short micro-play segments will be fun, rewarding, and continually interesting to the player.

Mid-Term: Completing Goals, Navigating, Finding Keys, Earning Money

The next type of gameplay loop involves completing a goal. The player typically should not play for more than around 15 minutes without achieving a major goal in the game. Even if your game is 10 hours long, you should really think of it as 40-50 or more small games all tied seamlessly and cohesively together. A mid-term loop could be about winning a game or match within an entire season, killing all the enemies in one base on one of five planets, etc. If you look at how a level within a game such as *Ratchet & Clank* is structured, each level is composed typically of three to four paths. Each path has a goal, and the player may complete the paths in any order. The player follows this pattern on each of the 10-20 levels in the game.

Sony Computer Entertainment America

In *Ratchet & Clank*, each level is composed typically of three to four paths, each of which has a goal and may be completed in any order.

Long-Term: Leveling Up, Spending Money, Skill-Building

Long-term segments are more about what the player gets to do every 3-4 mid-level loops. These segments usually encompass a level, chapter, or mission. In many games, other features such as spending money and learning new skills will also occur frequently.

Understanding how all of these micro-play segments work together is important to the overall structure of the game and to ensuring that the player is having fun from minute to minute but also has long-term goals that will continue to make the game fun. Keeping these segments in mind may help tremendously when you are trying to design the structure of your game.

Macro-Play

Long-term loops in which the player progresses, levels up, learns new skills, spends money, and accumulates more items are considered to be part of *macro-play*. For instance, in *Ratchet & Clank: Going Commando*, the player has the ability to mine areas for various resources. Mining is for the most part optional in the game, but players may spend hours mining, collecting, and building up their characters. This could be considered at some level a macro-game since it exists outside of the normal game, but it allows players to manage and expand their resources, thus affecting the main game.

Sony Computer Entertainment America

In *Ratchet & Clank: Going Commando*, the player has the ability to mine areas for various resources.

Meta-Play

Some games such as *Star Wars: Empire at War* and *EVE Online* contain an entire strategic *meta-game*. Players not only fight on planets and in space, but they have to manage all of their planets and resources across the galaxy. Even a game such as *Madden '07* or *Smackdown! vs. Raw 2006* has a season mode where the player manages a team.

In *Shogun: Total War* and the *Risk* computer game, players first play the "board game" part of the meta-game where they move their pieces around. When players land on a square where a battle needs to happen, the game changes and moves down to the battlefield where the players may then fight their battles.

CCP Games

EVE Online contains an entire strategic meta-game.

Risk® & ©2007 Hasbro, Inc. Used with permission.

In *Risk*, players first play the "board game" part of the meta-game where they move their pieces around.

A meta-game is a game on top of the regular game and exists at a much higher level. Meta-games are most commonly found in strategy games but may be found in action games as well.

Mini-Play

Mini-games, mini-mechanics, and *mini-play* gameplay are all the same. Any time the player must do something for a short period of time using a different interface or mechanic, this may be considered a mini-play mechanic. In *God of War* there are many mini-games related to combat, where the player must complete a small mini-game in order to get some additional benefit (e.g., matching a series of icons on the screen that appear in a random order which, if the player succeeds, will kill the enemy quietly and instantly). A game such as *Splinter Cell* has a lockpick mini-game that requires you to pick locks you want to open. Mini-games may add diversity and fun to your standard gameplay and is usually fairly easy to implement.

Sony Computer Entertainment America

In *God of War,* there are many mini-games related to combat where the player must complete a small mini-game in order to get some additional benefit.

Mega-Play

Not as common as mini-games are *mega-play* games that exist as a subset of the typical gameplay. Mega-play often involves things that are optional and utilizes some features of the game to create a game within a game. Sometimes the completion of these mega-play sections is important to the overall game, while other times it is just a diversion.

In *Ratchet & Clank*, players may go to arenas to fight many enemies. A series of competitions, opponents, and various rules are given to the player, along with various rewards for playing in the tournaments. There are also numerous races in which players may compete, either driving a vehicle of some sort, flying, or even using a hoverboard. The player must compete in the first race as part of the story but the other races are usually optional.

Other mega-play games could take the form of a card game, gambling, other video games, and distractions within the game. These differ from mini-games because players tend to play them for longer periods of time. While it is not

Sony Computer Entertainment America

In *Ratchet & Clank,* there are numerous races in which players may compete, either driving a vehicle of some sort, flying, or even using a hoverboard!

necessary that you have mega-play gameplay, it may be very useful to incorporate when appropriate. Anything that might lengthen your game, give players more to do, and keep them playing is desirable. Evaluate what core skills and optional features you may give the player and whether any of these could be tied together in different ways to incorporate additional gameplay.

Pouring the Solid Foundation

You now know that before you begin doing a lot of hard-core feature design, it is good to create a solid overview and understanding of the game that you are trying to design. It is very important to know what will be expected from you and your project as early as possible, even before you really get started. The same applies to knowing what information you will have to work with. You've also seen that it is important to structure your gameplay systems into many different layers that cover the minute-to-minute and long-term experience of the players to ensure they are constantly having fun.

As with building a house, if your foundation for the game is off, you could be in for a lot of redesign or adjustments on the fly, or you might need to tear down the whole structure and start over. While some foundation cracks and structural problems are inherent in game development, and you often do not know enough early on to create a solid design, it is good to at least try.

A critical part of being a good designer is knowing when you need to know something, when you should design something, when to keep the design or a part of the design fluid, and when to lock down aspects of the design. A little planning up front might save you a tremendous amount of time later on. This is where understanding the game development process is very important, and where having an established system in place for creating your game will make a huge difference.

Tutorials & Instructions

Another critical aspect of creating a complete game experience is deciding how to provide the player with instructions. This does not necessarily involve creating "tutorials," since these are often forced and lacking in fluidity. *God of War* is one of the best examples of a recent game that teaches the player very well throughout the game. You must think about how to do the following:

- initially instruct the player
- teach the player new things as needed
- help lost players
- ensure that the player knows what to do at all times

Sony Computer Entertainment America

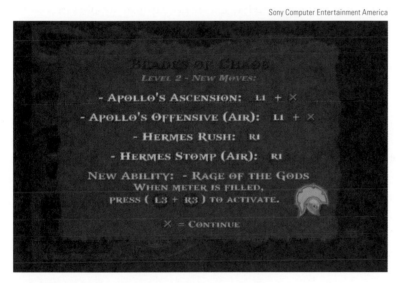

God of War does an exceptional job of teaching the player properly—which is critical in a game, especially if it targets casual players.

When designing how to teach the player new things, you must carefully consider how to ramp up the player slowly by not introducing too many new things at once. Players, especially casual ones, may be overwhelmed during gameplay. Even console games, which have easier controls than a computer, still involve eight main buttons, two analog sticks, and other complexities. Teaching players all the new things they need to know—while they get used to the controls, figure out the camera and navigation, and try to follow the storyline—is often far too confusing. Try to teach the player as few things as possible at any one time.

It is also essential to realize that human beings have limitations, and our memories are far from perfect. It is not critical that you fully understand the psychology behind human memory, but it might be extraordinarily helpful. Most of us may remember 3-4 new pieces of information at any one time. Additional items must then be transferred from short-term memory to long-term memory if we are to remember them permanently. People also remember new information better in chunks, or blocks of 3-4 items. This is the reason that telephone numbers are broken into blocks of numbers containing 3-4 numbers each, and why social security numbers are broken into blocks of three, two, and four numbers. Keep this in mind when introducing new information and try not to overwhelm the player with too many details at one time.

Reinforcing what the player has learned is also important. Players need to practice what you teach them and master it before trying to learn something new, if possible. Imagine trying to learn a new language when someone quickly tells you the numbers 1-10 in that language and then moves on to some other topic. Without some form of practice, you will never be able to remember those numbers, let alone use them in other ways. Learning the core fundamentals of playing games is similar to learning a new language in that the player must not only memorize many actions but commit them to muscle memory in order to perform most of the actions without consciously thinking about them. Therefore, the more that a player must utilize a skill, the more deeply it must be properly trained.

How you train players may be as important as *when* you train them. Are the instructions presented in a manner that makes the information interesting and easy to comprehend? Is the game using a traditional "tutorial" at the beginning that is set apart from the rest of the game, or is the information presented to the player as part of the overall game experience?

Another possible solution is to initially present players with only the new or more complicated features in the game so that they do not necessarily have to learn the most rudimentary or basic skills. This prevents experienced players from getting bored and moves them into the core of the game much more quickly. You could provide a tutorial focusing on only basic skills to players who are obviously having a tough time.

Some games also use text or voice prompts to teach the player new things, but they may become very repetitive and boring. Traditionally, most of these prompts are triggered when the player gets to a location. Consider adding a series of delays or if/then conditions that trigger the prompt only if the player is having trouble.

Finding out if players are having trouble and what they need to know is challenging, and it is very easy to overreact and feel that you need to teach players every little detail. Ensure that your systems for helping players learn the game are very well thought through and fully integrated into the macro design of the game as early as possible in the game design.

Case Study

This chapter focuses on how to develop the mechanics for a hypothetical game concept and how you might apply the process to your own game designs. The game will be a console action-adventure game with light RPG elements. In addition to coming up with some innovative game mechanics, we'll incorporate an original IP to go along with it that will be new and fresh but still familiar. Game ideas that are too "out there" are not as appealing for many players as those in which players feel that the events could happen to them.

Let's say that you want your game to be designed as a trilogy—epic in scope and scale, cinematic. You also want to utilize emergent gameplay system design so that you may reuse as many systems as possible. Keep in mind that this game design is still at the "blue sky" stage and has not been wrung through the sanity check for feasibility yet.

Seeing the Big Picture

It is quite difficult for most systems designers to understand how their feature fits into the practicalities of developing the overall game. This is not as obvious as it sounds. Since games have become so much harder to develop, it is not as easy to say that if something does not work, you will just redo it. There are some systems that a team with an agile mentality may be able to continually modify and change, while others might cost a tremendous amount of time and money to redo.

Building levels for some games used to take days or weeks, and may now take many months to complete. Many teams used to build numerous levels and throw out the bad ones; this may still work occasionally, but not for most game companies—even if you claim to be working with "agile" methodologies (which might emphasize iterations of "design, prototype, evaluate" throughout the lifecycle of project).

Since there is too much to understand, some designers do not even try to see how a feature will fit in. They will tend to initially implement a single feature; if it conflicts with another feature or system, they will redo whatever it is that is conflicting. This may require a minimal change or a complete redo, but is an acceptable risk to working more agile.

Other designers do not know the big picture because they are given a small section of the design to work on. Some designers such as Miyamoto take the approach of just getting one feature correct, such as jumping, before moving on to the next feature. This is a lot easier to do if you are very familiar with the type of game you are making, such as a sequel.

It is critical to understand the big picture of the game design so that your designs are solid and require as little reworking as possible. This does not mean that you should write massive design documents and design every single system up front, but you should have a basic understanding of the totality of the system you are designing, even if you do not work out all the details ahead of time. The goal is to minimize the amount of additional work while still allowing some design flexibility.

The Game Concept

Merged Destinies is a third-person action-adventure that takes place a hundred years in the future after a comet passes very close to the Earth and merges an evolved prehistoric world back into our dimension. Imagine a world where dinosaurs still rule the Earth; they never died out and continued to evolve. Now intelligent and city builders, the dinosaurs ruled their version of the Earth until they are somehow merged into our time line and fused into our lives. A few ragtag human armies are desperately battling advanced prehistoric armies for control of the Earth. Human cities and massive dinosaur cities must now share the same space as they are slammed together. What would a player do when faced with giant man-eating creatures that also use laser guns and other advanced weapons?

Designing the Mechanics

The first step is to look at some games that are exciting and contain game mechanics you enjoy, or those that you would consider your competition. Since you want to create an open world or sandbox game, such as *GTA* and *Mercenaries,* you might decide to first take a look at Microsoft's *Crackdown,* since it is a sandbox game set in a science fiction world.

Reprinted with permission from Microsoft Corporation

Crackdown is a sandbox game set in a science fiction world.

Our goal is to allow the player to be able to travel around the world and explore it, while also taking several paths through the world. The player should have the ability to work with the humans or the various factions of dinosaurs and utilize means that are "good" and "evil" or somewhere in between in order to accomplish the goal of finding his or her brother and somehow allowing humanity to survive.

You must remember that this game concept is not necessarily the hook for the game. You need to find the really cool hook for the game that all of your mechanics will focus on (as much as possible). For instance, the hook for *Crackdown* is that the player is a cybernetic agent with superhuman abilities. However, a mechanic that you like in another game may not be right for your game concept. The superhuman running, jumping, and picking up of objects in *Crackdown* is fun—but for this game concept, it does not fit.

The hook for *Crackdown* is that the player is a cybernetic agent with superhuman abilities.

Another good way to accelerate your evaluation of the competition is to utilize magazine and website reviews, hint books, and other material about the game you might find. This may make it much easier to evaluate some games and save you a lot of time. Normally, you would break down the mechanics like this for several different games, but for the scope of this book, let's look only at *Crackdown*.

Crackdown Features Breakdown

Here is a basic breakdown of the core features of *Crackdown*:

Movement

Driving cars, swimming, running, super jumping (increasing with agility increase), platforming, and may grab hold of small ledges and jump around. Players may teleport from supply point to supply point as well.

Combat

Melee, many weapons, subtarget enemies to hit exact locations; players gain accuracy the longer they target an enemy; players may visit supply points to rearm or get ammo, use grenades, etc.

Equipment

Need to resupply yourself by capturing supply points.

Special Abilities

Gain "cybernetic" (superhero) powers. Pick up almost any item, carry it and use it as a weapon. More strength allows players to pick up heavier items. Armor regenerates. Stats increase through use and players gain orbs for one to five different skills for everything they do, which offers collectables throughout the game.

Other Features

Enemies steal unattended vehicles, find stat increase power-up orbs, eliminate gangs and bosses, and upgrade agency vehicles. Players take damage if they fall too far. If players die, they may regenerate at a home base or at any supply point. Enemy gangs will send out more characters and tougher groups (including hit squads) to deal with players if they do too much damage to them in a short time period (similar to the police response system in *GTA*). If the player kills too many civilians, the police will attack the player as well. A voice on the radio guides players through the game and helps them. Each time the player eliminates one general in a gang (there are seven generals protecting each gang leader), it weakens the leader so that leader is easier to take out in the end.

Take Away

Within *Crackdown,* there are many general concepts that work. Many of these are similar in *GTA* and *Mercenaries* as well:

- big open world that players are free to explore
- constant sense of danger
- driving all the vehicles
- supply points
- increasing abilities over time
- enemy factions that players must deal with in different ways
- subtargeting enemies
- upgrading vehicle

While *Crackdown* has some great near sci-fi features, there are elements in it that are not right for this game. Its major new hook is the player character's super powers. It also has almost no cinematics and no "Hollywood" essence. The story is somewhat superfluous when compared to the *GTA* series. *Crackdown* also seems much more linear than some of the other sandbox games. At any one time, there may be several gang leaders the player might take out, so the player has a choice of where to go;

however, each gang leader is really the same, just in a different location. This means that the game is actually quite linear and not as open as a sandbox game should be. *Crackdown* also offers very little variety in the missions.

Combat sequence from *Crackdown*.

The combat system, storyline, and open world structure work well together in *Grand Theft Auto: San Andreas*.

In the *GTA* series, it is great to be able to buy locations and own them. Players can also get missions from several different groups. In *Mercenaries,* the player also can get missions from many different factions, and who the player is working for really affects how the other factions treat the players. The weapon/vehicle purchasing and delivery system in *Mercenaries* is great, as well as the "super weapon" attacks players may summon to do major damage.

Mercenaries contains helicopters and a few other features, but these do not inspire a great gameplay hook. You need to make the game mechanics fit the theme. For instance, players in *Crackdown* may participate in races that make no sense in the story and world. Your mechanics should be fun but also fit the world you are trying to build.

In *Mercenaries 2,* the player receives missions from different factions.

In an open world game such as *Mercenaries 2,* players may explore the environment from the helm of helicopters and other vehicles.

Creating Cohesion: putting it all together   chapter 9

Take a look at ideas from other games, such as the cover system and squad control mechanics in *Tom Clancy's Rainbow Six: Vegas,* along with the player-weapon interface that allows players to hold down buttons to access more advanced weapon or player options. If you want to keep the pace of the game fairly fast but not hectic, avoid too many mechanics from games that force the player to slow down and play too tactically.

Tom Clancy's Rainbow Six: Vegas contains a cover system and squad control mechanics.

Inspiration & Competition

Early in the process, you should think about what kind of game you want to make and what the top competition would be. In some genres, this is very obvious. If you are making a first-person shooter (FPS), you know that *Halo, Gears of War, Resistance: Fall of Man, Tom Clancy's Rainbow Six: Vegas, Tom Clancy's Ghost Recon: Advanced Warfighter,* and *Call of Duty* are probably the games to beat. Even they may be narrowed down, depending on the setting (science fiction, fantasy, modern military, WWII). It is important that you have played your competition and understand it.

For *Merged Destinies,* there is no direct competition that is exactly the same. There are elements in *Crackdown, Mercenaries, GTA,* and others that incorporate similar combat, RPG, or gameplay mechanics. You might want to look at movies such as *War*

Gears of War is one game to beat if you are designing a first-person shooter.

of the Worlds, Planet of the Apes, Battlefield Earth, The Postman, King Kong, and others that deal with alien invasions, battling giant creatures, the apocalypse, war, and more. If you have read a lot of science fiction from great authors such as Robert Heinlein, David Brin, Philip K. Dick, Isaac Asimov, Richard Matheson, Larry Niven, and David Gerrold, you might find much inspiration. There are some other things you could look back on for inspiration, such as the *Rifts* pen-and-paper RPG, which deals with portals opening and massive wars against aliens from another dimension on the Earth.

Designing the Game

Now it is time for you to do the hard part of the design; you must determine how to start creating your mechanics and come up with a hook for the game. Throughout the book, we have discussed the need to design mechanics that will instantly hook players and keep them playing over time.

You might be envisioning a world that is partially post-apocalyptic and has lots of humans (who generally are not very well armed) fighting big nasty monsters. You might look at movies such as *Battlefield Earth,* where humans are enslaved by aliens; *Deep Impact,* where the world prepares for an oncoming catastrophe; and *The Sound of Thunder,* where the world changes as the time line is disturbed. (Better yet, read the superior short story by Ray Bradbury.)

Perhaps you are also inspired by David Gerrold's classic science fiction series, *The War Against the Chtorr*. In this series, the Earth is invaded by aliens—not green Martians in flying saucers, but strange creatures and fauna that transformed the Earth and are slowly terraforming the planet. By the time readers realize what is happening, it is almost too late. Some characters fight strange and deadly creatures, while scientists try to figure out what they are and how to stop them through science.

Imagine a set of goals where the player must not just defeat the dinosaurs but figure out what happened, while also finding his or her brother. In the spirit of allowing the player a little more free-form play and more options, you might want to explore giving the player several different paths to winning the game. Instead of dealing with different paths such as good and evil, what if the player had the option to explore gameplay paths dealing with combat, science, exploration, teamwork, unification, and reconstruction? These goals will offer not only different stories but a slightly different set of gameplay mechanics that all interrelate.

Think of these gameplay paths as alternate ways to play the game using different emergent tools. A great example may be found in *Deus Ex*, which uses an FPS engine, but at the core it is an RPG. It is possible, although very difficult, to play the game as an FPS where the player is primarily running and gunning, taking the macho way through the game. Players may also take the stealth route, where they use similar tools to very carefully move through the game. However, players may also take RPG-style paths through the game, where they may use their heads, do more exploring, and take the route of least resistance.

Eidos Interactive Ltd.

Deus Ex: Invisible War uses a first-person shooter engine, but at the core, it is a role-playing game.

Some of this may also be seen in a game such as *Star Wars: Knights of the Old Republic,* where the player is able to buy lots of different weapons, skills, and equipment. Depending on what players buy, who their teammates are, and how they want to play, their character arcs become not only "good or evil" but more aggressive, sneaky, or diplomatic. These gameplay system paths are the same concept but are taken to a new level.

The most obvious gameplay mechanics to develop are those that revolve around combat. At many levels this is the easiest, or at least more straightforward, set of mechanics, since players must combat the dinosaurs if they hope to survive. Eventually this path may become extremely difficult, but the players should be allowed to pursue it. Combat mechanics may be similar to many other games.

The next possible path to explore is that of science. At its heart, the scientific path is about finding new information and technology. While the combat path is about killing, the scientific path is about collection, discovery, and advancement. Taking a cue from games such as *Civilization IV* or *Age of Empires* where players advance their technology by performing research, the scientific path is about finding an answer to what has happened.

Sony Computer Entertainment America

Firaxis Games

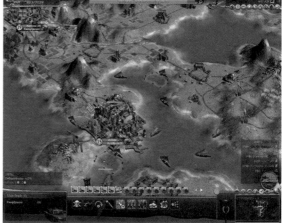

In *Rogue Galaxy*, the player is able to buy or create over 500 new different weapons and other specialized gear.

In *Civilization IV,* players advance their technology by performing research.

The exploration systems are all about discovery and access to information. The player needs to be rewarded for exploration. Information could serve many different purposes and help feed all of the other paths in the game. Exploration is also rewarded with discovery and collection, by being able to find items needed in the game, which could help the combat and science routes as well as the others. Exploration is about resources and trying to find the items needed to survive. Even the best army needs to eat and survive, and a good scrounge could be a lifesaver.

Another major goal in the game could be to unify the warring factions—not only of humans but potentially of some dinosaurs. Imagine a dinosaur culture similar to that of the ape culture in the *Planet of the Apes* movies—with gorillas (soldiers), chimpanzees (workers), and orangutans (scientists). Perhaps there are alliances to be made, politics to be played, and other related mechanics that may be pursued. Unification is also about teamwork. The player needs to be part of something bigger; the player needs allies.

The reconstruction systems are all about rebuilding the world—finding safe houses, bases, fortresses, and other locations that may be used as operation headquarters. It is not just about finding and buying places (such as in *GTA*)—but figuring out how to acquire, upgrade, and secure new places that may be used by the player or for a grander vision of rebuilding the world.

Brainstorming New Features

After you have done a little research on your game concept, it is time to begin brainstorming. Ultimately, you want to come up with a solid vision for the game, but you want to get an idea of the big picture before you dive in to any features design. While you could flesh out only the combat, other ideas may have a strong influence on the features and systems that should be included. You might try to understand how all of the different features are interrelated because you want to see if any one system is isolated, or if the various systems interact with each other in some kind of emergent way. Each of these five systems is really a conceptual catch-all for a wide variety of mechanics. It is still too early to say what features are feasible, so it is best to brainstorm as many ideas as possible.

Combat

Although it would be possible to rely on the same old combat mechanics of most other third-person shooters (where the player has a lock-on system, different guns to choose from, grenades, and all the usual suspects), it is important to explore possible new or original combat mechanics. The combat could be one area that is not as innovative, but it does involve minute-to-minute gameplay and needs to be as strong as possible.

First, look at what kind of game world is possible in order to define acceptable combat systems. Since this game takes place in a futuristic post-apocalyptic world filled with "dinosaur technology" that could be very alien in nature, it would be possible to use many modern to futuristic guns. This is the easy choice, but not the most innovative.

The game will require players to battle huge creatures (such as evolved T-Rexes), so modern guns would most likely not be terribly effective. Guns might be useful against humans and small creatures, but not against the larger creatures. Perhaps there is some alternative that could be explored later. You could also say that most weapons have been destroyed and are hard to find, broken down, and so forth. The player may need to assemble weapons and piece them together. The player might even create new combinations of weapons. For instance, perhaps players must use a lot of bows or crossbows—but they might rig up poison arrows, explosive arrows, rope arrows, and much more beyond the standard arrow.

The player may be able to utilize vehicles emergently as weapons. If you are making a game such as *GTA* where you plan on allowing players to drive vehicles, then you need to think about how to use vehicles in a combat situation. This might be accomplished as in *Mercenaries,* in which players may have allies enter into vehicles with them and shoot out of the windows or use mounted weapons. This idea ties to the unification theme, but it could also be done differently. Players might modify their vehicles; add weapons, armor, and other goodies to them so that they are more powerful; or strap explosives onto vehicles and then use them as car bombs, which could be effective against giant creatures.

As part of the combat system, the game also needs a robust response and escalation system, such as in *GTA,* where the player performs actions and the world reacts to the player. This system could be more robust than in *GTA* and much more advanced than the one in *Crackdown*. The question is how the dinosaurs and humans will react to players as they kill them or do other things to them, good or bad. You will not be able to answer this properly until you more fully realize the story, world, characters, and other features of the game, since you need to know how to respond just a little or a lot to what the player does. In other words, should the game send a raptor against the player first, and a T-Rex later, or are there "bigger and badder" enemies the player must deal with? Since you also do not know yet how many enemies will be in combat at once, it is hard to know what level of response may be sent to the player. At

Electronic Arts, Inc.

In *Mercenaries 2,* players may get allies to enter into vehicles with them and shoot out of the windows or use mounted weapons.

this point, you're probably not completely happy with the direction of the combat system—but you want to move on and think about the other systems in the game to try to understand them better, coming back to the combat systems later.

Grand Theft Auto: San Andreas contains a robust response and escalation system where the world reacts to the player's actions.

Science

Science could take several different forms and be used for a couple of different key purposes in the game. Directly fighting the dinosaurs may be an option for some players, but fighting them with science and technology could be another. This could involve trying to figure out how this whole event happened and how to reverse it (if possible); discovering how the dinosaur technology works, so that the humans may utilize it to their advantage somehow; or researching new technologies to help players either live with the dinosaurs or eliminate them in some way.

Instead of just finding new weapons randomly as the player progresses through the game, what if the player is forced to research new, more effective weapons in order to battle the dinosaurs? This could involve a tech tree such as that found in many real-time strategy (RTS) games, where the player may research different technologies in an attempt to get desired items.

You might tie science and combat together by making it possible (and maybe necessary) for players to collect specimens. Instead of just needing to kill creatures, what if players need to research them? This could include photographing them, capturing live specimens, or collecting samples. This may be more difficult, but it would involve a reasonable risk/reward structure. Therefore, the player must have access to tranquilizers, freeze weapons, nets, cages, or other kinds of equipment to help capture or study the dinosaurs. Players may also have access to additional scientific equipment that they must utilize to learn things about the dinosaurs themselves, their technology, their cities, and their politics.

Firaxis Games

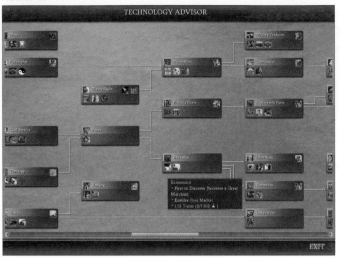

Tech trees, which are found in many real-time strategy games such as *Civilization IV,* allow the player to research different technologies in an attempt to get desired items.

Exploration and science could be combined because the player may be looking for a way to defeat the overall dinosaur threat. For example, the player may eventually find a powerful weapon but does not know where to place the bomb, use the device, or inject the chemical; the player then must not only build the science for the new weapon but also figure out how to assemble it and find the locations where it needs to be used. While a lot of this is story-related, it is really tied to many of the core mechanics of the game. Science could be a key part of the objectives and story in the game as well.

Exploration

Encouraging exploration could be as simple as just rewarding the player for looking around. The game could provide some alternate paths in the levels that might be easier or different for the player by hiding upgrades, special equipment, or secrets around levels. These are all fine, but you might want to consider new gameplay features that will facilitate some additional types of exploration.

What about some kind of scanner that could be used to look for hidden items in the environment? Maybe this ties into the science aspect of the game. However, this scanner could be used to identify hidden portals, secret passages, traps, and weak spots in the environment. Taking a cue from *Metroid Prime*, how could a scanner of some kind be used to make the world more interesting? What else could the scanner be used for?

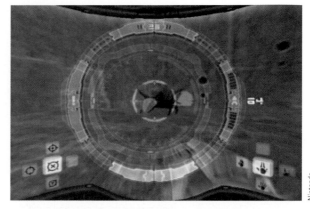

Exploration would also be more interesting in a more interactive environment. What if the world is more alive, more responsive, more destructible, and more subject to change by the player? LucasArts is using some amazing technology known as digital molecular matter (DMM) that allows most surfaces to take on a real-world physical property, such as wood or ice, and then behave like it. Even materials such as wood could be very different, from thin plywood to thick, hard oak. But what if other items took on these physical properties? It may not be practical to make every surface destructible, since you cannot control the player's movements, and you cannot afford to model every interior and exterior in an entire world, but you could create "weak points" that players could see or find with their scanner and then blow up, smash through, or interact with. These weak points could be treated like a door system, but instead of opening a door, the player could smash through a wall.

A scanner is used in *Metroid Prime* to make the world more interesting.

Perhaps the player could also interact with the environment by being able to move objects—like being able to roll boulders away from a cave entrance, or knock over a tree that could be used to climb up to a new level. Interactive objects are found in many games, but they could be taken to a whole new level and used to make the worlds far more interesting than those found in most of today's games.

Reconstruction

In *Diablo* and many action and RPG games, players have acquired almost everything they need by the time they get halfway through the game. The game often becomes tedious because players are in a seemingly never-ending loop where they are trying to upgrade themselves; they are then constantly grinding to earn a little more XP (experience points) to level up, some more money to buy something, or loot that they might sell for more money. This is one way you might hook some players, always keeping them striving for the new reward that is just minutes away or right around the corner. This system concept is also a way to give the player ownership and some additional customization that may be engaging in the long term. *Neverwinter Nights 2* incorporates a system where players may buy a castle and continue to upgrade it, along with their characters and team. This is an interesting mechanic, since it gives the player something else to focus on.

In *Diablo II*, players acquire almost everything they need by the time they get halfway through the game.

Neverwinter Nights 2 incorporates a system where players may buy castles and continue to upgrade them.

Ask yourself who your character is. Could the skills of your main character actually be applied to the game in some way? There are games in which the player character is supposed to be a car mechanic, yet when the player's car breaks, the player character cannot fix it. You could make the player character a special forces military type from the start, but this is sometimes cliché and not as appealing as a story about an average character who must save the world.

In this design concept, let's look at the idea of making the player character a construction worker. This means that you might want the character to do some type of construction, which ties into the entire reconstruction theme of the game. The character might possibly upgrade locations in different ways and repair them. Perhaps the buildings owned by the player character could also be attacked and damaged, which would require the player to repair them or risk losing them. This could tie into the meta-game aspect; players could also fix or upgrade other buildings that are owned by NPCs in order to meet objectives.

The real question is what happens at these locations and how they might be upgraded. Being able to buy, find, build, or acquire structures in the game could incorporate several gameplay mechanics beyond just providing ownership and upgrade abilities or new missions. These structures could be used as safe places to hide, heal, respawn, rearm, and store vehicles or other items.

Players might initially control but not "own" buildings and later be able to purchase them, which would give the players some additional benefits later in the game. The buildings may not only provide players with places to re-arm and equip themselves, but they could be fortified and used as direct weapons against the dinosaurs. They might also be used to control orbital super weapons or have other uses in relation to combat as well.

The buildings could tie to the science theme by providing additional research, storage locations, and much more. Each building the player owns may add some additional research and development (R&D) points, bonuses, technologies, or other aspects that could be beneficial.

The buildings could tie to the exploration systems in several ways. They could allow the player to move quickly from building to building using some travel analogy such as the subway and bus transportation systems in *GTA*, and give the player built-in radar or map bonuses for any surrounding areas containing buildings the

The transportation systems in *Grand Theft Auto: San Andreas* allow the player to move quickly through the environment.

player owns or controls. The buildings could also serve other purposes that relate to the unification theme; they could be "safe houses" not only for player characters but for non-player characters (NPCs) that need to be protected.

The player may have access to several levels of economy throughout the game. As the game progresses, the player may find a way to automatically generate more money (or whatever the economy uses) and shift the focus away from making money into other areas. However, players must deal with "cash" flow issues since their R&D from the science section requires a continual source of money, while other locations and items they purchase continually generate income.

In order to make the concept of "money" fit this game, it is important to explore its feasibility. Would money really be a factor in a world such as this? Probably not. But what about weapons? Maybe there is a big black market for weapons, where players may buy, sell, and trade them. There are many possibilities. You may also look at food, soldiers, or other items that would be logical to trade in your economy. The player may ultimately choose to delegate some missions and pay/fund/command allies or possibly mercenaries to do some jobs.

Unification

Another next-generation ability in games that you might want to leverage involves teams, groups, and crowds. This may be realized at many different levels. You might want to explore concepts of working in groups, which move beyond just having some artificial intelligence (AI) partners who follow the player around and shoot at enemies. Explore new ways to utilize team and crowd mechanics interactions. Keep in mind, though, that this is very risky and needs to be carefully understood and developed to minimize risk.

Wizards of the Coast

Neverwinter Nights 2 contains some very effective team mechanics.

It is easy for the main character do the quest alone. However, it is a lot more interesting for the player to work in groups, on a team, or with a partner. Having an AI character who works with your main character may be very difficult to pull off, but it might be very rewarding. Games such as *Tom Clancy's Rainbow Six: Vegas* and *Neverwinter Nights 2* contain some very effective team mechanics to look at for reference. Providing support for two (or more) characters on screen at the same time also makes way for some potentially creative co-op multiplayer gameplay.

Rescuing trapped and imprisoned humans is a theme worth exploring. If you're going to build squad interaction behaviors, then consider giving players the ability to locate and save other characters. This would include being able to find humans who are imprisoned, freeing them, and then bringing them to safety. Imagine that the dinosaurs have set up large prisons, detention camps, work camps, or other areas where humans are being kept as slaves.

If the player has the ability to drive or fly vehicles, characters may enter the vehicles and the player may transport them to safety. This could become a cool modern version of *Choplifter* in 3D. Exploration and unification are also closely linked together because players must use their exploration skills to find other humans in the game. Unification and reconstruction are important, since the closer the safe house, the less risk in extracting other characters to safety.

Summarizing the Features

After brainstorming new feature ideas, you will find that it is a good exercise to list the basic set of features your competition has by going over the back of their boxes and reading any other available marketing material or ads. Whether you realize it or not, you ultimately must sell your game and get marketing to sign off on it. From there, you might put together a basic list of features:

- Third-person action adventure for next-generation consoles
- Open "sandbox" post-apocalyptic world
- Advanced and evolved dinosaurs that utilize technology and weapons
- Single-player and co-op gameplay

- **Characters:** Players find characters to help them along their journey; rescue and free the enslaved people of Earth; search for brother
- **Dinosaurs:** Encounter a wide variety of friendly and hostile dinosaurs, both large and small. Imagine dinosaurs that have evolved for the last 50+ million years, gained intelligence, built cities, and become more advanced than the human race
- **Character Movement:** Walking, running, jumping, swimming, climbing, moving objects, swinging, and more
- **Character Weapons:** Shoot guns, use explosives, use grenades, use knives, use advanced technology weapons
- **Character Equipment:** Body armor, camouflage, dino scanner, GPS, rope, radio, health packs, laser cutter, and probably much more
- **Vehicles:** Cars, helicopters, boats, motorcycles; load others into vehicles and transport them or have them help players attack enemies
- **Vehicular Combat:** Use mounted weapons on vehicles, use turreted weapons, use vehicles to ram and crash into things, turn vehicles into car bomb
- **Upgrades:** Player characters gain new abilities and improve attributes over time; vehicles and weapons may be upgraded to include new abilities
- **Research:** New technologies to allow for equipment upgrades and new features
- **Economy:** Find and trade weapons and science information to get what is needed; buy and sell items on the black market

It is good to try to keep this to a one-page sheet or less. Some of this list may still need to be trimmed back, but it is important to include all of the features you think are critical on this list, if you know about them.

Pressures

Now that you have a list of features, you need to decide what to do next. There is no exact science here, and no real right or wrong way to proceed. Much of your work will have to do with who else is on your project and waiting for you.

Technology

The engine programmers on your team need to get some rough parameters in the first month so that they may gauge how far players need to see, how fast they need to move, how high they need to go, how many characters will be onscreen, and how players interact with the world. Some difficult questions should be answered in order to estimate how the engine should be created, whether the existing engine will work with your ideas, and whether it is best to license a new engine or create one from scratch. If you are holding up programmers, find out what additional information is needed and provide it sooner rather than later.

Art

If the artists on your team are eager to start, you may need to feed them more information so that they may safely begin. While it is possible for artists to work in a vacuum and create pretty pictures (and sometimes this is desirable), you generally want to create some details for them that revolve around what gameplay is needed. However, even this basic concept could probably keep a team of artists busy for a month or two figuring out some ideas for the world and dinosaurs. If artists are waiting for you, find out what they want to work on first (characters, environments, or other thematic art) and then spend some time designing the world, characters, or props for the game so that they might draw them well.

Executive

You also cannot ignore the fact that you may soon need to pitch the game. At some companies, you may get to initially pitch only a 1-2 page game concept before getting approval to bring more resources onto the project. Even after passing the initial hurdle, you may need to pitch the core game concept within a few months as well, which may be tricky. If this happens, you need to understand that most (not all) executives will be interested in the gameplay, story, characters, genre, and sales potential. It is very difficult to pitch new gameplay concepts to most executives. You'll need to be able to explain your game in a very short time. This means working on the overview of the game concept and character/environmental descriptions soon. If at all possible, you will also need some art concepts to go along with them. You'll then need to just keep refining the core vision for the game until you feel it sounds appealing and may be easily pitched to executives in a meeting.

No Pressure!

Sometimes you are working on your own to come up with a concept, so you might have more time to work out the core game mechanics first, without having to worry about external pressures. A way to approach the next step of the design is to assume that you are making a post-apocalyptic *GTA* with advanced dinosaurs who use guns. In fact, you could pitch it this way! The game concept for *Mercenaries* was pitched to executives as "military *GTA*." It was simple and easy for an exec to grasp the concept without having to worry about the details.

Next, try to refine the story concept (not the entire story, just its overall premise) and a few of the main characters—and try to nail down who the dinosaurs are, what they might do, and how their cities are built. This is what executives will want to see, but it is also unique for this concept and may be a little tricky to sell. Selling executives

on a post-apocalyptic *GTA* will probably be easier than selling them the
concept of "dinosaurs with guns," or
whoever your enemies turn out to
be. Try to identify the biggest risks to
the entire concept and work out their
details as early as possible, in case you
hit a snag and need to change a major
portion of your concept.

Electronic Arts, Inc.

The *Mercenaries* series (*Mercenaries 2*, shown) was
pitched to executives as "military *Grand Theft Auto*."

Designing the Mechanics

In this book, we began with a discussion of some higher-level concepts such as
cameras, movement, and controls. These are important topics to emphasize early
on, once you've decided on your vision of the game and how you want to innovate.
From there, diving deeper into the player character, enemies, interface, and other
core systems is important. You might also want to spend time determining the emergent systems for the game and how they will work together.

Getting a prototype of the game up and running as soon as possible is critical. The
longer it takes you to do this, the more risky the game development will be. It is best
to try to get the game playable as early as possible, or at least find a way to hack a
playable prototype using another engine or tools.

As you move forward in designing your game, keep in mind what is risky, what is
hard, what is new, what is unproven, and what will be the core of the game, which
you should develop as early as possible in the game design.

The Future of Gameplay Mechanics

You'll notice as you study the evolution of gameplay and genres over the years that
some mechanics have remained popular, while many others have become outdated.
Many of us who grew up playing the Atari 2600 and NES think back and remember
games such as *Defender* or *Super Mario Bros.* fondly. However, most games have
become increasingly more complex over the years, making it difficult for some
genres to truly thrive, at least for the hard-core player. Several projects that started
off as remakes of classic games have failed miserably because those who proposed
the project did not change the game mechanics, just the graphics and controls.

If you consider the mechanics in popular beat-em-up games such as *Double Dragon* and think you might make a next-generation game using it as a model, you would be mistaken. Players are much more savvy and demanding of games than ever before. Players want to see much deeper gameplay, and much longer games with more variety. Classic games may help you understand some basic single game mechanics, but you must be very careful in modeling a modern game after a classic game; if you are trying to remake a classic game, you should focus on improving the mechanics along with the graphics.

> At present, digital game designers are by and large ringing the changes on a limited subset of mechanics. The space of all possible mechanics is vastly larger than they seem aware, and designers are well advised to take a look at things like tabletop RPGs, the Eurogame movement, ARGs, etc., to expand their palette of the possible.
>
> —*Greg Costikyan*
> *(Chief Executive Officer, Manifesto Games)*

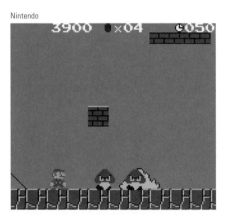
Nintendo

If you were to remake a classic game such as *Super Mario Bros.* or *Double Dragon,* you would need to alter the game mechanics, not just the graphics and controls.

While it is impossible to predict what will happen in the future, several trends are clearly emerging. Games are becoming more and more complicated all the time and relying on not only classic game mechanics but innovation and technology to drive them as well. Emergent gameplay, or sandbox game mechanics, is becoming all the rage and will be even more popular as time goes on and more designers determine how to utilize systemic game mechanic design rather than isolated mechanics.

Many publishers and developers, along with Microsoft and Sony, have been guilty of pushing visual look and cinematics over the pure fun of the gameplay mechanics and game experience. The Nintendo Wii challenges many publishers because it is distinct from the Sony PS3 and Microsoft Xbox 360 in focusing on gameplay and innovation over graphical performance. The Wii has a cool new controller that is very innovative and very appealing to the mass market, but its games do not look spectacular. The success of the Wii will possibly drive the industry and game designers, even those working on the other next-generation platforms, to think twice about how important it is to just make their games fun and engaging—and that pretty graphics and other next-generation features are less important to many on the mass market. The ultimate success of the Wii may also drive Microsoft and Sony to innovate more on the side of gameplay.

Thoughts on the Future

I think we've only scratched the surface of what's possible in game mechanics. We've been modeling a lot of physical and spatial mechanics, but there are many more human activities we can be looking at for inspiration. I'm particularly interested in games of social negotiation and interaction—these types of mechanics are intrinsically emergent, because players can use their natural social skills in very creative ways to solve game problems.

—*Tracy Fullerton*
(Assistant Professor, Interactive Media Division, USC School of Cinematic Arts)

I think we're going to see a lot of innovation at the 'Indie Games' level with all of the game building kits and new distribution methods available. If the risk is low, and the number of game makers high, this makes for exciting times. This is how we'll see the future of gameplay mechanics.

—*Frank Trevor Gilson*
(Senior Producer, Gas Powered Games)

Graphics will continue to improve, which will make games more believable and attractive; access will become more straightforward. Broadband, and more powerful broadband connections, will allow richer games to be more easily played from more locations; Modifications on the manufacturing side and the user/player side will become more seamless.

—*Titus Levi*
(Media Arts Consultant)

I believe that future gameplay machines will mostly come from changes in technology. The Nintendo Wii has proven this with their new controller. Other things like physics and new AI will allow game developers to inject new gameplay elements utilizing these new technologies.

—*John Comes*
(Lead Game Designer, Gas Powered Games)

Chris Taylor & Milan Petrovich on the Future of Gameplay Mechanics :::::

Chris Taylor
(Creative Director
& Owner, Gas
Powered Games)

For the past 18 years, Chris Taylor has been one of the game industry's most imaginative and dynamic visionaries. The creator of the first true next-generation RTS game, *Total Annihilation*, Chris enjoys an industry-wide reputation as an innovator who is able to push both technology and gameplay to their limits. In 1998, Chris founded Gas Powered Games—where he currently serves as the CEO and Creative Director. To date, Gas Powered Games has released *Dungeon Siege*, *Dungeon Siege II*, *Dungeon Siege II: Broken World*—and it oversaw the development of *Dungeon Siege: Throne of Agony* for the PSP. The company's newest release is the highly anticipated RTS game, *Supreme Commander*.

We'll see a lot of evolution, but we'll also occasionally get a revolution that has us all smacking our heads saying, "Why didn't I think of that!" It's what makes this business so much fun... you never know what someone will come up with... and if I dare say, these kinds of gameplay advancements are usually right under our nose! Whatever the future holds, I sure hope it continues to see the craft of game making continue to move in the direction of rewarding the players, and not punishing them. This is essential to growing our market and bringing more players into the world of video games. And last, I hope we continue to find ways to exploit the interactive side of games and not try to mimic or duplicate what the other popular entertainment artforms are good at... we have our own very important and unique characteristics, and we should spend more time focusing on that instead of jealously looking over the fence at film and television.

Milan Petrovich
(Associate Dean of
Academic Affairs, Art
Institute of California
– San Francisco)

Prior to becoming Associate Dean of Academic Affairs at the Art Institute of California – San Francisco, Milan Petrovich was Academic Director for Game Art & Design at the Art Institute of Las Vegas. He has taught game design theory and development at the Art Institute since 2003. Prior to the Art Institute, he was Director of Production for the pioneering Internet television studio WireBreak Entertainment. He has over 17 years of professional experience in design and multimedia. He received his MFA from the USC School of Cinema-Television where he studied the development of online games under the Sega Interactive Fellowship.

Innovation is not dead. Just when you begin to think that today's games are just fancier wrappings around the same-old tired gameplay, along comes something like *Katamari Damacy* to shake things up. On the hardware side, the Wii console has added an entirely new dimension to how designers think about games. Currently, I think the resurgence of casual games and the emergence of the mobile market will both spur developments in gameplay mechanics. The simple fact that more people are developing for these (relatively-speaking) graphics-handicapped devices means that the likelihood of new types of gameplay will increase.

Becoming a Designer

It is difficult to give advice on how to get into game design. You may want to go to school to learn game design, or you may already be in the game industry or work in another industry and hope to become a game designer. The question is where you should begin.

Many will advise you to learn everything about being a game designer; they will try to get you to learn how to do every job, from building levels to scripting, writing code, writing design docs, writing stories, and everything else. Although it is great to have experience across the entire field of game design, you must realize that there is a tremendous amount to learn—and, in order to get a job, you should be really good at a few things initially. Many schools also try to teach a great deal of art or programming skills that might be unnecessary, while other schools are too theoretical and do not incorporate enough practical and real-world teaching.

No matter where you go, or how you plan on learning how to become a game designer, you must realize that those who also spend much of their own time practicing, building their own games, and learning things outside of class will be the most successful.

To be a great designer, you cannot overlook your general education and other non-game-related classes. While it is hard enough just to take all the computer and game design classes you need, it is still invaluable to learn subjects such as mathematics, physics, chemistry, biology, history, sociology, psychology, English, creative writing, film studies, marketing, and business. Math and science have direct applications in the game industry, and many game projects also deal with history, military, and cultural studies. Psychology and sociology also come into play, especially in simulation and online multiplayer games.

> When I was in college, I had two roommates. One of them had three master's degrees in computer science but had only taken classes at school and had never done anything outside of class. My other roommate was in his senior year getting his first BS degree. You can guess who got a job first. My roommate with all the degrees had a lot of trouble getting a job because he couldn't apply his skills and actually do any real-world work. My other roommate spent every night writing games, tools, and other stuff he wanted to make; he had an impressive demo reel by his senior year and was hired at Intel before he graduated.
>
> —*Troy Dunniway*

The moral of this story? Do not overlook the basics. Many game designers skipped school, became testers, and worked their way up to become designers. While this may be a viable career path, don't take it unless you have no other route. If you don't like school and studying, you will probably hate being a game designer. Taking the dark path on your way to becoming the Jedi Design Master will only lead to long-term problems and will ultimately cause you to fail because you lack the skills to advance. Half of your job as a designer will involve communication. Being able to write great design documents and present your ideas to others is critical. In the ETC program at Carnegie Mellon University, game design students must take improvisational acting because it teaches them how to think on their feet.

The reality is that almost nobody will hire you to be a designer without some experience as a level designer. There are many different design jobs, but most designers tend to start off as level designers or some kind of technical designer, and then work their way up to becoming a game systems designer and eventually a senior or lead designer. If you want to get into the industry, you need to first determine how to become a great level designer.

Advice for Future Designers

Play lots of games of all types. Hunt down older computer games of styles that the narrow constraints of the current industry no longer find commercially viable; play lots of non-digital games, too.

—Greg Costikyan
(Chief Executive Officer, Manifesto Games)

Work hard. Learn as much as you can (from everyone who'll teach you). Communicate well. Be a professional. And have fun!

—Jeremy McCarron
(Academic Director, The Art Institute of Vancouver)

Play a lot of games. Take notes. What do you think is good? bad? why? Read the blogs of game designers. React to what they are saying and justify it.

—Frank T. Gilson
(Senior Producer, Wizards of the Coast)

Build a mod. There's nothing like experience and proving you can create something that is plausibly shippable. Mods not only give you that experience but they give you something to show off to prospective employers.

—John Comes
(Lead Game Designer, Gas Powered Games)

Stay close to users/players. Serve the market and don't get too caught up in the numbers game. Quality content is what drives popularity and economic success.

—Titus Levi
(Media Arts Consultant)

Play as many games as you can. Analyze each game thoroughly. Ask yourself how you would improve the game but don't give the easy answer of adding more content. Also get your hands on some good game tools like Source or the *Neverwinter Nights* (Aurora) editor and make as many levels as you can. Get them out to the public and listen to their feedback. Read lots of books. Think of how you can take things in those books into the games you will make. For instance, there are missions in the game I am working on that were inspired by chapters from a science fiction book I read called *Fallen Dragon*.

—*Starr Long*
(Producer, NCsoft Corporation)

Get a job working with a game designer you respect, and find a position on their team doing anything you can to learn from them. Don't worry about getting that big 'lead role' until you have some time under your belt. And you have to remember to play lots of different games, not just your favorites. It took me a long time to learn that I can steal great ideas from almost any game, and not just those that match my favorite genres.

—*Chris Taylor*
(Creative Director & Owner, Gas Powered Games)

Study the classics...chess, *Monopoly*, *Risk*, poker, *Pac-Man*...and thoroughly try to understand the impact of these games. The human emotions that feed these gameplay experiences will continue to play a vital role in game design. The current obsession with the art, style, and technological capability of games will take a backseat to elements that feed the emotions. Gaming is becoming the next literary movement. Challenge yourself to find out what makes audiences emotionally invested in the experience.

—*Roby Gilbert*
(Academic Department Director, Game Art & Design/
Media Arts & Animation, Art Institute of Seattle; Commercial Illustrator)

First and foremost, get out there and actively make your own games. Use whatever tools you have available: Flash, existing game engines/tools such as Source or Unreal, pen/paper, card games, board games, etc. School is great, but all the education in the world can't replace passion and real-world experience. As with anything in life, you are going to get out of your education what you put into it. Learn everything you can and then go out and apply it. Start small and work your way up. Make maps for your favorite games, then play and refine them so that you can get a feel for what works and what doesn't. Once you are ready, move on to creating missions or scenarios. Explore new challenges and play more games (the fun part!), both good and bad, learn from their successes and pitfalls, be open to expanding beyond your favorite 2-3 game genres, then critique them with friends. Try designing for single-player games—then take a stab at multiplayer games, co-op and adversarial. Nothing looks better to a prospective employer than presenting samples of work in the form of your own games or, better yet, a successful mod that you helped build as part of a team.

—*Randy Greenback*
(Creative Director, Red Storm Entertainment/Ubisoft)

Learn to program, take a lot of math courses, and take a lot of writing courses. If you can program (or at the very least script), then you'll be able to prototype your own idea: not only will this give you more control over the development of gameplay, it will make you much quicker and more productive at it. Math knowledge (especially of advanced algebra, probability, and statistics) is also invaluable for a game designer—ultimately game mechanics are substantially about equations and curves, and if you can quickly visualize the kinds of curves that equations produce (or the kind of equation you need to produce the curve you want) then you've got a lot more tools at your disposal. Finally it's important to take a lot of writing courses, because as a game designer you'll need extremely high written communications skills to survive. Game designers do a lot of writing.

—Brian Reynolds
(Chief Executive Officer, Big Huge Games)

The best way to learn is to design and, more importantly, implement as many systems yourself as you can. There are plenty of game editors on the market for many genres of games—whether real-time strategy (RTS), first-person shooters, or even role-playing games (Neverwinter Nights 2 comes with an editor that allows you to build your own characters, modules, creatures, and items). Each editor can give you the power to tweak weapon statistics, create new weapons, design crafting and spell systems, and so on. Get hold of these editors and just start messing around with them—and once you've implemented some systems, find a way to release these for public consumption so people can jump up and down on them to break them. When they do, learn from whatever errors you made (or successes), then try again. Try to prototype the system early, if you can. Not all systems have to look beautiful to start testing them and seeing how they work in practice. On our Aliens project, our lead system designer, Paul Boyle, tries to mock up prototypes of combat and tactics as early as possible and integrates the systems into a 2D model that simulates how the systems would work in the final version of the game. Gameplay is an iterative process, and implementation aside, play as many games and pay attention to the systems they use—study what units work well in an RTS game, which ones seem to be unbalanced, why X spell has Y drawback, or why X spell has Z advantage. Read forum posts on various games and isolate balance problems that other players find with existing games on the market and store them in the library in your head for future consideration. And don't just play console or PC games—board games, flash games, card games, pen-and-paper games, and other non-computer games rely heavily on systems for their fun factor, so they are worth studying as well. Many mechanics from those systems are applicable in a computer game environment. One last word of advice—try to avoid 'fire and forget' design for gameplay systems ('It seems to work great on paper, so implement it, and then move on to the next thing'). Balance is extremely important for each system, and if a system isn't tested by a variety of people with different playstyles, you may find an error in your system far too late to correct it.

—Chris Avellone
(Chief Creative Officer & Lead Designer, Obsidian Entertainment)

Level Designer

The most important element of being a game designer is doing what you love. It is important to remember that it is a job, and that you must work long hours doing it, so you had better enjoy it and feel confident you might do it day in and day out. You must also realistically assess your skills and interests in order to decide what kind of designer you ultimately want to be.

To become a great level designer, you must have several different skills. Game level design might be approached from one of two different directions, either artistic or technical (programming). To be a great level designer, you need to know how to make games fun, but you also need to know how to build them. Some companies hire level designers who are supposed to do every-

> See *Game Level Design* (Castillo/ Novak), part of the *Game Development Essentials* series, for more information on becoming a level designer.

thing—including building, scripting, and aesthetically improving the level. Some companies employ several designers, each of whom has specialized skills.

A great level designer understands what it will take to make levels fun. This is a skill that may be learned by using level editors that ship with games such as *Neverwinter Nights 2, Half-Life 2, Age of Empires 3*, or *Dungeon Siege* to practice building levels and letting others play them.

Level designers must also be proficient at scripting. Programming languages such as Lua, C#, and Python are the most popular scripting languages, but almost any kind of scripting language can be found. Many games use proprietary languages as well. However, getting a good foundation of Lua, C#, or Python will go a long way toward being able to pick up and learn a new tool later.

You should also consider brushing up on your art skills. Do not only learn Photoshop, Max, Maya, and/or popular level editors; also take some foundation classes on composition, color theory, and drawing. These are important for several reasons. First, some teams use existing programs such as Max and Maya as their editors. It is also easier to communicate your ideas to the rest of the team visually, so having art skills is important. Finally, some teams expect you to create some of the art in a level, so you will be better off in the long run if you're able to create great-looking levels. The good news is that there are many games with editors just waiting to be modded, which will allow you to practice and gain lots of practical experience.

Valve

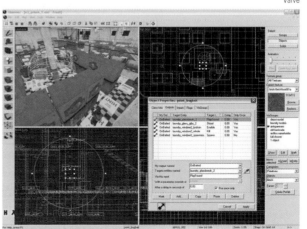

Creating mods using level editors such as Valve's Hammer Editor (shipped with *Half-Life*) will give you some valuable level design experience.

Travis Castillo, Roby Gilbert & Jim McCampbell on Becoming a Gameplay Designer:::::

Travis Castillo
(Level Designer &
Environmental Artist,
InXile Entertainment;
Professor, Art Center
College of Design)

Travis Castillo began his career in the game industry in 2002 while still in school when he landed an internship at Activision's Central Technology where he worked under the art director and art team. With a year left still to graduate he then landed a job with Paramount Studios creating top-secret military simulations in the Unreal engine in partnership with the Army and USC. Graduating in 2004 with a BA in Game Art and Design, he was offered a job teaching level design at Santa Monica College and helped form the game curriculum for the school's blossoming program. Since then he has taught and helped form curriculums for Art Institute Online and Westwood College, and he is currently teaching Unreal level design at the Art Center College of Design. He was the lead level designer and consultant on the highly acclaimed Tactical Language games; Tactical Iraqi and Tactical Pashto. He currently works as a level designer and environmental artist for InXile Entertainment creating games on the Unreal 3 engine for the Xbox 360 and the PlayStation 3.

Playing lots of games is a given. Anyone who will design gameplay will need to know and understand games! Note what is fun and what is not when you play. Your job will be to create these mechanics and make them fun. Besides this, you should also be observant for inspiration at anytime in life. Immerse yourself in the subject matter of your game. If it is based on human history, how did the people of the time deal with achieving the same goals that are in your game? Watch movies and documentaries and read books. Design your mechanics based off of this and most importantly, make sure they are fun.

Roby Gilbert
(Academic Department
Director, Game Art &
Design/Media
Arts & Animation,
Art Institute of Seattle;
Commercial Illustrator)

Roby Gilbert is a commercial animator/ illustrator with over 20 years of experience in educational media, broadcast, and illustration. He is a regular contributor to *Ranger Rick Magazine*. Clients have included Disney Interactive, Nikelodeon, PBS, Sesame Street, WWF, Whispering Coyote Press, and Broderbund Software. Roby is currently Academic Department Director for the Media Arts & Animation and Game Art & Design Programs at the Art Institute of Seattle.

Study the classics—chess, *Monopoly*, *Risk*, poker, *Pac-Man*—and thoroughly try to understand the impact of these games. The human emotions that feed these gameplay experiences will continue to play a vital role in game design. The current obsession with the art, style, and technological capability of games will take a backseat to elements that feed the emotions. Gaming is becoming the next literary movement. Challenge yourself to find out what makes audiences emotionally invested in the experience.

Jim McCampbell received his BFA from the University of Tennessee and began his professional career as a graphic designer, then as Senior Art Director for several advertising agencies. In 1986, he was fortunate to be at the forefront of the burgeoning 3D Animation industry where he developed his skills as a 3D animator while working for several film and video production companies. His national clients have included notable names such as TNN, A&E, HGTV, The Discovery Channel, Electronic Arts, CMT, GAC, Time Warner, CBS, NBC, and ABC. McCampbell has been with Ringling College of Art and Design since 1995, and is the head of the Computer Animation Department, which houses Ringling's internationally renowned Computer Animation major, as well as the newly formed Game Art & Design major. He also owns the 3D animation production company Peculiar Pictures, a Sarasota-based business specializing in animation for film, broadcast, and video games.

Jim McCampbell
(Department Head,
Computer Animation,
Ringling College of
Art + Design)

Two things... first, recognize the incredible value of the Liberal Arts classes in your curriculum. Believe it or not, those are most likely the places where you will learn to understand the audience you are making games for, and how to manipulate the way they think. History sociology, and psychology classes are the places that will empower you to control minds.

Second (and this is going to be really hard to do), don't think about what games are today. I know... it's almost impossible... but consider the potential of the medium and try to break free. Don't fall prey to the 'templates of creativity' that the industry perpetuates. Impress recruiters with your creativity and originality. The big opportunities lie in the next great thing, and the next great thing lies within you.

Gameplay System Designer

This book is focused on the next step of the game design career, which is becoming a game system designer. A system designer is someone who designs gameplay systems (mechanics). When trying to learn how to be a game system designer, you need to learn how to start small. Find some simple games to design, start small, practice and practice some more. If you are working on a game team as a level designer, see if you might get a chance at taking over a small part of the system design and owning it. Read as many as you can of the design documents for the project you are on, other projects you may find, or anything you might get your hands on that will show you examples of how game systems are designed. Some schools do teach a lot about designing gameplay mechanics, so it is possible to learn about gameplay mechanic design at a school or possibly even by reading a book, but you ultimately will learn the most from just practicing.

Exercise Your Game Design Muscle

I advise students to design a lot of little game prototypes to practice their skills. Try to design a game with the objects sitting on your desk right now. Or come up with another game design challenge for yourself and try to answer it. Game design skills are like a muscle you need to exercise, and the way to do this is to practice designing games. I also tell students not to worry too much about specific technologies, because these technologies change. Learn the basics of game design and be ready to continually learn new tools all the time.

—Tracy Fullerton
(Assistant Professor, Interactive Media Division. USC School of Cinematic Arts)

Know What Works—and What Doesn't

One piece of advice for students who are interested in becoming gameplay designers is that they should spend a lot of time playing games, analyzing game mechanics, and trying to determine what works and what doesn't work. There should be a large focus on board games and card games, and not just computer games. Students should play and analyze games that earn awards, along with the games that turn out to be busts. Those who can design a board game that plays well and has good game mechanics will understand and have a better success demonstrating their knowledge and skills of game mechanics in general.

—Chris Rohde
(Assistant Director, Game Art & Design / Visual & Game Programming, The Art Institute of Portland)

Mark Skaggs on "Idea" vs. "Numbers" Designers :::::

Mark Skaggs
(CEO & Executive Producer, Funstar Ventures, LLC)

Mark Skaggs is best known for his work in the RTS genre—leading award-winning products such as *Command & Conquer: Red Alert 2*, *Command & Conquer: Generals*, and *Lord of the Rings: The Battle for Middle-Earth.* With a game career spanning over 13 years, Mark has been responsible for production, game design, technical direction, and art direction on hit products that have sold over 10 million units since 2000.

An 'idea designer' is usually great at coming up with amazing out-of-this-world types of ideas, while a 'numbers designer' usually has better skills at creating and working with all the numbers that go behind making the game work. It's a continuum; numbers designers can have great creative ideas and idea designers can do the number crunching and stats design, but people usually have their individual strengths and I encourage them to lead into those strengths while partnering with someone else to help shore up their weaknesses.

With people who are stronger in the numbers area, I suggest that they instantly tear into an existing game and start playing with the stats. For an RTS game, it would be as simple as cracking up the files exposed by the development team and changing weapons, movement and other attributes of game elements. Starting simple with ideas like 'I think this tank should have more armor' and then getting everyone you know to play your version of the game will give the designer a chance to get instant feedback and at the same time, probably give him or her ideas for new things to try. It's possible for new designers to radically change up some existing games just by using the game editor and tweaking the numbers, and using an existing game allows the designers to focus 100% of their efforts on doing design work within the constraints of the game (something they will have to do when they get into the industry).

For 'idea' designers, I would advise that they spend time practicing how to quickly and easily articulate their great ideas in a way that anyone can 'grok' in one minute or less. I suggest that they start with their idea and write it down and get it organized. Next step is to then 'boil it' two or three times to get rid of all the fluff so that only the key, simple and central ideas of their idea remain. The next step is to create simple diagrams, which explain the idea in pictures and a few words. From there they should show that idea to as many people as possible so they can get feedback and figure out how to improve. The idea designer type of person can also focus their thinking on how to improve existing games. If they do this, they may be able to use the game's editor to implement their ideas or get a friend to help out.

My basic approach for anyone interested in making games is to 'get into the game' of making games as simply and easily as possible. There will always be classes to take at school to help educate you, but there is no substitution to immersing yourself in what you want to do by reading websites, getting onto forums, working with mod teams, going to game conventions, talking to friends, etc. Just get started and realize that your first great game ideas might not be all that great, but you'll be able to get better quickly if you immerse yourself every way possible in the business you want to work in.

Advancing as a Designer

No matter what job position you are in, you always need to learn new skills. If you hope to get a job as a game designer or become a better game designer, you must realize that you will constantly need to learn new things and practice them to get better. Even if you are a working game designer, it is easy to stop using some skills and to get very rusty. Remember that to be a great designer, you also must be a great leader, manager, mentor, and executive. You must eventually take on a role of responsibility and ownership if you are to advance in your career, so if you don't have great communication, presentation, leadership, management, and overall people skills, keep taking classes and learning more about these areas while you develop as a designer. Don't wait until the last minute to improve, since it takes years for some to build and practice these skills.

Wrapping It All Up

Keep in mind how important it is to look at the big picture of the design as often as possible and not to work in a bubble. Games are usually made in teams, and you must learn how to work in one. This is especially true for game designers. Even if you're not the lead designer, or if you are a designer working on writing game design documents (GDDs), you must remember that at some level, most things are connected if you are doing your job right. Some designers have plenty of time and money and might afford to redo a lot of art, code, and design as often as needed. These designers do not need to think through everything to avoid rework.

Designing next-generation games in today's development environment is a lot harder than you think, and significantly harder than the last generation, amazingly enough. As much as you may thirst to bring your own new and original IP to life, hopefully you're lucky the first time and may take on a sequel or franchise that is a little easier.

Innovation is not everything. Some of the most successful games for the next-generation systems, such as *Resistance: Fall of Man,* are innovative in a few key areas but beautiful, highly polished, and solid all around. You do not need to reinvent the wheel to be successful. Sometimes just taking a few bumps out of the wheel, making it look different and innovative, and ensuring that every aspect of the game is highly polished is far more important than making a game unlike anything else.

Sony Computer Entertainment America

Resistance: Fall of Man is innovative in only a few key areas but beautiful, highly polished, and solid all around.

The *Merged Destinies* game design case study is very different and innovative at the game mechanics level and somewhat original at the story concept level. It could just as easily have been an FPS that now has a cover system, co-op multiplayer, online multiplayer, and highly cinematic values. This sounds like any other FPS, but if you consider games such as *Gears of War,* you will see that there is not much to sell either; this does not make it any less of a game. Many games tried to innovate a lot more than *Gears of War*, had teams twice as large, sold half as many copies, and were never successful because their designers and creative directors tried to do too much. Great game designers will know what they and their team are capable of, what their engine might do, and where to push the envelope. This is a hard skill to learn.

Many teams try to inject innovative gameplay into a genre and spend a tremendous amount of time and resources trying to incorporate features such as FPS hand-to-hand combat (martial arts), vehicles, and other elements that are eventually cut from the game. On the one hand, the game may be much more innovative if they succeed. It is always easier to look back and see the mistakes you made. But, spending too much time on things that are risky may kill your project or severely handicap it. On the other hand, many teams put together a great prototype that is highly polished and fun, but the vision for the game is not big enough and a competitive game cannot be created in the time needed, so the game ultimately is known as a great rental but not worth buying. The opposite has also happened, where teams focus on getting mechanics working that are fun in and of themselves but do not form a cohesive game experience; this ultimately kills the game because it feels like many disparate features are slammed together rather than forming a seamless game experience.

Many games tried to innovate a lot more than *Gears of War* but were not as successful because their designers and creative directors tried to do too much.

Decide what you want to make, get the big picture of the game clear, and then work on defining and refining the key features before you dive into the little details. If you get caught up on minor points or invest time in things that may not work, you could be in trouble. You must ultimately ensure that the game is highly polished and fun minute to minute.

:::CHAPTER REVIEW:::

1. Play at least three electronic games that are currently on the market and identify their gameplay structures in terms of micro, macro, meta, mini, and mega play. How do these forms of gameplay mechanics work together to create a solid game experience? Take a look at the gameplay features you've developed for your original game so far and structure them based on these categories. (If you feel that additional features are still needed, use the brainstorming techniques discussed in this chapter to create more.)

2. Choose one of the games you played in Exercise 1 and discuss the effectiveness of the game's tutorial. How did the tutorial provide instructions on how to play the game without taking you out of the immersiveness and excitement of the game? How did the game continue to instruct and guide you outside of the tutorial? How will you incorporate a tutorial and other instructional techniques into your original game idea?

3. What are your thoughts on the future of gameplay mechanics? Do you agree or disagree with any of the opinions in this chapter? Why or why not?

Resources

There's a wealth of information on game development and related topics discussed in this book. Here is just a sample list of books, news sites, organizations, and events you should definitely explore!

News

Blues News—www.bluesnews.com
Computer Games Magazine—www.cgonline.com
Game Daily Newsletter—www.gamedaily.com
Game Developer Magazine—www.gdmag.com
Gamers Hell—www.gamershell.com
Game Music Revolution (GMR)—www.gmronline.com
Game Rankings—www.gamerankings.com
GamesIndustry.biz—www.gamesindustry.biz
GameSlice Weekly—www.gameslice.com
GameSpot—www.gamespot.com
GameSpy—www.gamespy.com
Game Industry News—www.gameindustry.com
GIGnews.com—www.gignews.com
Internet Gaming Network (IGN)—www.ign.com
Metacritic—www.metacritic.com
Music4Games.net—www.music4games.net
Next Generation—www.next-gen.biz
1UP—www.1up.com
PC Gamer—www.pcgamer.com
Star Tech Journal [technical side of the coin-op industry]—www.startechjournal.com
UGO Networks (Underground Online)—www.ugo.com
Video Game Music Archive—www.vgmusic.com
Wired Magazine—www.wired.com

Directories & Communities

Apple Developer Connection—developer.apple.com
Betawatcher.com—www.betawatcher.com
Fat Babies.com [game industry gossip]—www.fatbabies.com
Gamasutra—www.gamasutra.com
GameDev.net—www.gamedev.net
Game Development Search Engine—www.gdse.com
GameFAQs—www.gamefaqs.com
Game Music.com—www.gamemusic.com
Games Tester—www.gamestester.com
GarageGames—www.garagegames.com

Machinima.com—www.machinima.com

Moby Games—www.mobygames.com

Overclocked Remix—www.overclocked.org

PS3—www.ps3.net

Wii-Play—www.wii-play.com

Xbox.com—www.xbox.com

XBOX 360 Homebrew—www.xbox360homebrew.com
[includes XNA developer community]

Organizations

Academy of Interactive Arts & Sciences (AIAS)—www.interactive.org

Academy of Machinima Arts & Sciences—www.machinima.org

Association of Computing Machinery (ACM)—www.acm.org

Business Software Alliance (BSA)—www.bsa.org

Digital Games Research Association (DiGRA)—www.digra.org

Entertainment Software Association (ESA)—www.theesa.com

Entertainment Software Ratings Board (ESRB)—www.esrb.org

Game Audio Network Guild (GANG)—www.audiogang.org

International Computer Games Association (ICGA)—www.cs.unimaas.nl/icga

International Game Developers Association (IGDA)—www.igda.org

SIGGRAPH—www.siggraph.org

Events

Consumer Electronics Show (CES)
January—Las Vegas, NV
www.cesweb.org

Game Developers Conference (GDC)
March—San Francisco, CA
www.gdconf.com

Serious Games Summit (SGS)
March (San Francisco, CA at GDC) & October (Washington, DC)
www.seriousgamessummit.com

D.I.C.E. Summit (AIAS)
March—Las Vegas, NV
www.dicesummit.org

SIGGRAPH (ACM)
Summer—Los Angeles, CA; San Diego, CA; Boston, MA (location varies)
www.siggraph.org

Tokyo Game Show (TGS)
Fall—Japan
tgs.cesa.or.jp/english/

E3 Business & Media Summit
July—Santa Monica, CA
www.e3expo.com

Austin Game Developers Conference
September—Austin, TX
www.gameconference.com

IndieGamesCon (IGC)
October—Eugene, OR
www.indiegamescon.com

E for All Expo
October—Los Angeles, CA
www.eforallexpo.com

Colleges & Universities

Here is a list of schools that have strong game degree or certificate programs:

Academy of Art University—www.academyart.edu

Arizona State University—www.asu.edu

Art Center College of Design—www.artcenter.edu

Art Institute of Pittsburgh - Online Division—www.aionline.edu

The Art Institutes—www.artinstitutes.edu

Carnegie Mellon University/Entertainment Technology Center—www.cmu.edu

DeVry University—www.devry.edu

DigiPen Institute of Technology—www.digipen.edu

Expression College for Digital Arts—www.expression.edu

Full Sail Real World Education—www.fullsail.edu

Guildhall at SMU—guildhall.smu.edu

Indiana University - MIME Program—www.mime.indiana.edu

Iowa State University—www.iastate.edu

ITT Technical Institute—www.itt-tech.edu

Massachusetts Institute of Technology (MIT)—media.mit.edu

Rensselaer Polytechnic Institute—www.rpi.edu

Ringling College of Art & Design—www.ringling.edu

Santa Monica College Academy of Entertainment & Technology—academy.smc.edu

Savannah College of Art & Design—www.scad.edu

Tomball College—www.tomballcollege.com

University of California, Los Angeles (UCLA) - Extension—www.uclaextension.edu

University of Central Florida - Florida Interactive Entertainment Academy—fiea.ucf.edu

University of Southern California (USC) - Information Technology Program—itp.usc.edu

University of Southern California (USC) School of Cinematic Arts—interactive.usc.edu

Vancouver Film School—www.vfs.com

Westwood College—www.westwood.edu

Books & Articles

Adams, E. (2003). *Break into the game industry.* McGraw-Hill Osborne Media.

Adams, E. & Rollings, A. (2006). *Fundamentals of game design.* Prentice Hall.

Ahearn, L. & Crooks II, C.E. (2002). *Awesome game creation: No programming required. (2nd ed).* Charles River Media.

Ahlquist, J.B., Jr. & Novak, J. (2007). *Game development essentials: Game artificial intelligence.* Thomson Delmar.

Aldrich, C. (2003). *Simulations and the future of learning.* Pfeiffer.

Aldrich, C. (2005). *Learning by doing.* Jossey-Bass.

Allison, S.E. et al. (March 2006). "The development of the self in the era of the Internet & role-playing fantasy games. *The American Journal of Psychiatry.*

Atkin, M. & Abercrombie, J. (2005). "Using a goal/action architecture to integrate modularity and long-term memory into AI behaviors." *Game Developers Conference.*

Axelrod, R. (1985). *The evolution of cooperation.* Basic Books.

Bates, B. (2002). *Game design: The art & business of creating games.* Premier Press.

Beck, J.C. & Wade, M. (2004). *Got game: How the gamer generation is reshaping business forever.* Harvard Business School Press.

Bethke, E. (2003). *Game development and production.* Wordware.

Brandon, A. (2004). *Audio for games: Planning, process, and production.* New Riders.

Brin, D. (1998). *The transparent society.* Addison-Wesley.

Broderick, D. (2001). *The spike: How our lives are being transformed by rapidly advancing technologies.* Forge.

Brooks, D. (2001). *Bobos in paradise: The new upper class and how they got there.* Simon & Schuster.

Business Software Alliance. (May 2005). "Second annual BSA and IDC global software piracy study." www.bsa.org/globalstudy

Campbell, J. (1972). *The hero with a thousand faces.* Princeton University Press.

Campbell, J. & Moyers, B. (1991). *The power of myth.* Anchor.

Castells, M. (2001). *The Internet galaxy: Reflections on the Internet, business, and society.* Oxford University Press.

Castronova, E. (2005). *Synthetic worlds: The business and culture of online games.* University of Chicago Press.

Chase, R.B., Aquilano, N.J. & Jacobs, R. (2001). *Operations management for competitive advantage (9th ed).* McGraw-Hill/Irwin

Cheeseman, H.R. (2004). *Business law (5th ed).* Pearson Education, Inc.

Chiarella, T. (1998). *Writing dialogue.* Story Press.

Christen, P. (November 2006). "Serious expectations" *Game Developer Magazine.*

Cooper, A., & Reimann, R. (2003). *About face 2.0: The essentials of interaction design.* Wiley.

Cornman, L.B. et al. (December 1998). A fuzzy logic method for improved moment estimation from Doppler spectra. *Journal of Atmospheric & Oceanic Technology.*

Cox, E. & Goetz, M. (March 1991). Fuzzy logic clarified. *Computerworld.*

Crawford, C. (2003). *Chris Crawford on game design.* New Riders.

Crowley, M. (2004). "'A' is for average." *Reader's Digest.*

Csikszentmihalyi, M. (1991). *Flow: The psychology of optimal experience.* Perennial.

DeMaria, R. & Wilson, J.L. (2003). *High score!: The illustrated history of electronic games.* McGraw-Hill.

Egri, L. (1946). *The art of dramatic writing: Its basis in the creative interpretation of human motives.* Simon and Schuster.

Erikson, E.H. (1994). *Identity and the life cycle.* W.W. Norton & Company.

Erikson, E.H. (1995). *Childhood and society.* Vintage.

Escober, C. & Galindo, J. (2004). Fuzzy control in agriculture: Simulation software. *Industrial Simulation Conference 2004.*

Evans, A. (2001). *This virtual life: Escapism and simulation in our media world.* Fusion Press.

Feare, T. (July 2000). "Simulation: Tactical tool for system builders." *Modern Materials Handling.*

Index

Friedl, M. (2002). *Online game interactivity theory.* Charles River Media.

Fruin, N. & Harrigan, P. (Eds.) (2004). *First person: New media as story, performance and game.* MIT Press.

Fullerton, T., Swain, C. & Hoffman, S. (2004). *Game design workshop: Designing, prototyping & playtesting games.* CMP Books.

Galitz, W.O. (2002). *The essential guide to user interface design: An introduction to GUI design principles and techniques.* (2nd ed.). Wiley.

Gamma, E., Helm, R., Johnson, R. & Vlissides, J. (1995). *Design patterns: Elements of reusable object-oriented software.* Addison-Wesley.

Gardner, J. (1991). *The art of fiction: Notes on craft for young writers.* Vintage Books.

Gee, J.P. (2003). *What video games have to teach us about learning and literacy.* Palgrave Macmillan.

Gershenfeld, A., Loparco, M. & Barajas, C. (2003). *Game plan: The insiders guide to breaking in and succeeding in the computer and video game business.* Griffin Trade Paperback.

Giarratano, J.C. & Riley, G.D. (1998). *Expert systems: Principles & programming (4th ed).* Course Technology.

Gibson, D., Aldrich, C. & Prensky, M. (Eds.) (2006). *Games and simulations in online learning.* IGI Global.

Gladwell, M. (2000). *The tipping point: How little things can make a big difference.* New York, NY: Little Brown & Company.

Gladwell, M. (2007). *Blink: The power of thinking without thinking.* Back Bay Books.

Gleick, J. (1987). *Chaos: Making a new science.* Viking.

Gleick, J. (1999). *Faster: The acceleration of just about everything.* Vintage Books.

Gleick, J. (2003). *What just happened: A chronicle from the information frontier.* Vintage.

Godin, S. (2003). *Purple cow: Transform your business by being remarkable.* Portfolio.

Godin, S. (2005). *The big moo: Stop trying to be perfect and start being remarkable.* Portfolio.

Goldratt, E.M. & Cox, J. (2004). *The goal: A process of ongoing improvement (3rd ed).* North River Press.

Gordon, T. (2000). *P.E.T.: Parent effectiveness training.* Three Rivers Press.

Hamilton, E. (1940). *Mythology: Timeless tales of gods and heroes.* Mentor.

Heim, M. (1993). *The metaphysics of virtual reality.* Oxford University Press.

Hight, J. & Novak, J. (2007). *Game development essentials: Game project management.* Thomson Delmar.

Hsu, F. (2004). *Behind Deep Blue: Building the computer that defeated the world chess champion.* Princeton University Press.

Hunt, C.W. (October 1998). "Uncertainty factor drives new approach to building simulations." *Signal.*

Jensen, E. (2006). *Enriching the brain: How to maximize every learner's potential.* John Wiley & Sons.

Isla, D. (2005). "Handling complexity in the *Halo 2* AI." Game Developers Conference.

Johnson, S. (1997). *Interface culture: How new technology transforms the way we create & communicate.* Basic Books.

Johnson, S. (2006). *Everything bad is good for you.* Riverhead.

Jung, C.G. (1969). *Man and his symbols.* Dell Publishing.

Kent, S.L. (2001). *The ultimate history of video games.* Prima.

King, S. (2000). *On writing.* Scribner.

Knoke, W. (1997). *Bold new world: The essential road map to the twenty-first century.* Kodansha International.

Koster, R. (2005). *Theory of fun for game design.* Paraglyph Press.

Krawczyk, M. & Novak, J. (2006). *Game development essentials: Game story & character development.* Thomson Delmar.

Kurzweil, R. (2000). *The age of spiritual machines: When computers exceed human intelligence.* Penguin.

Laramee, F.D. (Ed.) (2002). *Game design perspectives.* Charles River Media.

Laramee, F.D. (Ed.) (2005). *Secrets of the game business. (3rd ed.)* Charles River Media.

Levy, P. (2001). *Cyberculture.* University of Minnesota Press.

Lewis, M. (2001). *Next: The future just happened.* W.W.Norton & Company.

Mackay, C. (1841). *Extraordinary popular delusions & the madness of crowds.* Three Rivers Press.

McConnell, S. (1996). *Rapid development.* Microsoft Press.

McCorduck, P. (2004). *Machines who think: A personal inquiry into the history and prospects of artificial intelligence (2nd ed).* AK Peters.

McKenna, T. (December 2003). "This means war." *Journal of Electronic Defense.*

Mencher, M. (2002). *Get in the game: Careers in the game industry.* New Riders.

Meyers, S. (2005). *Effective C++: 55 specific ways to improve your programs and designs (3rd ed).* Addison-Wesley.

Michael, D. (2003). *The indie game development survival guide.* Charles River Media.

Montfort, N. (2003). *Twisty little passages: An approach to interactive fiction.* MIT Press.

Moravec, H. (2000). *Robot.* Oxford University Press.

Morris, D. (September/October 2004). Virtual weather. *Weatherwise.*

Morris, D. & Hartas, L. (2003). *Game art: The graphic art of computer games.* Watson-Guptill Publications.

Muehl, W. & Novak, J. (2007). *Game development essentials: Game simulation development.* Thomson Delmar.

Mulligan, J. & Patrovsky, B. (2003). *Developing online games: An insider's guide.* New Riders.

Mummolo, J. (July 2006). "Helping children play." *Newsweek.*

Murray, J. (2001). *Hamlet on the holodeck: The future of narrative in cyberspace.* MIT Press.

Negroponte, N. (1996). *Being digital.* Vintage Books.

Nielsen, J. (1999). *Designing web usability: The practice of simplicity.* New Riders.

Novak, J. (2007). *Game development essentials: An introduction. (2nd ed.).* Thomson Delmar.

Novak, J. & Levy, L. (2007). *Play the game: The parents guide to video games.* Thomson Course Technology PTR.

Novak, J. (2003). "MMOGs as online distance learning applications." University of Southern California.

Oram, A. (Ed.) (2001). *Peer-to-peer.* O'Reilly & Associates.

Patow, C.A. (December 2005). "Medical simulation makes medical education better & safer." *Health Management Technology.*

Peck, M. (January 2005). "Air Force's latest video game targets potential recruits." *National Defense.*

Piaget, J. (2000). *The psychology of the child.* Basic Books.

Piaget, J. (2007). *The child's conception of the world.* Jason Aronson.

Pohflepp, S. (January 2007). "Before and after Darwin." *We Make Money Not Art.* (http://www.we-make-money-not-art.com/archives/009261.php)

Prensky, M. (2006). *Don't bother me, Mom: I'm learning!* Paragon House.

Ramirez, J. (July 2006). "The new ad game." *Newsweek.*

Rheingold, H. (1991). *Virtual reality.* Touchstone.

Rheingold, H. (2000). *Tools for thought: The history and future of mind-expanding technology.* MIT Press.

Robbins, S.P. (2001). *Organizational behavior (9th ed).* Prentice-Hall, Inc.

Rogers, E.M. (1995). *Diffusion of innovations.* Free Press.

Rollings, A. & Morris, D. (2003). *Game architecture & design: A new edition.* New Riders.

Rollings, A. & Adams, E. (2003). *Andrew Rollings & Ernest Adams on game design.* New Riders.

Rouse, R. (2001) *Game design: Theory & practice (2nd ed).* Wordware Publishing.

Salen, K. & Zimmerman, E. (2003). *Rules of play.* MIT Press.

Sanchanta, M. (2006 January). "Japanese game aids U.S. war on obesity: Gym class in West Virginia to use an interactive dance console." *Financial Times.*

Sanger, G.A. [a.k.a. "The Fat Man"]. (2003). *The Fat Man on game audio.* New Riders.

Saunders, K. & Novak, J. (2007). *Game development essentials: Game interface design.* Thomson Delmar.

Schildt, H. (2006). *Java: A beginner's guide (4th ed).* McGraw-Hill Osborne Media.

Schomaker, W. (September 2001). "Cosmic models match reality." *Astronomy.*

Sellers, J. (2001). *Arcade fever.* Running Press.

Shaffer, D.W. (2006). *How computer games help children learn.* Palgrave Macmillan.

Standage, T. (1999). *The Victorian Internet.* New York: Berkley Publishing Group.

Strauss, W. & Howe, N. (1992). *Generations.* Perennial.

Strauss, W. & Howe, N. (1993). *13th gen: Abort, retry, ignore, fail?* Vintage Books.

Strauss, W. & Howe, N. (1998). *The fourth turning.* Broadway Books.

Strauss, W. & Howe, N. (2000). *Millennials rising: The next great generation.* Vintage Books.

Strauss, W., Howe, N. & Markiewicz, P. (2006). *Millennials & the pop culture.* LifeCourse Associates.

Stroustrup, B. (2000). *The C++ programming language (3rd ed).* Addison-Wesley.

Trotter, A. (November 2005). "Despite allure, using digital games for learning seen as no easy task." *Education Week.*

Tufte, E.R. (1983). *The visual display of quantitative information.* Graphics Press.

Tufte, E.R. (1990). *Envisioning information.* Graphics Press.

Tufte, E.R. (1997). *Visual explanations.* Graphics Press.

Tufte, E.R. (2006). *Beautiful evidence.* Graphics Press.

Turkle, S. (1997). *Life on the screen: Identity in the age of the Internet.* Touchstone.

Van Duyne, D.K. et al. (2003). *The design of sites.* Addison-Wesley.

Vogler, C. (1998). *The writer's journey: Mythic structure for writers. (2nd ed).* Michael Wiese Productions.

Welch, J. & Welch, S. (2005). *Winning.* HarperCollins Publishers.

Weizenbaum, J. (1984). *Computer power and human reason.* Penguin Books.

Williams, J.D. (1954). *The compleat strategyst: Being a primer on the theory of the games of strategy.* McGraw-Hill.

Wolf, J.P. & Perron, B. (Eds.). (2003). *Video game theory reader.* Routledge.

Wong, G. (November 2006). "Educators explore 'Second Life' online." *CNN.com* (http://www.cnn.com/2006/TECH/11/13/second.life.university/index.html)

Wysocki, R.K. (2006). *Effective project management (4th ed).* John Wiley & Sons.

Friedl, M. (2002). *Online game interactivity theory.* Charles River Media.

Fruin, N. & Harringan, P. (Eds.) (2004). *First person: New media as story, performance and game.* MIT Press.

Fullerton, T., Swain, C. & Hoffman, S. (2004). *Game design workshop: Designing, prototyping & playtesting games.* CMP Books.

Galitz, W.O. (2002). *The essential guide to user interface design: An introduction to GUI design principles and techniques.* (2nd ed.). Wiley.

Gamma, E., Helm, R., Johnson, R. & Vlissides, J. (1995). *Design patterns: Elements of reusable object-oriented software.* Addison-Wesley.

Gardner, J. (1991). *The art of fiction: Notes on craft for young writers.* Vintage Books.

Gee, J.P. (2003). *What video games have to teach us about learning and literacy.* Palgrave Macmillan.

Gershenfeld, A., Loparco, M. & Barajas, C. (2003). *Game plan: The insiders guide to breaking in and succeeding in the computer and video game business.* Griffin Trade Paperback.

Giarratano, J.C. & Riley, G.D. (1998). *Expert systems: Principles & programming (4th ed).* Course Technology.

Gibson, D., Aldrich, C. & Prensky, M. (Eds.) (2006). *Games and simulations in online learning.* IGI Global.

Gladwell, M. (2000). *The tipping point: How little things can make a big difference.* New York, NY: Little Brown & Company.

Gladwell, M. (2007). *Blink: The power of thinking without thinking.* Back Bay Books.

Glcick, J. (1987). *Chaos: Making a new science.* Viking.

Gleick, J. (1999). *Faster: The acceleration of just about everything.* Vintage Books.

Gleick, J. (2003). *What just happened: A chronicle from the information frontier.* Vintage.

Godin, S. (2003). *Purple cow: Transform your business by being remarkable.* Portfolio.

Godin, S. (2005). *The big moo: Stop trying to be perfect and start being remarkable.* Portfolio.

Goldratt, E.M. & Cox, J. (2004). *The goal: A process of ongoing improvement (3rd ed).* North River Press.

Gordon, T. (2000). *P.E.T.: Parent effectiveness training.* Three Rivers Press.

Hamilton, E. (1940). *Mythology: Timeless tales of gods and heroes.* Mentor.

Heim, M. (1993). *The metaphysics of virtual reality.* Oxford University Press.

Hight, J. & Novak, J. (2007). *Game development essentials: Game project management.* Thomson Delmar.

Hsu, F. (2004). *Behind Deep Blue: Building the computer that defeated the world chess champion.* Princeton University Press.

Hunt, C.W. (October 1998). "Uncertainty factor drives new approach to building simulations." *Signal.*

Jensen, E. (2006). *Enriching the brain: How to maximize every learner's potential.* John Wiley & Sons.

Isla, D. (2005). "Handling complexity in the *Halo 2* AI." Game Developers Conference.

Johnson, S. (1997). *Interface culture: How new technology transforms the way we create & communicate.* Basic Books.

Johnson, S. (2006). *Everything bad is good for you.* Riverhead.

Jung, C.G. (1969). *Man and his symbols.* Dell Publishing.

Kent, S.L. (2001). *The ultimate history of video games.* Prima.

King, S. (2000). *On writing.* Scribner.

Knoke, W. (1997). *Bold new world: The essential road map to the twenty-first century.* Kodansha International.

Koster, R. (2005). *Theory of fun for game design.* Paraglyph Press.

Krawczyk, M. & Novak, J. (2006). *Game development essentials: Game story & character development.* Thomson Delmar.

Kurzweil, R. (2000). *The age of spiritual machines: When computers exceed human intelligence.* Penguin.

Laramee, F.D. (Ed.) (2002). *Game design perspectives.* Charles River Media.

Laramee, F.D. (Ed.) (2005). *Secrets of the game business. (3rd ed).* Charles River Media.

Levy, P. (2001). *Cyberculture.* University of Minnesota Press.

Lewis, M. (2001). *Next: The future just happened.* W.W.Norton & Company.

Mackay, C. (1841). *Extraordinary popular delusions & the madness of crowds.* Three Rivers Press.

McConnell, S. (1996). *Rapid development.* Microsoft Press.

McCorduck, P. (2004). *Machines who think: A personal inquiry into the history and prospects of artificial intelligence (2nd ed).* AK Peters.

McKenna, T. (December 2003). "This means war." *Journal of Electronic Defense.*

Mencher, M. (2002). *Get in the game: Careers in the game industry.* New Riders.

Meyers, S. (2005). *Effective C++: 55 specific ways to improve your programs and designs (3rd ed).* Addison-Wesley.

Michael, D. (2003). *The indie game development survival guide.* Charles River Media.

Montfort, N. (2003). *Twisty little passages: An approach to interactive fiction.* MIT Press.

Moravec, H. (2000). *Robot.* Oxford University Press.

Morris, D. (September/October 2004). Virtual weather. *Weatherwise.*

Morris, D. & Hartas, L. (2003). *Game art: The graphic art of computer games.* Watson-Guptill Publications.

Muehl, W. & Novak, J. (2007). *Game development essentials: Game simulation development.* Thomson Delmar.

Mulligan, J. & Patrovsky, B. (2003). *Developing online games: An insider's guide.* New Riders.

Mummolo, J. (July 2006). "Helping children play." *Newsweek.*

Murray, J. (2001). *Hamlet on the holodeck: The future of narrative in cyberspace.* MIT Press.

Negroponte, N. (1996). *Being digital.* Vintage Books.

Nielsen, J. (1999). *Designing web usability: The practice of simplicity.* New Riders.

Novak. J. (2007). *Game development essentials: An introduction. (2nd ed.).* Thomson Delmar.

Novak, J. & Levy, L. (2007). *Play the game: The parents guide to video games.* Thomson Course Technology PTR.

Novak, J. (2003). "MMOGs as online distance learning applications." University of Southern California.

Oram, A. (Ed.) (2001). *Peer-to-peer.* O'Reilly & Associates.

Patow, C.A. (December 2005). "Medical simulation makes medical education better & safer." *Health Management Technology.*

Peck, M. (January 2005). "Air Force's latest video game targets potential recruits." *National Defense.*

Piaget, J. (2000). *The psychology of the child.* Basic Books.

Piaget, J. (2007). *The child's conception of the world.* Jason Aronson.

Pohflepp, S. (January 2007). "Before and after Darwin." *We Make Money Not Art.* (http://www.we-make-money-not -art.com/archives/009261.php)

Prensky, M. (2006). *Don't bother me, Mom: I'm learning!* Paragon House.

Ramirez, J. (July 2006). "The new ad game." *Newsweek*.

Rheingold, H. (1991). *Virtual reality*. Touchstone.

Rheingold, H. (2000). *Tools for thought: The history and future of mind-expanding technology.* MIT Press.

Robbins, S.P. (2001). *Organizational behavior (9th ed)*. Prentice-Hall, Inc.

Rogers, E.M. (1995). *Diffusion of innovations*. Free Press.

Rollings, A. & Morris, D. (2003). *Game architecture & design: A new edition*. New Riders.

Rollings, A. & Adams, E. (2003). *Andrew Rollings & Ernest Adams on game design*. New Riders.

Rouse, R. (2001) *Game design: Theory & practice (2nd ed)*. Wordware Publishing.

Salen, K. & Zimmerman, E. (2003). *Rules of play*. MIT Press.

Sanchanta, M. (2006 January). "Japanese game aids U.S. war on obesity: Gym class in West Virginia to use an interactive dance console." *Financial Times*.

Sanger, G.A. [a.k.a. "The Fat Man"]. (2003). *The Fat Man on game audio*. New Riders.

Saunders, K. & Novak, J. (2007). *Game development essentials: Game interface design.* Thomson Delmar.

Schildt, H. (2006). *Java: A beginner's guide (4th ed)*. McGraw-Hill Osborne Media.

Schomaker, W. (September 2001). "Cosmic models match reality." *Astronomy*.

Sellers, J. (2001). *Arcade fever*. Running Press.

Shaffer, D.W. (2006). *How computer games help children learn*. Palgrave Macmillan.

Standage, T. (1999). *The Victorian Internet*. New York: Berkley Publishing Group.

Strauss, W. & Howe, N. (1992). *Generations*. Perennial.

Strauss, W. & Howe, N. (1993). *13th gen: Abort, retry, ignore, fail?* Vintage Books.

Strauss, W. & Howe, N. (1998). *The fourth turning*. Broadway Books.

Strauss, W. & Howe, N. (2000). *Millennials rising: The next great generation*. Vintage Books.

Strauss, W., Howe, N. & Markiewicz, P. (2006). *Millennials & the pop culture*. LifeCourse Associates.

Stroustrup, B. (2000). *The C++ programming language (3rd ed)*. Addison-Wesley.

Trotter, A. (November 2005). "Despite allure, using digital games for learning seen as no easy task." *Education Week*.

Tufte, E.R. (1983). *The visual display of quantitative information*. Graphics Press.

Tufte, E.R. (1990). *Envisioning information*. Graphics Press.

Tufte, E.R. (1997). *Visual explanations*. Graphics Press.

Tufte, E.R. (2006). *Beautiful evidence*. Graphics Press.

Turkle, S. (1997). *Life on the screen: Identity in the age of the Internet*. Touchstone.

Van Duyne, D.K. et al. (2003). *The design of sites*. Addison-Wesley.

Vogler, C. (1998). *The writer's journey: Mythic structure for writers. (2nd ed)*. Michael Wiese Productions.

Welch, J. & Welch, S. (2005). *Winning*. HarperCollins Publishers.

Weizenbaum, J. (1984). *Computer power and human reason*. Penguin Books.

Williams, J.D. (1954). *The compleat strategyst: Being a primer on the theory of the games of strategy*. McGraw-Hill.

Wolf, J.P. & Perron, B. (Eds.). (2003). *Video game theory reader*. Routledge.

Wong, G. (November 2006). "Educators explore 'Second Life' online." *CNN.com* (http://www.cnn.com/2006/TECH/11/13/second.life.university/index.html)

Wysocki, R.K. (2006). *Effective project management (4th ed)*. John Wiley & Sons.

Index